AUDRE LORDE'S TRANSNATIONAL LEGACIES

AUDRE LORDE'S TRANSNATIONAL LEGACIES

EDITED BY

Stella Bolaki and Sabine Broeck

University of Massachusetts Press
Amherst and Boston

ISBN 978-1-62534-139-6 (paperback); 138-9 (hardcover)

Designed by Sally Nichols
Set in Monotype Dante Std
Printed and bound by Maple Press, Inc.

Library of Congress Cataloging-in-Publication Data

Audre Lorde's transnational legacies / edited by Stella Bolaki and Sabine Broeck.
pages   cm
Includes bibliographical references and index.
ISBN 978-1-62534-139-6 (pbk. : alk. paper) — ISBN 978-1-62534-138-9 (hardcover : alk. paper)
1. Lorde, Audre—Criticism and interpretation. 2. Lorde, Audre—Influence. I. Bolaki, Stella,
editor. II. Broeck, Sabine, editor.
PS3562.O75Z57 2015
818'.5409—dc23

2015009737

British Library Cataloguing-in-Publication Data
A catalogue record for this book is available from the British Library.

CONTENTS

ACKNOWLEDGMENTS

It has been a pleasure to be involved in the collaboration that has become *Audre Lorde's Transnational Legacies*. We have learned so much from our contributors, and without their work and commitment this book would not have been possible. We offer special thanks to Dagmar Schultz, Marion Kraft, Katharina Gerund, Lester C. Olson, Tiffany N. Florvil, Peggy Piesche, Ika Hügel-Marshall, Sara Ahmed, Gail Lewis, Melba Wilson, Aishah Shahidah Simmons, and the Centre for the Study of Sexual Dissidence at the University of Sussex for their organization and participation in the following conference panels and events: Audre Lorde's Legacy: A Film and Cultural Festival at the Women's Library, London, May 2012; "Audre Lorde's Transnational Legacies" at the British Association for American Studies annual conference, University of Exeter, April 2013; "Audre Lorde and the Afro-German Feminist Movement" at the Feminist and Women's Studies Association conference, University of Nottingham, June 2013; "Audre Lorde's Queer International Feminisms" at the annual conference sponsored by the *International Feminist Journal of Politics,* University of Sussex, May 2013; "Audre Lorde and Europe" at the Afroeurope@ns IV: Black Cultures and Identities in Europe conference, Institute of Advanced Studies, University of London, October 2013; and "Audre Lorde's Transnational Sisterhood and the Black German Experience," at the Modern Language Association annual convention, Vancouver, January 2015. We are also grateful to all who attended these panels and events and gave us valuable feedback.

Many friends and colleagues have generously assisted with various aspects of the project. We are particularly grateful to Sara Lennox, Derek Ryan, Caroline Rooney, David Stirrup, the members of the Centre for Postcolonial Studies at the University of Kent, Macarena Gómez-Barris, Sue O'Sullivan, Michelle Mckenzie, Cora Leibowitz (also known as Corasón), Suzanne Bellamy, and Alan Rice. Many thanks to Paula von Gleich for her invaluable help in editing the manuscript.

We thank Marion Kraft for giving us permission to reprint "The Creative Use of Difference: Interview with Audre Lorde," which was first published in *EAST. Englisch Amerikanische Studien. Zeitschrift für Unterricht, Wissenschaft und Politik*, no. 3/4 (December 1986): 549–56; and Pratibha Parmar and Jackie Kay for permission to reprint "Frontiers: Interview with Audre Lorde," which was first published in *Charting the Journey: Writings by Black and Third World Women*, ed. Shabnam Grewal, Jackie Kay, Liliane Landor, Gail Lewis, and Pratibha Parmar (London: Sheba, 1988), 121–31. We would also like to acknowledge the support of our institutions, the University of Kent and the University of Bremen; the Spelman College Archives (especially the help of the late Taronda Spencer); the British Academy, which funded Stella Bolaki's visit to the Audre Lorde Papers at Spelman in 2012; the British Association for American Studies; and the Collegium for African American Research.

Finally, we were extremely fortunate to work with the University of Massachusetts Press, and we owe a great debt to the anonymous readers for their insights and direction, the editorial team for its guidance, and especially to Brian Halley for his continuing encouragement and faith in our project.

ACKNOWLEDGMENTS

FOREWORD
Sara Ahmed

What an honor it is to write this foreword to *Audre Lorde's Transnational Legacies*. Each time Lorde's words reach me, they teach me. Every time I encounter her work, I feel a ripple of hope. This is a collection of essays about her reach: about how she managed to travel widely, through both the alliances she built and the places she went. As these essays show, Lorde addressed so many of us—African Americans, black Europeans, indigenous Australians . . . I could go on; she *will* go on.

All of the authors featured in this collection show remarkable care and appreciation for the "special fragility" of Lorde's archive (to borrow Stella Bolaki and Sabine Broeck's beautiful expression) as part of a wider black feminist transnational archive. We need to keep building the archive. We need to preserve and remember Lorde's work so that her words will stay alive and reach those who have yet to encounter her. This book is important because it expands the ways in which we can encounter and re-encounter Audre Lorde. The collection includes various kinds of writing—interviews, reflections, and shared memories from authors around the world. It is a moving, powerful book that tells us what we, too, can do if we follow Lorde and take the risk of naming ourselves; if we follow Lorde and refuse to be silent about racism, sexism, and the institutions designed to kill some of us prematurely; if we follow Lorde and build our communities with our hands, from the ground up.

In this foreword, I want to follow Lorde's example and describe how her work came to matter to me personally. She asks us to be personal, to refuse the refuge of distance and abstraction. I think of her and I think of those moments when a lifeline has been thrown to me; those moments when what I have received has given me a chance, a breathing space. A lifeline can be the quiet words of an encouraging friend, an unexpected alliance with a stranger, the sounds of a familiar or unfamiliar landscape. A lifeline can be the words sent out by a writer, gathered in the form of a book; words that I hang on to, that pull me out of an existence; words that can, perhaps later, on another day, pull me into a more livable world.

I read Audre Lorde's work, including *Sister Outsider* and her extraordinary memoir *Zami,* as a student of color in the early 1990s. For me, her words were a lifeline. Here is just one example on their power. In *Zami* she shares a memory of her mother, who explained to her that people were spitting into the wind because they were ill-mannered and rude. Her mother wanted to protect Audre, her black child, from the knowledge that people were spitting at her because she was black. When I read Lorde's words, I understood that racism can be what happens right in front of us but that we learn not to see it. When others try to protect us from racism, we are not protected. This is why, in saying *racism,* in naming an event *racism,* we are always doing something. We need to use this difficult word, even if others judge us as creators of the problem we are describing.

Lorde's memories helped me face my own. When I read her words, I reoccupied not only the spaces in which I was living and working but also my own past. I had grown up as a brown mixed-race child in a very white neighborhood in Australia, and I went to a very white school. (There is something "very" about whiteness.) I was called names and stopped by police: I experienced the difficult sensation of being a problem, and I had not wanted to think too much about it. But Audre Lorde did not let me get away with this, which meant she did not let me get away from myself; and that was a gift. By reading her work, I began to think about what it means to be stranger. This was a way of coming to terms with my own past, however different it was from hers. Lorde was so generous with her words that I could make the connections. She helped me find my way back to the self

SARA AHMED

I had been and reach toward a self that I could become. I think this is one reason why her work has such reach: when it touches you, it brings you to a new place. I have learnt from Audre Lorde that optimism does not require us to blunt our tools. We can be optimistic *because* of the sharpness of our critiques; we can be optimistic *because* we attend to the relations of violence and power that wear us down.

So how can we work together to create less wearing worlds? Lorde helps us answer that question. As the essays in this book demonstrate, the transnational is an actual lived space populated by real bodies. It is not a glossy word in a brochure but one that requires work. We have to work to learn from others who do not share our language. We have to travel out of our comfort zones, to open our ears. What can happen when African American and Afro-German women speak to each other, or when women of color throughout the diaspora speak to each other across generations, time, and space? We learn from differences about differences. We learn also that the national is transnational: that the very ground of nations is shaped by histories of empire and colonialism. As Lorde says in "The Dream of Europe," reproduced in this collection, "Black Europeans are not foreigners to you, not strangers. Yet I do not hear the voice of one Black European writer here and so I wonder how serious this dreaming can be." For her, a future without black voices is no future at all.

By bearing witness to Audre Lorde's transnational legacy, this book creates a collective. Even when we single her out, we still end up with a "we" because she taught us how to build a "we" from the shattered pieces of our dwelling places, how to build a "we" to survive being shattered. Reading this book reminds me that an individual life does matter; Lorde is asking us to ask ourselves what our life is and can be. Her work teaches us that what people dismiss as "identity politics" is a politics that we need to claim as women, as people of color, as lesbians or queers in a world that still tends to equate human with male, white, and straight. Lorde reminds us that identity as a political art is a way of inventing ourselves.

As I read this book, I thought of Lorde's much quoted sentence: "the master's tools will never dismantle the master's house." To create new dwellings, we have to make our own feminist tools. I think of her as a feminist killjoy, willing to name sexism, for example, by calling attention to violence against women *wherever* it happens. She spoke out as an angry woman of color, willfully exposing racism within feminism. I love the expression she uses in "Frontiers," an interview reproduced here: "the monstrosity of racism." She was committed to demonstrating the necessity of this exposure so that white women and women of color would be able to work together.

This book has also reminded me that writing may become even more important when there is so much resistance to hearing what we have to say. In the film *A Litany for Survival* Lorde says that she started writing because of "a need to create something that was not there": "what I leave behind has a life of its own." Writing, like bearing children, was for her an unflinchingly optimistic gesture. Words that are sent out may end up anywhere.

Audre Lorde suggested that poetry can be revolutionary because it can move us, can make us feel, can allow us to be vulnerable. She invited us to stay with the hard feelings: to refuse to be silenced by anger, to speak out of anger, to inhabit the despair of knowing the world we aim for will not be achieved in our life time. She invited us to inhabit the hope of passing that aim to others. There can be warmth in struggle; there can be kindness and patience in survival. Lorde showed us that survival is a radical project for those who "are not meant to survive." Even her approach to cancer, to death, embraced life as a struggle. Perhaps this very struggle against injustice is what gives us the resources we need to build a more just world. These resources might include a certain willingness to cause trouble, but they also include humor, love, freedom of spirit, and wit. We lighten our loads as well as our moods when we create spaces to be with each other.

This book lightens my spirit. With Audre Lorde, we begin again.

SARA AHMED

AUDRE LORDE'S TRANSNATIONAL LEGACIES

INTRODUCTION
Audre Lorde's Transnational Legacies

STELLA BOLAKI AND SABINE BROECK

> What is our real work as Black women writers of the Diaspora? Our responsibilities to other Black women and their children across this globe we share, struggling for our joint future?
>
> Audre Lorde, "A Burst of Light: Living with Cancer"

Seeking and forging connections and challenging silence and invisibility were organizing principles of Audre Lorde's life and work. "What are the words you do not yet have? What do you need to say?" she famously asked in "The Transformation of Silence into Language and Action." Her answer never ceases to inspire new visions and struggles: "Your silence will not protect you."[1] In her well-anthologized essay "The Master's Tools Will Never Dismantle the Master's House," she asserted that "without community there is no liberation."[2] In her foreword to *Showing Our Colors: Afro-German Women Speak Out* (the first anthology of writings by Black German women, which Lorde was instrumental in publishing), she wrote that "the essence of a true global feminism is the recognition of connection."[3] But as she explained at "I Am Your Sister: Forging Global Connections across Difference," a 1990 Boston conference organized in her honor, and as she repeated throughout her work, "to recognize that we move against a common enemy does not mean that we beat the same drum or play the same tune. It means that we are committed to a future."[4] Creating the space to grow in the sharing of differences and working toward liberation, survival, and creativity are elements of the distinctive legacy that she has left us.

Audre Lorde's Transnational Legacies explores the depth and range of Lorde's literary, intellectual, and activist commitments by situating her life and work within transatlantic and transnational perspectives. Although both the research and nonacademic communities have documented her involvement in the African American civil rights and black arts movements and in feminist and lesbian/gay movements in the United States, the transnational dimensions of her legacy have not yet been systematically researched. We can grasp a sense of this legacy by considering the coalitions she founded with black diasporic women during her travels in Europe and around the world and her contribution to the reception of the Black Revolution of the 1960s, whose effects, as she suggested, "are sometimes more obvious in other countries than in America."[5] The essays in this book bear witness to Lorde's many enduring legacies by reconstructing little-known transnational histories and critically reflecting on her speeches, essays, journals, and poetry. Yet at the same time we acknowledge that it is impossible, in a single volume, to do full justice to a major figure in American literature, culture, and politics who has attained such iconic status among so many diverse audiences.[6]

Audre Lorde never stopped crossing boundaries in her life and work. Likewise, our book seeks to broaden the interdisciplinary study of American cultures in a transnational context, to move beyond disciplinary and geographic boundaries that have confined the field of American and African American studies to the U.S. context. By focusing on the multiple intersections and exchanges across such borders, *Audre Lorde's Transnational Legacies* attests to the wider "transnational turn" in American studies, to borrow a phrase from Shelley Fischer Fishkin's 2004 presidential address to the American Studies Association.[7] Conceptually and methodologically, the book is particularly indebted to work such as Paul Gilroy's, which powerfully argues for a complex history of African diasporic intellectual culture that is specifically transnational, as well as to growing interest in the histories of black diasporic communities from outside the Americas, particularly in Europe.[8] Drawing attention to the enduring transnational manifestations of African American diasporic knowledges and struggles is one of our key objectives, and the book's contributors form a truly international group of scholars of literature, communication, and history as well as cultural theorists, artists, filmmakers, writers, activists, educators, publishers, and translators.

By way of this book, we also want to highlight the European and transnational dimensions of black women's intellectual culture, which in comparison to work on major figures such as Frederick Douglass, W. E. B. Du Bois,

STELLA BOLAKI AND SABINE BROECK

and Richard Wright, has been understudied. More than twenty years after her death, Lorde's legacies have not been systematically accounted for on either side of the Atlantic. For example, Lorde's official biography, Alexis De Veaux's 2004 *Warrior Poet,* includes only sparse mention of her travels in Europe. Similarly, Rudolph P. Byrd, Johnnetta Betsch Cole, and Beverly Guy-Sheftall's 2009 edited volume *I Am Your Sister* is primarily concerned with situating her work within the tradition of U.S. black feminist thought.[9] In contrast, by reflecting and theorizing on Lorde's writing and work in various contexts, our contributors suggest the importance of a wider international recognition.

We are, of course, grateful for and committed to work that has laid the foundations for documenting the transnational feminist histories to which the essays in this book contribute. Among them are *Conversations with Audre Lorde* (2004), which includes many rare interviews with Lorde, including international ones. Another is the groundbreaking 1986 collection *Showing Our Colors: Afro-German Women Speak Out,* which put Afro-German women on the map of black diasporic studies in Europe and acknowledged Lorde's important influence in Germany. Also important is *"Euer Schweigen schützt euch nicht": Audre Lorde und die Schwarze Frauenbewegung in Deutschland,* an anthology of both published and previously unpublished work accompanied by essays and creative work by Peggy Piesche (a contributor to our volume) as well as other Black German scholars, activists, and artists.[10]

Audre Lorde's Transnational Legacies accompanies the 2012 film documentary *Audre Lorde—The Berlin Years, 1984 to 1992,* directed and produced by Lorde's German publisher and close friend Dagmar Schultz (another of our contributors). It was produced seventeen years after another film, *A Litany for Survival: The Life and Work of Audre Lorde,* directed by Ada Gay Griffin and Michelle Parkerson, who collaborated with Lorde for eight years to create this work.[11] *Litany* focuses on Lorde's activism in the United States, Mexico, the Caribbean, Europe, and Africa. Lorde herself was the narrator, telling viewers that "the battles we fight in this country as Black Americans against racism, police brutality, unemployment, miseducation, destruction of our children, history, earth, planet, are not our battles alone. We are, as members of an international community of people of color, connected with these battles all over the world." Schultz's *The Berlin Years,* which premiered at the sixty-second Berlin International Film Festival, has continued *Litany's* important documentation of Lorde's transnational legacies. While the films overlap to some extent, *The Berlin Years* has raised awareness of her key role in the Afro-German movement and has introduced worldwide audiences to a little-known chapter of her active life. More recently, in February 2014 documentary filmmaker, producer, writer, and activist Aishah Shahidah Simmons curated and lead-edited a two-week global forum commemorating Lorde's eightieth birthday. The forum, which appeared in *The Feminist Wire*, an online publication that "celebrates a multiplicity of feminist expressions from a variety of writers that span genders, sexualities, professions, races, and ethnicities," featured short essays, poems, remembrances, and testimonials from a wide range of feminist scholars, activists, artists, and cultural workers based in North America, Europe, Africa, and the Caribbean.[12]

Rather than constructing a unitary response and reception of Lorde's work, the essays in this book reconstruct the parallel yet various ways in which her work circulated in Europe and elsewhere. Using a diverse range of approaches, the contributors consider her influence and impact in Germany, Britain, France, Belgium, the Netherlands, Switzerland, Austria, Greece, Mexico, Canada, the Caribbean, South Africa, Australia, and New Zealand. Topics include the role of publishers and translators in Lorde's reception in various circles outside of the United States; her interactions and alliances across national, racial, and gender boundaries and her theoretical articulations of solidarity, difference, and responsibility as an African American woman; her contribution to the rise of black feminist consciousness movements, grass-roots organizations, and political and social movements against racism and violence, especially in Europe; and an examination of community art projects and feminist collectives inspired by Lorde that document the relevance and lasting impact of her work. Because academic response to Lorde's writing spans multiple disciplines, the essayists' perspectives and methodologies draw on transatlantic studies, feminist studies and gender theory, black diaspora studies, oral history, cultural anthropology, public advocacy, queer studies, critical whiteness and comparative race studies, and postcolonial studies.

Responding to Lorde's evocative image of the "house of difference" in her biomythography *Zami: A New Spelling of My Name*, a text that embraces autobiography, mythology, and history, this book brings together critical material, personal reflections from key figures in Lorde's interactions with Europe, and interviews with her from the 1980s.[13] Published here for the

STELLA BOLAKI AND SABINE BROECK

first time in English is Lorde's speech for "The Dream of Europe: Authors Invite Authors" conference, which she delivered in Berlin in May 1988. Many of the essays move beyond conventional academic format and incorporate experimental approaches such as dialogue and conversation that were central to Lorde's own task of forging connections and approaching difference creatively. In the spirit of her work, we have included a variety of texts that honor her distinct ways of knowledge production, which while not exclusively academic have had a profound and lasting impact on women's studies, gender and queer studies, black studies, and postcolonial studies programs. We believe that a collection that blurs those generic lines "in the name of grand asymmetries," to echo Lorde, is the best way to study her multiple legacies.[14]

Because Audre Lorde's words will continue to "be there, incit[ing] thought and activity," no collection of essays on her transnational legacies can be definitive.[15] Moreover, there is no existing comprehensive scholarly archive of her travels and interactions with black diasporic communities, despite the wealth of material in the Audre Lorde Papers at Spelman College (which opened to scholars in 2009 and on which many of our contributors draw), the Lesbian Herstory Archives in Brooklyn, and resources in Europe such as the new Audre Lorde Archive at the Free University of Berlin. Contributors have collaboratively pieced together these scattered transnational histories by looking at Lorde's own work and consulting historical witnesses and researchers from a variety of contexts and backgrounds. Even though an alternative archive is hard to produce because it depends on oral histories, lived experiences, and ephemeral traces that are difficult to document and (as many of the contributors show) largely ignored, this is precisely the aim of our collection. We hope that it will stimulate further research into both Lorde's legacies and the broader field of transnational American and black diasporic studies.

Before we go on to describe the book's structure, we would like to turn to Audre Lorde's "A Burst of Light: Living with Cancer" from her essay collection *A Burst of Light*.[16] While the essay can be placed next to Lorde's other work on health in the United States and the politics of illness (in particular, *The Cancer Journals*), it also constitutes an important archive of transnational encounters and reflections on several black diasporic communities.[17] By illustrating how Lorde's Atlantic crossings shaped her conception of the black diaspora, the essay is a valuable entry into considering the impact of her presence and her work on a number of discourses in Europe and elsewhere. In this way, it anticipates the transnational legacies explored by the essays in this book.

In the three years covered by the journal entries of "A Burst of Light" (1984 through 1987), Lorde discovered "the marvelous arithmetics of distance" (to borrow the title of her final collection of poems).[18] During those years she traveled to Germany, Switzerland, England, the Netherlands, and France, "determined to . . . see what Europe's all about," as well as to New Zealand, Australia, and her native Caribbean.[19] These trips gave her the opportunity to reflect on her responsibilities as an African American woman toward black diasporic women. Thus, they contributed to what her biographer De Veaux calls "the globalisation of her consciousness," which came "in her second life"—that is, the period following her discovery that she had cancer.[20] As Lorde explained, "I want to write down everything I know about being afraid, but I'd probably never have enough time to write anything else. Afraid is a country where they issue passports at birth and hope we never seek citizenship in any other country. The face of afraid keeps changing constantly, and I can count on that change. I need to travel light and fast, and there's lot of baggage I'm going to leave behind me. Jettison cargo."[21]

In her effort to resist the infantilization of patients, a tendency that *The Cancer Journals* indicts so powerfully, Lorde insisted on the need to make her own choices. Traveling to places that permitted alternative cancer treatments was one way of asserting her authority over a narrow medical culture. Just as her journal entries convey the lived experience of illness, "A Burst of Light" gives the reader a sense of the "transnational as an actual lived space populated by real bodies," as Sara Ahmed says in the foreword to this collection: "It is not a glossy word in a brochure but one that requires work. We have to work to learn from others who do not share our language. We have to travel out of our comfort zones, to open our ears." Seeking temporary citizenship in another country, then, helped Lorde overcome the powerlessness of fear while challenging a parochial American attitude: it helped her "stretch as far as I can go."[22]

Until her death in 1992, Lorde returned to Berlin every year for homeopathic treatment for liver cancer. As her partner Gloria Joseph acknowledges in Schultz's film *Audre Lorde—The Berlin Years*, the treatment

STELLA BOLAKI AND SABINE BROECK

prolonged her life; but the regularity of her visits also established a framework for conversations and mutual exchanges and prolonged and diversified the legacy of her activism. In both "A Burst of Light" and her foreword to the English edition of *Farbe bekennen,* Lorde made it clear that she went to Germany because she wanted to meet Afro-German women: "One of my aims for this trip was to meet Black German women. I'd been told there was quite a few in Berlin, but I had been unable to obtain much information about them in New York."[23] Several of this book's contributors review the story of her first trip to Germany and her various strategies for reaching out to white and Afro-German women. Many Afro-German women have spoken of the isolation they experienced before they began organizing into a more concrete movement. Though Lorde was an important mentor, they were truly surprised that she wanted to meet them in person. In her memoir *Invisible Woman: Growing Up Black in Germany* (which won an Audre Lorde Literary Award), Ika Hügel-Marshall described her first meeting with Lorde, which took place in 1987 at the Frankfurt airport: "Audre Lorde walked through the cordoned-off arrival area and straight toward me. She put her arms around me and hugged me to her and said my name. I was stunned . . . that she knew my name. It turned out she'd seen pictures from the first Afro-German conference held in Munich. She had asked the name of each participant and remembered us all."[24]

Such intimate connections have ethical and political implications. "Who are they, the German women of the Diaspora? . . . What can we learn from our connected differences that will be useful to both, Afro-German and Afro-American?" Lorde asked in "A Burst of Light." In a later entry she repeated, "Who are we? What are the ways in which we do not see each other? And how can we better operate together as a united front even while we explore our differences?"[25] Extending the work of Adriana Cavarero and Hannah Arendt but writing in the context of modernism, Jessica Berman has drawn attention to the "reciprocal exposure of the self to others through the mutual question 'who are you?'" as a way of proposing a transnational ethics and politics—an idea that Lorde, too, seems to pose here.[26] Lorde, of course, did not cease to define herself in brave acts of public self-identification, thus constantly answering, "Who are you?" with "black, lesbian, feminist, mother, poet, warrior." By asking, "Who are they, the German women of the Diaspora?" she united herself and these women in what Berman calls "a mutual relationship of responsibility" but, as the essays in this book demonstrate, "not necessarily in similarity, normativity, or consensus."[27] Lorde's emphasis on "the connected differences" between Afro-Germans and African Americans is reflected in recent critiques of theoretical models of the African diaspora that perpetuate black America's hegemonic role. By drawing attention to the asymmetries of power across and within black diasporic communities, scholars of the African diaspora, like Lorde, have affirmed the need to continually explore the intersection between the transnational and the local.[28]

Lorde worked with Afro-German women as they put together *Showing Our Colors,* which was published in German in 1986. Edited by May Opitz, Katharina Oguntoye, and Dagmar Schultz, it traced "the little-known history of white racism in Germany and its influence upon Black German men and women from the first African arrival to the present" and offered insights into the complexities of a future global feminism.[29] The book's publication triggered the formation of the *Initiative Schwarze Deutsche* (ISD), the first national organization of Black Germans. With Lorde, the women coined the term *Afro-German,* which, like the analogous *Afro-American,* was an attempt to define themselves instead of being defined by others as "half-breed," "mulatto," or "colored."[30]

As Lorde extended her stay in Europe, she deepened her perspectives about such hyphenated identities:

> Whatever our differences are that make for difficulty in communication between us and other oppressed peoples, as Afro-Americans, we must recognize the promise we represent for some new social synthesis that the world has not yet experienced. I think of the Afro-Dutch, Afro-German, Afro-French women I met this spring in Europe and how they are beginning to recognize each other and come together openly in terms of their identities, and I see that they are also beginning to cut a distinct shape across the cultural face of every country where they are at home.[31]

Similarly in her 1988 speech, "The Dream of Europe," Lorde told listeners that Europe had been a nightmare for her and that her dream, her vision of Europe's future, depended on "the hyphenated people of Europe who represent a last chance for Europe to learn how to deal with difference creatively."[32]

Lorde's Atlantic and global travels helped her reflect on the label *black.* While she was in the Netherlands, for example, and speaking with many women from Indonesia and Suriname who identified as both Dutch and symbolically black, she observed:

STELLA BOLAKI AND SABINE BROECK

> I see certain pitfalls in defining Black as a political position. It takes the cultural identity of a widespread but definite group and makes it a generic identity for many culturally diverse peoples, all on the basis of a shared oppression. This runs the risk of providing a convenient blanket of apparent similarity under which our actual and unaccepted differences can be distorted or misused. This blanket would diminish our chances of forming genuine working coalitions built upon the recognition and creative use of acknowledging difference, rather than upon the shaky foundations of a false sense of similarity.[33]

As she did later in her Melbourne address, "The Language of Difference," Lorde cautioned against the false sense of similarity that a common term such as *black* can create.[34] In her foreword to *Showing Our Colors* she also clarified that even when the term is not adopted symbolically, black diasporic experiences are heterogeneous.

Lorde actively sought and forged connections with people who were not seen as part of a recognizable black diasporic community or whom African Americans considered to be virtually nonexistent. She recognized that their experiences could not be articulated through dominant models of diaspora that revolve around ideas of displacement (the trope of the Middle Passage) or collective migration and of a shared home or culture according to the contemporary scholarship on the "Black Atlantic." As Lorde stressed in *Showing Our Colors*, "first we must recognize each other. Some of these [Black European] women have sustained and nurturing relationships with their African relatives. Others have grown into Blackness in the almost total absence of a Black community. What does it mean to be defined negatively from birth in one's own country because of a father who one may never see or know? How do you come to define a cultural identity when there has been no other Black person seen throughout your childhood?"[35] Lorde acknowledged a conversation with Ika Hügel-Marshall in relation to this point, but she could have equally spoken of Afro-Scot poet Jackie Kay, one of our contributors, who has written extensively about the loneliness of growing up black in Glasgow.[36] In a 2008 article for *The Guardian* Kay wrote, "I remember first reading *The Black Unicorn* in Brixton in 1981 (when Brixton was burning in the riots), before I'd ever met Audre, and then asking Sisterwrite bookshop in Upper Street, Islington, to order everything they could by her. It was like finding a friend."[37]

Such moments of sisterly solidarity were mutual. Lorde's travels filled her with energy and courage to fight cancer; and like *Zami* and *The Cancer*

Journals, "A Burst of Light" recognized the importance of a female network of friends and lovers to whom she owed her survival. In a 1986 entry from Bonnieux in southern France, she wrote, "How incredibly rich to be here in the south of France with the Zamani Soweto Sisters from South Africa . . . I learn tremendous courage from these women, from their laughter and their tears, from their grace under constant adversity, from their joy in living which is one of their most potent weapons, from the deft power of their large, overworked bodies and their dancing, swollen feet."[38] The Zamani Soweto Sisters were one of the two women's self-help groups in South Africa that had developed a relationship with Sisterhood in Support of Sisters in South Africa (SISA), established by Gloria Joseph in 1984. Lorde was among the founding mothers of SISA, whose goals included resisting apartheid, fighting poverty and illiteracy in the country, and promoting bonds between black American and black South African women. South African activist and author Ellen Kuzwayo, who became a close friend of Lorde, addressed her and the audience of the "I Am Your Sister" conference with the following words: "Let me say to you, Audre, that your name is known in Soweto. You are greatly thought of for the work that you have done . . . The struggle in South Africa is so much interwoven with the struggle of your own country."[39]

As Lorde traveled, her reflections on her responsibility as an African American woman extended to concerns closer to home:

> Sitting with Black women all over the earth has made me think a great deal about what it means to be indigenous, and what my relationship as a Black woman in North America is to the land rights struggles of the indigenous peoples to this land, to Native American Indian women, and how we can translate that consciousness into a new level of working together. In other words, how can we use each other's differences in our common battles for a livable future?[40]

Nevertheless, not all of her travel experiences and international activities were positive. For example, in her foreword to *Showing Our Colors,* she wrote of a poetry reading in Dresden in 1990, where "for the first time in six years I [was] afraid as I read my poetry in Germany."[41] Some of the better-known poems inspired by her stay in Berlin express her concern about Black Germans, especially after Germany's reunification, which led to many violent racist actions toward not only Afro-Germans but also Turkish and Pakistani people. Among those poems are "Berlin is Hard on Colored Girls" from *Our*

Dead Behind Us (1986) and "East Berlin" from the posthumously released *The Marvelous Arithmetics of Distance* (1993), which mentions an "Afro-German woman stomped to death / by skinheads in Alexanderplatz."[42] In a letter to Adrienne Rich in September 1992, Lorde described the climate in Berlin and the antiracist campaigns held in response. Subtly alluding to her deteriorating health, she noted, "I cannot help but be engaged, but am doing so in a way that is possible for me."[43] As an example, she enclosed the protest letter that she and Gloria Joseph had sent to Chancellor Helmut Kohl, protesting the well-publicized violent attacks against migrants in Rostock: "We watch Rostock and our hearts grow heavy with fear for our own safety, and for the safety of our Afro-German sisters and brothers, as well as for the safety of Jews, and foreigners, and all others who white German reactionaries may decide are unacceptable because of how they are, and therefore suitable objects of social fury and destruction. Is this the new German version of 'ethnic cleansing'?"[44]

Lorde also had problematic experiences elsewhere in Europe. After a poetry reading in Zurich in May 1984, Lorde described Swiss women as "insular, . . . more interested in gazing at the lives of black women in America than focused upon the need for change in their own environment and ignoring, therefore, the fact that cancer was on the rise in the cities of Basel and Zurich."[45] Several entries in "A Burst of Light," written in 1985 and 1986 while she spent three weeks in the Lukas Klinik in Arlesheim for cancer treatment, continue to criticize Swiss insularity:

> Good morning, Christmas. A Swiss bubble is keeping me from talking to my children and the women I love. The front desk won't put my calls through. Nobody here wants to pierce this fragile, delicate bubble that is the best of all possible worlds, they believe. So frighteningly insular. Don't they know good things get better by opening them up to others, giving and taking and changing? Most people here seem to feel that rigidity is a bona fide pathway to peace, and every fibre of me rebels against that.[46]

Lorde was disappointed by the first International Feminist Book Fair held in London in June 1984, which she called "a monstrosity of racism." As she noted, she was "accused of brutalizing the organizers by simply asking why Black women were absent" from the audience.[47] However, through different channels, she managed to make contact with the black feminists of England, which was her original reason for coming to London. In an article for *The Guardian* titled "My Hero: Audre Lorde," Kay fondly recalled her first meeting with Lorde in London, just after Sheba Feminist Publishers had released *Zami* in the United Kingdom to coincide with the Feminist Book Fair: "I first met Audre in 1984, when I was 22. She told me her grandfather had been Scottish, and that I didn't need to choose between being Scottish and being black. 'You can be both. You can call yourself an Afro Scot,' she said in her New York drawl."[48] In December of that year, Kay, along with Dorothea, a black poet of Afro-Caribbean descent living in South London, and Uma, a black feminist and political activist of Indian descent who had grown up in the South Pacific, interviewed Lorde for the feminist magazine *Spare Rib*. In that interview Lorde expressed her frustration at not being able to meet with black women privately at the book fair: "You're the women to whom I am writing, you're the women I need to contact and to touch, . . . and hey, what am I here for? What am I here for in this rainy place . . . doing this doing that?" Emphasizing Lorde's wide sisterhood across Britain as well as the rest of the world, the interviewers noted, "We're doing this interview for the one Black woman sitting out in the . . . Welsh countryside say who's gonna read this . . . in the Pacific . . . or even in some other part of the world."[49]

A few years later, Kay and filmmaker Pratibha Parmar interviewed Lorde for *Charting the Journey*, a collection of writing by black and "Third World" women. In that interview, reprinted as "Frontiers" in this book, Lorde stressed the need for an international black feminist movement but was careful not to obscure differences: "Now your history as Black women in England is a very complex one, and I certainly do not know enough to generalize." She closed by expressing her wish to continue to aid the living of "political lives": "I'm so impressed . . . with the press [that published *Charting the Journey*], with how you work together . . . I love to see Black women achieving on so many levels, and you're doing it. That's really wonderful. I would like to inject even more of that into Black women's groups everywhere."[50]

Lorde's transnational connections extended beyond Europe. In addition to her work with SISA and the South African women's groups, she had the chance to meet Maori and Pacific Island women during a 1985 stop in New Zealand before going on to Australia, where she had been invited to be a keynote speaker at the Women 150 Writers' Week in Melbourne. In her address, "The Language of Difference," she cautioned against the seductive

STELLA BOLAKI AND SABINE BROECK

belief that sharing a common language also means sharing the same experience: "It is when language appears most similar that it becomes most dangerous, for differences may pass for a time, unremarked." Expressing solidarity with her aboriginal black sisters and their land struggles, she urged her audience to "learn to hear and to feel" their language "without sentimentality and without the impotence of guilt: And remember these women are not exotic oddities. Do not objectify them. They are not instruments of your education. They are joint inheritors of this land. Learn their anger and their pain as well as your own." She concluded, "We are alien and particular from each other, but we can learn each other's tongue. And as we learn the language of difference, we will someday be able to speak of a true feminism."[51]

In 1980, Lorde visited Saint Croix in the U.S. Virgin Islands for a conference on violence against women organized by the Sojourner Sisters and helped to establish the Saint Croix's Women's Coalition, a counseling and advocacy community group focused on domestic violence. In 1986, she visited the island again for two conferences: "Caribbean Women: The Historical and Cultural Ties That Bind," organized by her partner Gloria Joseph; and the first "Conference of Caribbean Women Writers," organized by the Sojourner Sisters. As she wrote in "A Burst of Light," Lorde was "proud to speak and read [her] work as a Caribbean woman."[52] The following year, Lorde and Joseph returned to Saint Croix, where Lorde had decided to live and continue her work until the end of her life. As her 1990 interview with Charles H. Rowell made clear, she had ongoing concerns about the colonial relationship that Saint Croix maintains with the United States, an issue that also arose in her essay "Grenada Revisited: An Interim Report" about the 1983 U.S. military invasion of Grenada.[53]

Zami, in which Lorde describes her coming of age as the daughter of Caribbean immigrants from Grenada, may be the text that best addresses the Afro-Caribbean identity that she both inherited and fashioned for herself. The film Litany also captures this identity powerfully. In its beautiful opening sequence, we see the image of sea, later identified with the title "St. Croix, U.S. Virgin Islands," and archival footage of people disembarking from ships in the West Indies juxtaposed with color images of Lorde standing on cliffs looking out to sea. We hear her voice saying, "There is a point here where the Atlantic meets the Caribbean," that standing here "as an African Caribbean American woman, I could feel flowing through me Africa, the horrors of the Middle Passage, those fathers and mothers of mine who survived that, who came to these shores here, who came to Grenada, Barbados, the connection there with the indigenous people of these islands, and who I am as I sit in this place. It felt as if there was a total consciousness for one moment of all of these threads."

In the first stanza of her unpublished poem "Legacy," Lorde expressed her fear that nothing of her work would be left after her passing:

> No one can say what I have to say
> in my own way of saying it
> if the song freezes
> it will never be sung.[54]

There is no doubt about the singularity of Lorde's contribution, but voices from around the world continue to sing her song. As she wrote in "A Burst of Light,"

> We all have to die at least once. Making that death useful would be winning for me . . . Just writing those words down snaps everything I want to do into a neon clarity. The European trip and the Afro-German women, the Sister Outsider collective in Holland, Gloria's great idea of starting an organization that can be a connection between us and South African women. For the first time I really feel that my writing has a substance and stature that will survive me.[55]

The essays in this book are organized around three separate but interrelated themes. Part I, "Archives," includes contributions by people who were both historical witnesses and members of Lorde's personal community of transnational friends and sisters. The section also includes a speech by Lorde and two interviews with her from the 1980s. The majority of the pieces in this section weave the authors' biographical trajectories and their recollections of Lorde's interactions in Europe during the 1980s into larger questions of Europe's cultural, historical, and political identity. They also address the reception and ongoing impact of her work in different European countries, especially within black diasporic and feminist/queer communities and international organizations. All of them demonstrate the importance of transatlantic and transnational archives and remind us that memory, oral history, and personal reflections can be, in Ann Cvetkovich's words, "loaded with emotional urgency and need" that speak to the present and the future.[56]

Part II, "Connections," draws on a range of academic perspectives to discuss the reception and circulation of Lorde's work in various contexts and communities. An important focus is her theorization of sisterhood, solidarity, and difference and the ways in which they materialized through her activism and the formal aesthetics of her writing. Essays in the section consider Lorde's approach to the concept of sisterhood; her complex connections to specific sisterhoods and geopolitical contexts; the way in which encounters with diasporic communities shaped her thinking, poetic practice, and commitment to mutual struggles; her ideas about the intimate economies of geopolitics and the way in which the erotic may function as a counter-hegemonic force; and her thoughts about the black transnational feminist praxis in relation to the majority black spaces of South Africa and the Caribbean.

Part III, "Work," pays homage to a word that recurs throughout Lorde's speeches and writings, both as a verb ("work together") and as a noun: "I am a Black feminist lesbian warrior poet doing my work, and a piece of my work is asking you, how are you doing yours?"[57] The essays in this section focus on the diverse forms of work that Lorde has inspired and influenced: in literature and art, community action, grass-roots organizing and activism, teaching, and thought and theory. These ideas and practices are Lorde's transnational legacies, "the intimate exchange that takes place when true learning—teaching—occurs, of feeling myself and the perception of and reacting to the feelings of other human beings. Because of course we all must realize that it is this exchange which is the most strongly prohibited, or discouraged, human exercise of our time."[58]

Toward the end of the film *A Litany for Survival*, Lorde addresses the camera: "When you open and read something that I wrote, the power that you feel from it doesn't come from me; that's the power that you own." She goes on to explain that, for each of us, identifying this power and putting it to use matters more than anything. Her statement raises the question of legacy and its relationship to the future. As Sara Ahmed has written in *The Cultural Politics of Emotion*, "when we think [of] the question of feminist futures, we also need to attend to the legacies of feminist pasts, what we have inherited from past feminists." Examining the link between feminism and hope, she continues, "It is in the present that the bodies of subjects shudder with an expectation of what is otherwise; it is in the unfolding of the past in the present. The moment of hope is when the 'not yet' impresses upon us in the present, such that we must act, politically, to make it our future."[59] In their various unfoldings of Lorde's life and writings, the essays in our book demonstrate precisely how her transnational legacies involve multiple present impressions of the "not yet." As Lorde so eloquently wrote in "A Burst of Light,"

> This is why the work is so important. Its power doesn't lie in the me that lives in the words so much as in the heart's blood pumping behind the eye that is reading, the muscle behind the desire that is sparked by the word—hope as a living state that propels us, open-eyed and fearful, into all the battles of our lives. And some of those battles we do not win.
> But some of them we do.[60]

Notes

1. Audre Lorde, "The Transformation of Silence into Language and Action," in *The Audre Lorde Compendium: Essays, Speeches, and Journals,* introduced by Alice Walker (London: Pandora, 1996), 13.
2. Audre Lorde, "The Master's Tools Will Never Dismantle the Master's House," in *Audre Lorde Compendium,* 159.
3. Audre Lorde, "Foreword to the English Language Edition," in *Showing Our Colors: Afro-German Women Speak Out,* ed. May Opitz, Katharina Oguntoye, and Dagmar Schultz (Amherst: University of Massachusetts Press, 1992), xiii.
4. Lorde's speech appears in *The Edge of Each Other's Battles: The Vision of Audre Lorde,* dir. Jennifer Abod (New York: Women Make Movies, 2002).
5. Audre Lorde, "A Burst of Light: Living with Cancer," in *Audre Lorde Compendium,* 283.
6. A glance at the program for Lorde's memorial service in New York City's Cathedral of Saint John the Divine in January 1993 suffices to make this point. Thousands of people from around the globe gathered in remembrance of her life and legacy. The printed tributes on the program were from close friends, colleagues, publishers, and organizations in Hawaii, South Africa, Cuba, Germany, England, the Caribbean, and New Zealand. They included the Saint Croix Women's Coalition, the Union of Palestinian Women's Association in North America, the Disabled Persons Liberation Front, MADRE, Jews for Racial and Economic Justice, Asian Lesbians of the East Coast, the Asian and Pacific Islander Coalition on HIV/AIDS; and Other Countries: Black Gay Men Writing and Gay Men of African Descent.
7. Shelley Fisher Fishkin, "Crossroads of Cultures: The Transnational Turn in American Studies—Presidential Address to the American Studies Association, November 12, 2004," *American Quarterly* 57, no. 1 (2005): 17–57.
8. Paul Gilroy, *The Black Atlantic: Modernity and Double Consciousness* (London: Verso, 1993). For a selection of histories, see Michelle Wright, *Becoming Black: Creating Identity in the African Diaspora* (Durham, N.C.: Duke University Press, 2004); Tina

STELLA BOLAKI AND SABINE BROECK

Campt, *Other Germans: Black Germans and the Politics of Race, Gender, and Memory in the Third Reich* (Ann Arbor: University of Michigan Press, 2005); Tina Campt, *Image Matters: Archive, Photography, and the African Diaspora in Europe* (Durham, N.C.: Duke University Press, 2012); Yara-Colette Lemke Muniz de Faria, *Zwischen Fürsorge und Ausgrenzung: Afrodeutsche "Besatzungskinder" im Nachkriegsdeutschland* (Berlin: Metropol, 2002); Maria Diedrich and Jürgen Heinrichs, eds., *From Black to Schwarz: Cultural Crossovers between African America and Germany* (Münster: LIT, 2011); Jacqueline Nassy Brown, *Dropping Anchor, Setting Sail: Geographies of Race in Black Liverpool* (Princeton: Princeton University Press, 2005); Tyrel Stovall, *Paris Noir: African Americans in the City of Light* (Boston: Houghton Mifflin, 1996); Brent Edwards, *The Practice of Diaspora: Literature, Translation, and the Rise of Black Internationalism* (Cambridge, Mass.: Harvard University Press, 2003); Heike Raphael-Hernandez, ed., *Blackening Europe: The African American Presence* (New York: Routledge, 2004); Darlene Clark Hine, Trica Danielle Keaton, and Stephen Small, eds., *Black Europe and the African Diaspora* (Champaign: University of Illinois Press, 2009); and Fatima El-Tayeb, *European Others: Queering Ethnicity in Postnational Europe* (Minneapolis: University of Minnesota Press, 2011).

9. Alexis De Veaux, *Warrior Poet: A Biography of Audre Lorde* (New York: Norton, 2004); Rudolph P. Byrd, Johnnetta Betsch Cole, and Beverly Guy-Sheftall, eds., *I Am Your Sister: Collected and Unpublished Writings of Audre Lorde* (Oxford: Oxford University Press, 2009). Also see Lester C. Olson, "Review of Rudolph P. Byrd, Johnetta Betsch Cole, and Beverly Guy-Sheftall, eds., *I Am Your Sister: Collected and Unpublished Writings of Audre Lorde*," *Quarterly Journal of Speech* 96 (2010): 338–42.

10. Joan Wylie Hall, ed., *Conversations with Audre Lorde* (Jackson: University Press of Mississippi, 2004); May Opitz, Katharina Oguntoye, and Dagmar Schultz, eds., *Showing Our Colors: Afro-German Women Speak Out* (Amherst: University of Massachusetts Press, 1992); Peggy Piesche, ed., *"Euer Schweigen schützt euch nicht": Audre Lorde und die Schwarze Frauenbewegung in Deutschland* (Berlin: Orlanda Frauenverlag, 2012).

11. *Audre Lorde—The Berlin Years 1984 to 1992*, dir. Dagmar Schultz (New York: Third World Newsreel, 2012); *A Litany for Survival: The Life and Work of Audre Lorde*, dir. Ada Gay Griffin and Michelle Parkerson (New York: Third World Newsreel, 1995).

12. Aishah Shahidah Simmons, "Afterword: Standing at the Lordean Shoreline," *The Feminist Wire*, March 1, 2014, http://thefeministwire.com.

13. Audre Lorde, *Zami: A New Spelling of My Name* (London: Sheba, 1982), 226.

14. Audre Lorde, "The Cancer Journals," in *Audre Lorde Compendium*, 46.

15. Audre Lorde, "My Words Will be There," in *I Am Your Sister*, 163.

16. Portions of this section appear in Stella Bolaki, "Illness and Transatlantic Sisterhoods in Audre Lorde's 'A Burst of Light: Living with Cancer,'" *Symbiosis* 17, no. 1 (April 2013): 3–20, and are reprinted with permission of the journal.

17. Audre Lorde, *The Cancer Journals* (London: Sheba, 1985).

18. Audre Lorde, *The Marvelous Arithmetics of Distance: Poems, 1987–1992* (New York: Norton, 1993).

19. Lorde, "A Burst of Light," 273.

20. De Veaux, *Warrior Poet*, 340.

21. Lorde, "A Burst of Light," 272.

22. Ibid., 335.

23. Ibid., 275.

24. Ika Hügel-Marshall, *Invisible Woman: Growing Up Black in Germany*, trans. Elizabeth Gaffney (London: Continuum, 2001), 112.

25. Lorde, "A Burst of Light," 276, 281.
26. Jessica Berman, *Ethics, Politics, and Transnational Modernism* (New York: Columbia University Press, 2011), 75.
27. Ibid., 18.
28. On the asymmetries of power in diasporic studies, see, for example, Tina Campt, "The Crowded Space of Diaspora: Intercultural Address and the Tensions of Diasporic Relation," *Radical History Review* 83 (Spring 2002): 94–113; and Jacqueline Nassy Brown, "Black Liverpool, Black America, and the Gendering of Diasporic Space," *Cultural Anthropology* 13, no. 3 (August 1998): 291–325.
29. Lorde, "Foreword," ix.
30. Ibid., xxiii.
31. Lorde, "A Burst of Light," 282–83.
32. Audre Lorde, "The Dream of Europe," speech, Berlin, May 1988, box 17, Audre Lorde Papers, Spelman College Archives (hereafter cited as Lorde Papers). Also see chapter 1.
33. Lorde, "A Burst of Light," 283.
34. Audre Lorde, "The Language of Difference," speech, Women 150 Writers' Week, Melbourne, September 1985, box 21, Lorde Papers.
35. Lorde, "Foreword," ix–x.
36. This acknowledgment appears in an earlier version of the foreword. See Audre Lorde, "Showing Our True Colors," *Callaloo* 14, no. 1 (1991): 71, n.1.
37. Jackie Kay, "The Enemy of Silence," *The Guardian*, October 13, 2008, www.theguardian.com.
38. Lorde, "A Burst of Light," 309–10.
39. The speech is depicted in *Vision of Audre Lorde*. See also Audre Lorde, "Apartheid U.S.A.," in *Audre Lorde Compendium*, 253–61.
40. Lorde, "A Burst of Light," 289.
41. Lorde, "Foreword," xiii.
42. Audre Lorde, "Berlin Is Hard on Colored Girls," in *Our Dead Behind Us* (New York: Norton, 1994), 22–23; Audre Lorde, "East Berlin," in *The Marvelous Arithmetics of Distance*, 50.
43. Audre Lorde, letter to Adrienne Rich, September 20, 1992, box 1, Lorde Papers.
44. Ibid.
45. De Veaux, *Warrior Poet*, 341.
46. Lorde, "A Burst of Light," 301.
47. Ibid., 280–81.
48. Jackie Kay, "My Hero: Audre Lorde," *The Guardian*, November 18, 2011, www.theguardian.com.
49. Audre Lorde, Dorothea, Jackie Kay, and Uma, ". . . No, We Never Go Out of Fashion . . . for Each Other!" *Spare Rib* 149 (December 1984): 27, 29.
50. See chapter 5.
51. Lorde, "The Language of Difference."
52. Lorde, "A Burst of Light," 306.
53. This colonial relationship was evident after Hurricane Hugo. At a time when Saint Croix was in need of electricity, water, and food, the U.S. government brought in military personnel to guard Hess Oil, the largest oil refinery in the western hemisphere. See Audre Lorde and Charles H. Rowell, "Above the Wind: An Interview with Audre Lorde," *Callaloo* 14, no. 1 (Winter 1991): 84–85.
54. Audre Lorde, "Legacy," unpublished poem, box 31, Lorde Papers.

STELLA BOLAKI AND SABINE BROECK

55. Lorde, "A Burst of Light," 279.
56. Ann Cvetkovich, *An Archive of Feelings: Trauma, Sexuality, and Lesbian Public Cultures* (Durham, N.C.: Duke University Press, 2008), 166.
57. Audre Lorde, "Commencement Address: Oberlin College," in *I Am Your Sister*, 214.
58. Audre Lorde, "Poet as Teacher—Human as Poet—Teacher as Human," in *I Am Your Sister*, 183.
59. Sara Ahmed, *The Cultural Politics of Emotion* (Edinburgh: Edinburgh University Press, 2004), 183, 184.
60. Lorde, "A Burst of Light," 293.

I
ARCHIVES

I
The Dream of Europe—Remarks

❦

AUDRE LORDE

Introduction by Sabine Broeck and Stella Bolaki

If one searches for the phrase "The Dream of Europe" online, a long list of notable white men appears—from British prime ministers Winston Churchill and David Cameron, through various European parliamentarians, to economic and social theorist Jeremy Rifkin. In a 2013 speech at Sofia University, reprinted on the news portal *Voxeurop*, political scientist Ivan Krastev asks with dramatic flair, "What happened to the European dream?"[1] But Audre Lorde's speech "The Dream of Europe" does not come up anywhere in the search results.[2]

Lorde delivered the speech at the conference "Der Traum von Europa: Schriftsteller laden Schriftsteller ein" ("The Dream of Europe: Authors Invite Authors"), which took place between May 25 and 29, 1988, at the House of the Cultures of the World in Berlin. In their letter of invitation, the organizers told her that the aim of the conference was "to discuss questions of Europe's cultural, historical, and political identity" and to "examine . . . at what point and in what way writers can intervene to provoke changes."[3] As Dagmar Schultz has noted, however, not everyone involved in the conference was convinced that Lorde, a black lesbian feminist, would make a crucial contribution to a debate about Europe:

> The panel Audre was invited to take part in was moderated by Green party politician Daniel Cohn-Bendit. Audre was told that the panel would be a loose discussion and that she did not need to prepare a speech. When she

was on the podium, she realized that all the other participants had prepared speeches, which of course angered her. She did have her notes and made a very strong statement. When there was no reaction to her statement, she got up and left the panel in protest.[4]

Today politicians and intellectuals concerned about Europe, including Green party activists and feminists, continue to overlook Lorde's contribution to the conversation. For example, Rosi Braidotti, who promotes and disseminates feminist multicultural agency in debates about the future of Europe and the European Union, has not addressed Lorde's ideas. One reason may be general racist disinterest or ignorance of the urgency of Lorde's project and her work in Europe. Another may be the particularly un- or anti-European message of her speech, which interrupted a white-on-white debate about the chances and pitfalls of European democratization.

Lorde's black knowledge intervention radically recalled and intertextually answered Aimé Césaire's post-Shoah anticolonial *Discourse on Colonialism*, first published in 1955, which indicted Europe as rotten to the core. Césaire wrote of "societies drained of their essence, cultures trampled underfoot, institutions undermined, lands confiscated, religions smashed, magnificent artistic creations destroyed, extraordinary possibilities wiped out" and went on to contend that "'Europe' is morally, spiritually indefensible."[5] In her speech Lorde described a rotten Europe, what she called a "nightmare," visible in the discourses and practices of fascist/racist violence against black immigrants, acts that were exacerbated by the white German state apparatus and the public's broad indifference. A new vision would be possible only if European countries owned up to their ongoing coloniality and acknowledged the crucial role of black Europeans in building a continent that respected past history and present difference.

While, time and again, such black epistemic critiques of Europe have gone unrecognized in white pronunciations of Europeanness, the organizers of an evening held in London in February 1993 to celebrate her life and work concluded their memorial statement with an acknowledgment of Lorde's relevance to the debate on Europe's future:

> In the context of the Europe of the "New World Order": in which unification means fortification; in which there is an alarming increase in racist violence and murder; in which organized and systematic mass rape is carried out in the name of an "ethnic cleansing" process reminiscent of another sinister period of European history, there is clear and present danger that silence and inactivity will yet again not protect us from horrors worse than our combined imaginations may muster. In this context Audre's physical absence only defines our task more sharply. She summons us to dare the journey toward wholeness.[6]

Audre Lorde at "The Dream of Europe" conference, held at the House of the Cultures of the World, Berlin, May 1988. PHOTOGRAPH © DAGMAR SCHULTZ.

I am an African-American poet and believe in the power of poetry. Poetry, like all art, has a function: to bring us closer to who we wish to be, to help us vision a future which has not yet been, and to help us survive the lack of that future. If we were reading our literature here tonight, we would be exchanging the real stuff of dreams, our visions, the essence of our future. But instead, we sit discussing a dream of Europe, rather than evoking that dream so it may become a reality. And that, for me, is a very European approach to dreaming.

For most of my life I did not dream of Europe at all except as nightmare. Some here say that Europe civilized the world. To me and two thirds of the world's population, People of Color, it is more like Europe enslaved the world. Seventeenth, eighteenth, and nineteenth century Europe came to the shores of Africa and bought my ancestors, packed them into floating sardine-cans, and sold them to other Europeans in the New World. In the early twentieth century Germany practiced in South West Africa the techniques of genocide later perfected in the Holocaust. Pass Laws were invented by Germans in South West Africa.

I was fifty years old before I came to Europe. When I did, I found people there that now compose my dream of Europe. They are Afro-European and other Black Europeans, those hyphenated people who, in concert with other people of the African Diaspora, are increasing forces for international change. We concentrate difference inside of us in ways that can illuminate the future with a light the world has not yet seen. I am an outsider, dreaming of Europe. But Black Europeans are not foreigners to you, not strangers. Yet I do not hear the voice of one Black European writer here and so I wonder how serious this dreaming can be.

I believe it is the hyphenated people of Europe who represent a last chance for Europe to learn how to deal with difference creatively, rather than pretending it does not exist, or destroying it.

Those of us who feel our star is in the ascendant do not need to diminish the efforts of others who wish to examine their own decline with grace. I bear no one here ill will. We have learned useful tools from Europe—and by "we" I mean that two thirds of the world's population that are People of Color. Our survival means learning to use difference for something other than destruction. So does yours.

And, with or without you, we are moving on.

Audre Lorde
A2 Judith's Fancy
Christiansted, Saint Croix 00820
U.S. Virgin Islands
U.S.A.

Notes

"The Dream of Europe," © by the Estate of Audre Lorde, used by permission of the Charlotte Sheedy Literary Agency.

1. Ivan Krastev, "What Happened to the European Dream?" *Voxeurop,* April 25, 2013, www.voxeurop.eu.
2. The only other published version of the speech appears in German: Dagmar Schultz, ed., *Macht und Sinnlichkeit: Audre Lorde und Adrienne Rich; Ausgewählte Texte* (Berlin: Orlanda Frauenverlag, 1993, 1983), 216–17.
3. Dieter Esche, letter to Audre Lorde, March 22, 1988, box 17, Audre Lorde Papers, Spelman College Archives.
4. Dagmar Schultz, personal correspondence with Sabine Broeck and Stella Bolaki, September 8, 2013.
5. Aimé Césaire, *Discourse on Colonialism,* trans. Joanne Pinkham (New York: Monthly Review Press, 2001), 43, 32.
6. "Audre Lorde: Reflections," *Feminist Review* 45 (Autumn 1993): 7.

2
Audre Lorde—The Berlin Years, 1984 to 1992

Transnational Experiences, the Making of a Film, and Its Reception

DAGMAR SCHULTZ

In 1980, I met Audre Lorde for the first time at the United Nations' "World Women's Conference" in Copenhagen in a discussion following her reading. I was spellbound and very much impressed with the openness with which she addressed us primarily white women. She talked about the importance of her work as a poet, about racism and differences among women, about women in Europe, the United States of America, and South Africa, and stressed the need for a vision of the future to guide our political practice. On that evening it became clear to me: Audre Lorde must come to Germany for German women to hear her, though at that point in time I had no idea of the role she would play for Black Germans and what that would mean for my own development. In the early 1980s, the autonomous women's movement had begun to show divisions between those who turned toward newly found spiritual and body-related aspects of women's lives, those who were committed to struggling against the abuse of women and confronting institutions of oppression, and those who found a new focus in the peace movement. Racism was even less a topic in Germany at large and in the women's movement than anti-Semitism was, and contact with women of foreign origin was largely restricted to certain social projects.[1] I had lived in the United States for a decade since 1963, studying, teaching, and being involved in the civil rights movement, the anti-war and the women's movements. Therefore, I had the advantage of being particularly conscious of the white predominance in the German women's movement and wanted to spur a critical reflection on structural and internalized racism.[2]

As an assistant professor at the John F. Kennedy Institute of North American Studies at the Free University of Berlin, I was in a position to propose Audre for a visiting professorship for a semester. In addition, as the copublisher of Orlanda Press (then known as sub rosa Frauenverlag), I decided in 1983 to edit the book *Macht und Sinnlichkeit* (which translates as *Power and Sensuality*), a collection of poems and essays by Audre Lorde and Jewish poet Adrienne Rich, Audre's close friend and colleague. This book not only helped launch a self-critical analysis of racism and anti-Semitism among white women in Germany but also prepared them for the encounter with Audre Lorde.

One of Audre's first questions on arriving in Berlin in 1984 was "Where are the Black Germans?" She soon established close contact with a number of black women, some of whom attended her classes that year. Thus began a political movement—and an awareness-building journey—that lasted until the end of her life. During that time she initiated work on the book *Farbe bekennen: Afro-deutsche Frauen auf den Spuren ihrer Geschichte,* which Orlanda published in 1986. (It was later published in English as *Showing Our Colors: Afro-German Women Speak Out.*)[3] That book had a decisive effect on the formation of a Black German movement as well as a surge of transatlantic research projects on Afro-Germans. We also published Audre's biomythography *Zami, The Cancer Journals,* a number of her essays, and part of her poetry, including a bilingual volume of forty-two poems she herself selected in 1992 during her last summer in Berlin.[4] Audre particularly encouraged Afro-German women to write of their experiences. As a result, several authors were published, the first being Katharina Oguntoye, May Ayim, and Ika Hügel-Marshall.[5] I was able to get two books translated into English and thus contribute substantially to transnational research on and contact between Black Germans and black Americans.[6]

Through her publications, but above all through her critical public stance about society's ignorance and obliviousness about racism, anti-Semitism, and discrimination of immigrants within and outside the women's movement, Audre made lasting contributions to the German political and cultural scene before and after the fall of the Berlin Wall. Her recurrent presence in Germany (she returned to Berlin in 1986 and after that each year until her death in 1992) gave impulse, for instance, to several

DAGMAR SCHULTZ

Audre Lorde near the Free University of Berlin, in the park next to the street Im Schwarzen Grund, where she lived during her guest professorship, 1984.
PHOTOGRAPH © DAGMAR SCHULTZ.

conferences of black, Jewish, and immigrant women confronting the state of their different communities and their interrelationships.[7] Audre did not stop challenging white German women to examine their relations to and with black women, migrant women, and Jewish women. From her conversations and readings held in the Federal German Republic, Switzerland, the Netherlands, East Berlin, and Dresden, many white women learned to be more conscious of their privileges and more responsible in the use of their power, as is also reflected in the reception of the film *Audre Lorde—The Berlin Years, 1984 to 1992*.

In November 1992, Audre's partner Gloria I. Joseph called us from Saint Croix, and my partner Ika Hügel-Marshall, May Ayim, and I went there to be with Audre when she passed away.

DEVELOPING THE IDEA OF MAKING A FILM

While Audre was in Berlin, I accompanied her to all her speaking and teaching engagements, and I felt compelled to record, both on audio and video-tape as well as through photography, as much as my amateur gear could hold. Audre described herself as "a photo bug" and did not mind at all my taking pictures. Sometimes she even posed for pictures or talked directly to the video camera. She considered me her house photographer, and it was clear to us both that I would eventually do something with these photos and videos.

In 1989, I worked closely with Michelle Parkerson and Ada Gay Griffin, the filmmakers of *A Litany for Survival: The Life and Work of Audre Lorde* (1995), who had come to Berlin to document Audre's time there and her unique role in igniting the Afro-German movement. Yet her life was so busy that *Litany* could do no more than mention the Berlin years. Thus, after her death, I realized that all my videotapes, audiotapes, and photographs could and should be used to tell this little-known chapter of her life so that her legacy would be complete.

In 1995, I recorded on video an interview with Gloria Joseph, sections of which eventually became part of *The Berlin Years*. But our journey to the completion of the film had many fits and starts. One major detour occurred in 1996, when May Ayim committed suicide at the age of thirty-six. This traumatic event inspired us to make sure that May's voice and legacy would not be lost. I therefore coproduced with director Maria Binder a film on her life, *Hope in My Heart: The May Ayim Story*.[8] In addition, May is an important protagonist in *The Berlin Years*.

TRANSLATING A VISION OF THE FILM INTO A PROJECT OF ARCHIVAL ACTIVISM

After finishing *Hope in My Heart,* I turned again to the film about Audre. I wanted it to serve as a project of archival activism—that is, to be a personal, individual, sociopolitical document that also generates activism. My vision was to show Audre on and offstage in the many different contexts that made up her life in Berlin and beyond. Because I had been in a position to introduce her to Germany and put her in touch with people who would benefit from her insights, I had served as a catalyst. My goal was to capture Audre's ability to empathize with, motivate, and empower women and men and, at the same time, convey the significance that her life in Berlin and her encounters with black and white women had held for her.

Reviewing all the material at my disposal, I began to see a series of themes crystallize, most of which had a transnational dimension: Audre's relationship with and influence on Black Germans and her ideas about the role of what she called the "hyphenated people" of Europe; the significance that the notion of difference had for her, especially in her interactions with white Germans; the importance she attached to a positive concept of power; her understanding of her multiple identities, including her identity as a black lesbian as she applied it to herself and as she discussed it with women of color and white women; and her views on racism, anti-Semitism, homophobia in Germany and beyond, and political strategies, alliances, and networking. The film would also focus on her interactions with her partner Gloria (who frequently accompanied her to Berlin and played a crucial role in her political and personal activities with black and white women) and Gloria's views on the time Audre spent in the city. Finally, I wanted to focus on cancer as a personal experience as well as both a medical and a political issue in a profit-centered economy. Audre neither denied her illness nor placed it at the center of her life, which I communicated in the film by showing her courage, fears, and fierce determination to live a joyful life despite her illness.

The offstage aspect became an important part of the film. Fun activities at the lake and in Berlin's cafés, shopping at the market, buying flowers, dancing in 1991 at her last party in my home, bedside conversations, and interactions between Audre and Gloria—all found their way into the film. As many viewers, including Audre's daughter, have confirmed, these scenes show an intimate side of her life without taking away from her tremendous political influence. Kim Hester Williams, an African American professor at Sonoma State University, once related that her students often find Audre Lorde intimidating and that she herself had always thought of her as a very serious person: "Yet [*The Berlin Years* offers] a very different and complementary side of her . . . This film fills in a gap."[9] This may be why Warren Crichlow, professor at York University in Toronto, has argued that the film "will certainly jump start new thinking in 'Lorde studies' . . . I left the screening of *Audre Lorde,* with its home-made honest aesthetic, feeling really provoked emotionally and intellectually."[10]

THE MAKING OF THE FILM

Third World Newsreel (TWN), the distributor of *A Litany for Survival,* let me purchase copies of material they had filmed with Audre in Berlin and had used only in parts. Because I had studied film and television in the 1960s, I knew how to write a scene log, and that is what I did for all my videotapes and for those from TWN that I considered to be useful. After getting the necessary permissions for including such material, I transcribed more than thirty audiotapes of readings with discussions, interviews, and talks so that I could develop the themes that I wanted to address. During this time I was also looking for a filmmaker, preferably a woman of color, who would work with me closely. I eventually chose one, but our collaboration ended in a conceptual difference as she was not willing to use any interviews with contemporaries in the film.

On the advice of a friend, a professional editor, I gave up looking for a filmmaker and found an editor, Aletta von Vietinghoff, who agreed with my ideas and was able to make my material cinematically interesting. Having already recorded the interviews with contemporaries, I had concluded that the story would best be told if those who, indeed, had been part of that historic time would write the script with me. Two Afro-German friends— my partner Ika and our close friend Ria Cheatom—took up the challenge, and both also feature in the film as interviewees and protagonists. During several intense weeks we reviewed the material, evaluated the interviews, and cowrote a four-hour script based on the themes I had generated as well as additional ones we had extrapolated from interviews.

Our film editor, Aletta, then helped us consolidate our script into a manageable seventy-nine minutes. This process involved streamlining interviews to avoid repetition, deciding if poor-quality archival material or private scenes such as bedtime conversations should be included, and considering how and when the film should deal with Audre's cancer experience. In reference to this last point, we had lengthy discussions about the extent to which her relationship with white naturopath Manfred Kuno, whom I had introduced to Audre, should be incorporated. A few viewers have objected to his presence in the film, but it was clear to us that he had played an important role in the last years of Audre's life. We believed that she would have wanted to include him, and Gloria Joseph agreed. The ending of the film was also a difficult decision, but we thought that Audre would have liked our choice of a dance scene. While Ika, Ria, and I made choices that arose from our close connection with Audre, Aletta made use of her creative and professional skills in selecting sound, generating thematic links (for instance, threading the crucial poem "A Litany for

Survival" throughout the film), and matching decades-old images of the interviewees with their present-day interviews.[11]

For reasons of time and editorial coherence, we were not able to include footage of Audre's encounters with women from other countries. The DVD version, however, includes more than seventy minutes' worth of special features, including a segment in which I talk about her international influence beyond Germany's borders, more readings and offstage scenes that feature Audre, and her last meeting with her South African comrade, author, and friend Ellen Kuzwayo, which took place in the summer of 1992 in Berlin.[12] The special features also include Audre's reflections on her literary work, which she shared with members of Orlanda Press in September 1992. I find this addition particularly important because it can be used as teaching material in the future. In addition to the special features, the English-language DVD offers soft subtitling in German, French, and Spanish. A study guide developed by Marion Kraft, translator of Audre's poetry and a protagonist in the film, is available on the film's website. We have also set up a YouTube channel that includes clips from the special features as well as interviews with viewers during our film tours.

Financing the film was, of course, an enormous problem. Initially, I applied to a major public film funding agency and was denied support because, according to the agency, this was neither a typical documentary nor an art film and the organization preferred not to fund portraits of authors. I did not apply to any public broadcasting institutions as I was told that the reaction would be similar, and I was wary about losing control over the development of my project. I therefore relied on many small and large donations from individuals, women's projects, foundations, and universities. (The film credits list all persons and projects as donors, whether they gave twenty euros or three thousand.) Fortunately, in 2011 I received the Margherita von Brentano Award for my lifework in promoting women's equality in academia, which helped me to complete the film and partially fund the establishment of an Audre Lorde archive at the Free University of Berlin. That collection, another example of archival activism, includes full audio recordings of three courses that Audre taught at the university in 1984; audio recordings and transcripts of more than thirty readings, discussions, and interviews; personal correspondence; photos and videos; and reviews, articles, and material from Orlanda Press relating to her books and readings.

The Berlin Years was accepted into the Berlinale 2012, the first important indication of a public positive reception. But before submitting it to the Berlinale, I had to receive Gloria's consent to let us use scenes that feature her and Audre, and I needed to present an almost final version to Audre's daughter, Elizabeth Lorde Rollins, as well as to one of Audre's sisters and a number of Audre's close friends and colleagues. We wanted these people to confirm that the film was informative and conveyed the essence of Audre's ideas and convictions and that the personal scenes did not damage their privacy.

The film was shown four times at the Berlinale and received huge applause each time. Being screened at a major film festival is a great advantage because other festivals are more likely to consider taking the film. By mid-2014 it had been shown at sixty-two festivals in twenty countries (twelve European nations as well as the United States, Canada, Turkey, Israel, Guyana, Ecuador, Uruguay, and India).[13] Twenty-nine of the events were LGBT or lesbian festivals, seventeen were focused on black and other people of color, and nine were women's festivals. Only seven had no focus on a specific population group; in addition to the Berlinale, they included the Beyond Film Festival of the Goethe Institute in San Francisco. The film received five festival awards for best documentary: two in Spain, two in the United States, and one in Canada.[14]

Screenings outside of festivals has addressed a diverse public. Within a little more than two years the film has been screened at least 125 times in various institutions, not counting screenings at about 120 British and North American universities and colleges. It has also been shown at the sixth Congrès International des Recherches Féministes Francophones in Lausanne, Switzerland (2012); the African Literature Association's annual conference in Charleston, South Carolina (2013); the Feminist and Women's Studies Association conference in Nottingham, England (2013); the annual meeting of the Black Germans and Blacks in Germany Initiative in Herleshausen (2013); the Yari Yari Ntoaso conference of the Organization of Women Writers of Africa in Accra, Ghana (2013); and many other feminist- and black-focused events in Germany, England, the Netherlands, France, Italy, Denmark, Serbia, Switzerland, Canada, Mexico, and Australia.

The twentieth anniversary of Audre's death in 2012 was a good time to reintroduce her to today's young students, so I created a traveling Audre

Lorde's Legacy Cultural Festival. It consisted of several films, including *The Berlin Years* and *Hope in My Heart,* as well as a reading by Ika from her book *Invisible Woman.*[15] In March of that year Ika and I brought the festival to Spelman College in Atlanta, home of the Audre Lorde Archives, and to universities in North Carolina and the Brecht Forum in New York City. The University of Kent was the first in Europe to host the festival, and a diverse, highly interested audience attended the event at the Women's Library in London. In the fall of 2012, a second tour took us to ten universities, from the University of Hawaii, to institutions in California, Chicago, and Massachusetts, to Hunter College in New York City, where Audre had taught.

In March 2013, Marion Kraft and I brought *The Berlin Years* to the "Conference on the Contemporary Urgencies of Audre Lorde's Legacy" at the University of Toronto, an event that brought together students and the community and where Gloria Wekker, Audre's friend and a member of the black women's movement in the Netherlands, shared a panel with us. Presentations followed at the Rainbow Reels Queer Festival in Waterloo, Ontario; Indiana University; and the Goethe Institute in New York City. Everywhere we met a diverse public of students, faculty, and community members, some of whom had known Audre personally. In 2014, I traveled with the film to the California Institute of the Arts in San Francisco, to Berkeley University, and to the City University of New York, where it continued to provoke enthusiastic responses and often raised moving discussions about identity issues among people of color.[16]

As viewers have recognized, transnational and transcultural issues are crucial dimensions of the film, which Audre herself attests to in an early scene: "I feel myself sometimes in the tradition, in the old basic tradition of a traveling cultural worker. That's right, just like the troubadours crossed continents singing the things they felt and believed . . . that's how I often feel. To begin with, I love to travel. I love to experience new people in different places, in different ways . . . and to learn, to learn." This genuine desire for exchange characterized her interactions and gives breadth to the film.

According to Elaine Castillo, "the heart of the film" lies in Audre's "deep enthusiasm and commitment to fostering international solidarity, dialogue, and exchange between all women, in particular women of color, women of the African Diaspora, and queer women." She points out that

Audre did not come to Germany with the aim of exporting a version of American feminism but with "the hope of diversifying the landscape of feminism everywhere."[17] In April 2012 Sara Ahmed touched on this transnational dimension in her introductory talk at the Fringe! Queer Film and Arts Festival in London: "We learn especially of the importance of a transnational black feminist politics: of what can happen when African-American and Afro-German women speak to each other, when women of colour across the diasporas speak to each other; between generations, across time as well as space."[18] When asked what the gay movement can learn from other movements, Wieland Speck, director of Panorama, the section of the Berlinale in which the film was screened, said, "I believe that many movements can learn from each other. The documentary *Audre Lorde—The Berlin Years* . . . demonstrates this in a very vivid way."[19]

As the film makes clear, Audre's contribution to theory has been gravely underrated. The concept of intersectionality is often attributed to Kimberlé Crenshaw and Patricia Hill Collins—if black authors are credited with it at all.[20] But long before, Audre Lorde had talked and written about the intersections of various oppressions. She was also an early exponent of the idea of critical whiteness and the concepts of multiple identities and hyphenated people, of power and difference. As many of the essays in this book show, what has frequently become a fashionable academic exercise was for Audre a lived reality. She saw no use in any theory that was separate from practice.

Alexis Pauline Gumbs, a black author and critic from the United States, has addressed another major theme of *The Berlin Years,* namely Audre's impact on white women's consciousness: "Created by a white German feminist colleague and comrade of Lorde's, the film importantly includes many of Lorde's imperatives to white feminist would-be allies . . . Many women of color who are tired of telling white feminists what Audre Lorde and many other feminists of color have already stated so clearly hope that our would-be allies will pay special attention to these moments in the film."[21] Confirming Gumbs's hope, a number of white women have commented on the film website that they are learning from the film to acknowledge differences in their own and in black women's experiences, to confront their own racism, and take part in the struggle against all forms of it.

In the German context a more localized perspective reflecting another kind of transnationalism has emerged. Sandra Campe, who lives in the former German Democratic Republic, has recognized how white and

DAGMAR SCHULTZ

heteronormative both her project Ökodorf Sieben Linden (Ecological Village of Seven Linden Trees) and her region are, and how important it is to face her acquired racisms and overcome them.[22] Gabriele Zekina, another German feminist activist, has reflected self-critically on the era after Germany's reunification:

> I found it so interesting and understandable in the film that those years were very alarming years as far as racist violence is concerned. I could understand in a somewhat different way why we "East women" were met with so many feelings of resentment. The opening of the East seemed to call into question much of what Audre Lorde and you and many other women had been struggling for and you must have felt as if time was rewinding.[23]

Intergenerational aspects have arisen in review articles and comments we have received from people of various ages and ethnic and national backgrounds. Members of the older generation (age thirty-five plus) who are familiar with Audre's work have relished this new encounter with her in the film, emphasizing that "whether you're black / feminist / female / lesbian / into poetry, . . . generations of women continue to be influenced by her."[24] Younger viewers have written that "Audre Lorde's persistence inspired me to ask myself what I am doing to live a self determined life," and some have called on their peers "to see the film and go home right away to read Audre's books—and then translate the new realizations into action."[25]

German intergenerational perspectives often reflect on the past and critically look at the nation's present situation. For example, Gotlinde Magiriba Lwanga, a white German mother of an Afro-German son, has written, "What shocked me [in the film] is the up-to-dateness. On the one hand there are many more niches and much more space for Black identities and solidarity bridges. On the other hand so little has changed in the white 'German-German' self-conception of superiority, in the 'we' that excludes the 'others.'" Her son, Johnny Strange (also known as John M. Lwanga), is a member of the German band Culcha Candela. "I grew up as an Afro-German child of the generation after the young women shown in the film," he notes. "In my generation there were already many more of us, but above all we had the chance to grow up with more contact to our African parent. To see how difficult life was for Black Germans without this relation and above all without a respected identity in the public perception was quite fascinating for me and I could understand it very well through this film."[26]

Archival activism involves awareness of the past, readiness to evaluate the present, and purposeful willingness to move toward a vision of the future. Castillo has asked herself what Audre, who experienced the rise of the neo-Nazi scene in Germany in the late 1980s, would have to say about the multitude of reactionary developments in recent years. Wekker has stressed that an analysis of the ways in which gender, class, and ethnicity interact in our daily lives is still absent from Dutch public discourse.[27] Ahmed has made a similar statement in her introduction at the Fringe! Festival:

> We can also reflect on why this film matters now . . . Through watching Audre's Berlin years, through watching her at work, we can reflect on the politics of black, feminist, and queer activisms today . . . Audre showed us how feminism can be about new ways of being in the world, suggesting that if we do not use the master's tools, if we build with our own hands, we can create new dwellings . . . I do think of her as a feminist killjoy, . . . And we learn from this film that the life of a kill-joy can be a life full of joy, the joy of possibility, the joy of world creation.[28]

It has taken us twenty years to complete this project. Judging by the reactions, the film has come at the right time, touching many people deeply and moving them to reflect on their position in society, to live their manifold identities, and to become more active. As Peter J. Piercy wrote after the screening of the film at London's Fringe! Festival, "[it was] amazing, and [a] testament to [Audre's] awesome power that everyone I spoke to afterwards felt inspired to be bolder and more ambitious in their own work and activism, and [were] buzzing with ideas about things they wanted to do next."[29] Along with everyone who has been involved in making this film, I say, "Thank you, Audre, and may your spirit inspire us and many people in times to come."

Notes

1. Dagmar Schultz, "The German Women's Movement in 1982," in *German Feminism: Readings in Politics and Literature*, ed. Edith Hoshino Altbach, Jeanette Clausen, Dagmar Schultz, and Naomi Stephan (Albany: State University of New York Press, 1984), 368–77.
2. Dagmar Schultz, "Witnessing Whiteness—ein persönliches Zeugnis," in *Mythen, Masken, und Subjekte: Kritische Weißseinsforschung in Deutschland,* ed. Maureen Maisha Eggers,

DAGMAR SCHULTZ

Susan Arndt, Grada Kiloma, and Peggy Piesche (Münster: Unrast, 2005), 514–29; Dagmar Schultz, preface, *Macht und Sinnlichkeit: Audre Lorde und Adrienne Rich; Ausgewählte Texte*, ed. Dagmar Schultz, trans. Renate Stendhal (Berlin: Orlanda Frauenverlag, 1983), 9–11.

3. Katharina Oguntoye, May Opitz, and Dagmar Schultz, eds., *Farbe bekennen: Afro-deutsche Frauen auf den Spuren ihrer Geschichte* (Berlin: Orlanda Frauenverlag, 1986), published in English as *Showing Our Colors: Afro-German Women Speak Out*, trans. Anne V. Adams (Amherst: University of Massachusetts Press, 1991).

4. Audre Lorde, *Auf Leben und Tod: Krebstagebuch*, trans. Margarete Längsfeld (Berlin: Orlanda Frauenverlag, 1987); Audre Lorde, *Zami: Eine Mythobiographie*, trans. Karen Nölle (Berlin: Orlanda Frauenverlag, 1986); Audre Lorde, *Lichtflut*, trans. Margarete Längsfeld (Berlin: Orlanda Frauenverlag, 1988); Audre Lorde, *Die Quelle unserer Macht: Gedichte*, trans. Marion Kraft and Sigrid Markmann (Berlin: Orlanda Frauenverlag, 1993).

5. Katharina Oguntoye, *Eine afro-deutsche Geschichte: Zur Lebenssituation von Afrikanern und Afro-Deutschen in Deutschland von 1884 bis 1950* (Berlin: HoHo, 1997); May Ayim, *Blues in schwarz weiss* (Berlin: Orlanda Frauenverlag, 1995); May Ayim, *Grenzenlos und unverschämt* (Berlin: Orlanda Frauenverlag, 1997); May Ayim, *Nachtgesang* (Berlin: Orlanda Frauenverlag, 1997); Ika Hügel-Marshall, *Daheim unterwegs: Ein deutsches Leben* (Berlin: Orlanda Frauenverlag, 1998).

6. May Ayim, *Blues in Black and White*, trans. Anne V. Adams (Trenton, N.J.: Africa World Press, 2003); Ika Hügel-Marshall, *Invisible Woman: Growing Up Black in Germany*, trans. Elizabeth Gaffney (New York: Continuum, 2002).

7. May Ayim and Nivedita Prasad, eds., "Dokumentation: Wege zu Bündnissen (FrauenAnstiftung, 1992); "Conference by and for Ethnic and Afro-German Minorities," Bremen, June 8–10, 1990; "Congress by and for Female Immigrants, Black Germans, Jewish Women, and Women Living in Exile," Berlin, October 3–6, 1991.

8. *Hope in My Heart: The May Ayim Story*, dir. Maria Binder (New York: Third World Newsreel, 1997).

9. Dagmar Schultz, interview with Kim Hester Williams, Sonoma State University, September 25, 2012.

10. Warren Crichlow, comment, March 15, 2013, in "Film Comments," *Audre Lorde— The Berlin Years, 1984 to 1992* [film website], www.audrelorde-theberlinyears.com.

11. Audre Lorde, "A Litany for Survival," *The Black Unicorn* (New York: Norton, 1978), 31–32.

12. Audre had met Ellen Kuzwayo during her work with Sisterhood in Support of Sisters in South Africa (SISA) and again in Europe after Orlanda (as sub rosa) published the German translation of Kuzwayo's *Call Me Woman* (*Mein Leben: Frauen gegen Apartheid*, trans. Bruni Röhm [Berlin: sub rosa, 1985]).

13. Festivals included the Queer Film Festival Lisboa, where the film was nominated for best documentary; the Barcelona International Gay and Lesbian Film Festival, where it received the audience award for best documentary; the Identities Film Festival in Vienna; the Tel Aviv International LGBT Film Festival; the Langston Hughes African American Film Festival; the Subversive Film Festival in Zagreb, Croatia; the Bangalore Queer Festival; and the Kashish Queer Festival in Mumbai. Links to the complete list of festivals and screenings are available at *Audre Lorde— The Berlin Years, 1984 to 1992* [film website], www.audrelorde-theberlinyears.com.

14. Best documentary, Barcelona International Gay and Lesbian Film Festival, 2012; festival favorite, Cinema Diverse, Palm Springs Gay and Lesbian Film Festival, 2013; best documentary, Reel Sisters of the Diaspora Film Festival, New York City,

2013; audience award for favorite documentary, Muestra Internacional de Cine Realizado por Mujeres, Zaragosa, Spain, 2013; audience award for favorite documentary, Reelout Queer Film + Video Festival, Kingston, Ontario, 2014.

15. The other films were *A Litany for Survival: The Life and Work of Audre Lorde,* dir. Ada Gay Griffin and Michelle Parkerson (New York: Third World Newsreel, 1995); and *The Edge of Each Other's Battles: The Vision of Audre Lorde,* dir. Jennifer Abod (New York: Women Make Movies, 2002).

16. The interviews on YouTube illustrate the variety of responses, as does the "Film Comments" section on the website.

17. Elaine Castillo, "Survival, Feminist Killjoys, and the Making of Transnational Counterpublics: On Watching *Audre Lorde: The Berlin Years,*" *Big Other,* April 16, 2012, http://bigother.com.

18. Sara Ahmed, "Introduction to *Audre Lorde: The Berlin Years,* London, April 14 [2012] London," www.audrelorde-theberlinyears.com.

19. Wieland Speck, interview, 2012, *Panorama,* www.berlinale.del. The translation in the text is mine.

20. Kimberlé Crenshaw, "Demarginalizing the Intersection of Race and Sex: A Black Feminist Critique of Antidiscrimination Doctrine, Feminist Theory, and Antiracist Politics," *University of Chicago Legal Forum* (1989): 138–67; Patricia Hill Collins, *Black Feminist Thought* (New York: Routledge, 1990).

21. Alexis Pauline Gumbs, "Audre Lorde—The Berlin Years," *Make/shift* 13 (2013): 46.

22. Sandra Campe, comment, 2012, "Film Comments."

23. Gabriele Zekina, comment, 2012, ibid.

24. cnueva75 [U.S. reviewer], "Berlin and Beyond: Audre Lorde—The Berlin Years (2012)," October 2, 2012, *Leonine Films,* http://leoninefilms.com.

25. [U.K. reviewer], "Audre Lorde: Black, Feminist, Lesbian, Poet, Mother, Essayist, Activist . . . ," April 15, 2012, *Curved Marginz,* http://curvedmarginz.wordpress.com; halfjill [German reviewer], "Ein Abend mit Audre Lorde," February 18, 2012, *Afrika Wissen Schaft,* http://afrikawissenschaft.wordpress.com. The translation in the text is mine.

26. Gotlinde Magiriba Lwanga, comment, 2012, "Film Comments"; John M. Lwanga, comment 2012, "Film Comments."

27. Gloria Wekker, panel discussion, "Conference on the Contemporary Urgencies of Audre Lorde's Legacy," University of Toronto, March 15, 2013.

28. Ahmed, "Introduction."

29. Peter J. Piercy, comment, April 16, 2012, "Film Comments."

DAGMAR SCHULTZ

3
Bonds of Sisterhood / Breaking of Silences
An Interview with Audre Lorde

MARION KRAFT

Introduction by Marion Kraft

Audre Lorde influenced, inspired, and empowered many women from different backgrounds and different parts of the world. Her words continue to be a source of power for all of those committed to bringing about change and fighting for equality and survival, for all of those who acknowledge difference as a creative and progressive force. Above all, she worked to raise her voice for women of the African diaspora and for Afro-descendants and, in doing so, to encourage them to raise their own voices.

I am a black woman of white German and African American descent (what has pejoratively been called a "war baby" on both sides of the Atlantic) who is a scholar and a teacher. In the summer of 1986, when Audre was temporarily residing in Berlin, I had only recently discovered the power of black women's writings; so our first meeting was a landmark and a turning point for me because it confirmed the work I had already done. In the spring of 1985, I had written an essay on teaching the literature of black women writers, a topic that was entirely absent from the university-level English curriculum in Germany.[1] By then, I had been a member of the English faculty at the Undergraduate College at the University of Bielefeld for three years and had just joined a group of women colleagues who were about to initiate women's studies courses. I soon realized that this meant *white* women's studies; in other words, it didn't really include me. As a Black German woman who had grown up in postwar Germany, I may have been the only black teacher in the country at the time. Thus, while annoying, this experience was not new but had already shaped my life in many ways. I had begun to focus on studying and teaching the challenging and moving literature of black American women, and I had recently come across the Feminist Press anthology *But Some of Us Are Brave,* of which Lorde had written, "Exciting! Affirmations and the beginning of a new era, where the 'women' in women's studies will no longer mean 'white.'"[2] I felt encouraged and empowered to continue with my own research.

Shortly before I met Audre, I attended an international meeting on women's literature and politics in Hamburg and, once again, was struck by the fact that, although one section of the meeting addressed the issue of Eurocentrism, organizers had paid comparatively little attention to the works of women of color. Did we really feel so alien to one another? Or had we only just begun to recognize the importance of different cultural and social experiences in the lives of women? With those questions in mind, I published another essay on teaching black women's literature.[3] In the meantime, the female colleagues at my college were concentrating on the works of French poststructuralists such as Julia Kristeva, Jacques Lacan, and Jacques Derrida; and as a result, I sometimes felt as if I were dealing with an exotic subject. Our definitions of *desire* were different: I found mine reflected in the theory, fiction, and poetry of African American women writers, and I felt compelled to communicate this desire. Even before I met Audre, her words "your silence will not protect you" had become a source of inspiration for me, as they had also inspired others.

Fortunately, the 1986 women's conference in Hamburg turned out to be less homogeneous than I first had thought. I remember the presentation of two dissertations about African American women writers, but mostly I remember the shining face of May Ayim. She and coeditor Dagmar Schultz (founder of Orlanda Press) had come to Hamburg to read from the brand-new volume *Farbe bekennen: Afro-deutsche Frauen auf den Spuren ihrer Geschichte,* later published in English as *Showing Our Colors: Afro-German Women Speak Out.*[4] I was moved to meet women who also had a genuine interest in the politics and literature that concerned me. May, an Afro-German woman fifteen years younger than I was, had succeeded in publishing research work about black women in Germany! I was excited to learn that the book had been inspired by Audre Lorde, and I was even more excited when Dagmar Schultz asked me to come to Berlin to interview Audre, who had been there for some months to undergo alternative cancer treatment and to teach and summon a group of Afro-German women.

Before the interview, Audre and I had a long conversation, and immediately I felt a strong sense of commonality and mutual concern. In particular, I was impressed and affirmed by her definition of teaching as a survival technique and her honest conviction in the importance of recognizing each other's differences and learning from one another.[5] This awareness became even more potent later, after I had attended one of Audre's poetry readings. Not only did I hear the voice of the poet speaking to our hearts and minds, but I heard the teacher within her, not lecturing but communicating and inspiring her audience to reconsider notions of themselves and others.

Writing and speaking from who she was, Audre reached a variety of audiences—everybody, as she used to say, who could use her words. I organized a number of readings for her in Germany, and after one at Osnabrück University, where I was a visiting professor in 1990, a local journalist wrote enthusiastically, "Audre Lorde makes a translation of her works almost superfluous."[6] Nonetheless, because her bonds with Germany and Germany's black community were tight, she wanted her words to be understood in not only political but also poetic terms. As she says in the 2012 film *Audre Lorde—The Berlin Years, 1984 to 1992,* poetry is "the most subversive form of language." Thus, in 1988, she asked me if I might be willing to translate a selection of her poems. My initial reluctance was based on a lack of confidence in my ability to transfer the feelings in her poetry into German, a language that at the time had few available words for creating images of black women, their struggles, and their cultural heritage. But as Audre said at our first meeting, "we have to make the language our own and use it in the ways that we need to use it. In the same way that we reclaim the word *Black.*"[7] I also thought of her words about differences and the importance of coalitions.

In Sigrid Markmann, a colleague at Osnabrück University, I found a dedicated cotranslator who could work with me across racial and other separating lines. With the staff at Orlanda Press, we decided to prepare a bilingual edition that would keep the voice of the poet alive while conveying her thoughts and feelings to an audience with a different language and cultural background. Audre used the first drafts I sent to her at poetry readings in Germany and Switzerland, and I felt very proud when she wrote to me about how important these communications across language barriers were to her. The collection was published in 1994.[8] Although Audre did not live to see it in print, I have since used it in many of my English and literature classes, and I am glad I complied with her wishes and met the challenge of reclaiming my own language. Moreover, my deep and thorough occupation with her poems, in particular those that focus on African heritage, myths, legends, and survival, allowed me to refocus my dissertation, which was published a few months after the collection was published.[9]

To make use of Audre's words meant action and interaction. In 1990, after attending the "I Am Your Sister" conference in Boston, the two of us, along with our friends Helga Emde, Gloria Joseph, and Andrée Nicola McLaughlin, met in Saint Croix to begin organizing an international conference of women of color in Germany under the auspices of the International Cross-Cultural Black Women's Studies Institute. Founded by Andrée McLaughlin and supported by an advisory board of women writers, scholars, and activists of the African diaspora (among them Vinie Burrows as well as Gloria and Audre), the institute was a global network that organized world conferences, international forums, and study tours.[10] Between 1987 and 2006, conferences took place regularly in the United States, Europe, Aotearoa (New Zealand), Africa, South America, and the Caribbean, addressing topics such as communications, food, human rights, Afro-descendants, indigenous people, and empowerment.

It was Audre's idea to hold the fifth convention in Germany, and she suggested me as the director. Two years earlier I had attended the institute's meeting in Zimbabwe, and I was aware of the challenges of the task: how difficult it would be to work together toward common goals despite cultural differences and language barriers. Nonetheless, I consented, and the three-week event, Black People and the European Community, took place in Frankfurt am Main, Bielefeld, and Berlin in August 1991. The dedicated engagement and support of my close Black German friends, the psychologists Helga Emde and Bärbel Kampmann, were as indispensable as the cooperation of Ria Cheatom, Jasmin Eding, Judy Gummich, and Katharina Oguntoye, founding members of ADEFRA (Black German Women and Black Women in Germany). Despite my original hesitations, the convention was a success and gave a platform to many women of color from around the world. More than sixty had enrolled, and public plenaries, panels, and cultural events sometimes drew audiences of more than two hundred people. The keynote speakers at the opening in Frankfurt am Main were Andrée McLaughlin (from the United States), May Ayim (from Germany), and Philomena Essed (from the Netherlands). We had ensured simultaneous translations in five languages and cross-cultural dialogues in numerous workshops. Plenary and panel contributions were later published in an international collection of essays.[11] This convention was particularly important for the women of the Afro-German community, who had begun to organize themselves only a few years earlier. However, as I had noticed during the convention in Zimbabwe, it was not always easy to ensure that we were listening to one another and respecting our differences.

Although Audre's health made it impossible for her to attend these gatherings, she had learned about both our success and the struggles with listening and respect. In a personal letter on the subject, she asked me, "How *do* we deal with differences between us and not self-destruct in the process?" It would be counterproductive to deny that differences do exist in academic structures, women's movements, and black communities. But as Audre always pointed out, we need to examine these differences and use

MARION KRAFT

them creatively if we want to bring about change. Two decades after her passing, this need is more important than ever, given the political backlash we have witnessed in recent years. Twenty years ago, Audre and Gloria wrote an open letter to Chancellor Helmut Kohl, protesting racist violence in Germany after the fall of the Berlin Wall. In the fall of 2012, President Joachim Gauck paid tribute to the victims of such violence. Nonetheless, Nazi terrorists have recently committed a series of racist murders, partly because a blindness about rightwing violence has overtaken certain of our constitutional defense authorities. Twenty years ago, on my return from the Caribbean, I was temporarily arrested at the Munich airport under the assumption that I was an illegal immigrant. Today, racial profiling in public transportation and at Europe's international airports has become common, and I am reminded of what Audre said at our first meeting: that we must continue to be aware of the "enormity of the forces aligned against us."

Within the white feminist movement in Germany, a parallel blindness continues to prevail. Although the movement has not yet floundered, it has largely retreated to gender studies and the narrow academic structures that Audre criticized more than a quarter of a century ago. The Afro-German women's movement must continue to acknowledge our differences if we want to take Audre's visions seriously. Yes, we have different historical, social, and cultural backgrounds; different sexual orientations; different aspirations and visions; different skin colors and ages. But we share common experiences and a common goal. Our experiences are rooted in the oppressive forces of racism in various societies, and our goal is our mutual concern to work toward "a future which has not yet been," in Audre's words.[12] If we want to reach such a future, we need coalitions like the important one she initiated between Afro-Germans and African Americans. Audre defined herself as a cultural traveler who wanted to learn. This meant an exchange of experiences and ideas, an eye-to-eye dialogue; this meant enabling people, including women of the black diaspora, to move against their oppressors. African Americans, their struggles, and their achievements have had a positive impact on the political consciousness of black people in Germany. But as far as the German reception of African American history and African American writers is concerned, we also must acknowledge the contributions that Black German activists, writers, and scholars have made to set the record straight.

When you read the 1986 interview that follows, you will see that Audre Lorde's words remain as valid today as they were decades ago. But as we commemorate her and her work around the world, we must admit that we still have much to teach and learn. On a personal level, Audre taught me so many things that I was able to use in my teaching, research work, writing, and political activities—not least, how important the day-to-day struggle is as we work to define ourselves and acknowledge the creative use of difference. But as I browse through files of personal correspondence more than a quarter of a century after it was written, I realize that most important was our friendship and the sisterhood that governed our relationship. It was a friendship rooted in a shared notion of the world as it is and a shared vision of a world that could be. It was a friendship rooted in the recognition of our commonalities and the acknowledgment of our differences. It was a friendship that included joy over the discovery of a shell on the shores of Saint Croix, of a blossom in my German garden. Acknowledging the beauty of this world was as crucial to Audre as her commitment to fighting the powers of destruction and working for a better future.

I am still working and hoping for such a future. Perhaps I would do so without ever having met Audre Lorde, but certainly not with the great confidence and hope she instilled in me, in many other women, in all of those who still feel that they can make use of her words in order to bring about change.

THE CREATIVE USE OF DIFFERENCE

MARION KRAFT: Audre, you are an Afro-American woman of Caribbean descent, a mother and a lesbian, feminist, essayist, professor of English, and a poet. Is poetry the most important part of all these various aspects of your life?

AUDRE LORDE: Poetry is not the most important part of my life. Poetry is the strongest expression I have of certain ways of making, identifying, and using my own power. Because poetry is not a presentation, is not a product. Poetry—for me—is a way of living. It's the way I look at myself, it's the way I move through my selves, my world, and it's the way I metabolize what happens and present it out again. So, it is an inseparable part of who I am. All the other aspects of me, when I say "I am a Black lesbian feminist warrior poet mother," I am plucking out certain arbitrary pieces of me. I could pluck out different ones if I wanted to, but I find that those that are most problematic are usually also the sources of our strongest power, and so, for that reason, it is a ritual, it has always served me to underline for myself and for other people the sources of my power.

MK: In "Poetry Is Not a Luxury" you wrote that it could be something like an allusion to the architecture of our lives.

AL: Yes, poetry is, in fact, the skeleton architecture of our lives; because it helps to form the dreams for a future that has not yet been and toward which we must work when we speak of change. Then, to speak of change in the absence of vision is to court chaos forever.

MK: I've read in an essay by one of your critics that Audre Lorde is not per se a *black* poet; she is a woman poet who also happens to be black . . .

AL: There are some phrases that absolutely *tick me off*, and they usually start with "who happens to be." As a matter of fact, I have a brand new poem— in *Our Dead Behind Us*—the title of which is "To the Poet who happens to be Black and the Black Poet who happens to be a Woman." Very seriously, the reason I think this is so dangerous is because those of us who are committed to survival and to teaching—no, we don't *happen* to be anything. We are here, as Bernice Reagon says, over and over again, because somebody before us did something to bring us here. We are not ashored in our existence. So I didn't happen to be anything. Being Black is very important, and being a woman is very important. I have paid a great deal to be both, consciously.

MK: In one of your poems, that I like very much, there is that image of your mother as a woman with two faces who actually is *two* women borne on the poet's back, "one dark and rich . . . the other pale as a witch . . ." And then, there is this outcry, "Mother . . ."

AL: That's from "From the House of Yemanjá" [in *The Black Unicorn*]. Yemanjá is the mother of us all. She is the aura of goddess, of rivers, of love, and of war. And that poem really deals not only with the split consciousness that so many light skinned Black women from the islands have but also how it is necessary for each one of us to claim all of the parts of our ancestry and at the same time to recognize the great nourishment and the great power of our Blackness. The Black mother being the source of nourishment, the source of power for us all—Black, white, male, and female.

MK: In some of your essays you have also used this image of the black mother in opposition to the "white father."

AL: Yes, the white fathers are the ones who have said "I think, therefore I am," having the concept that it is only through our thoughts, through our intellectual, rational processes that we gain freedom. This is not true. I speak of the Black mother as that part of us which is chaotic, messy, deep, dark, ancient, old, and freeing. And, the struggle is constantly one to harness the left brain with the rational parts to do the service of what is original and deep, which is the right brain, the emotions. We think with tools that have been given to us. If we are to create a new order, we must go back, back, back to what is primary, and those are our feelings; and take those feelings and bring them forward enough, so we can cobble a new way out of them. In other words, a *screeaam* is just a feeling—but it is not a poem, it's not a piece of art. We must take the emotion behind that scream and make something out of it that is articulate and powerful and communicative.

MK: So, it is not that old stereotype: Women are emotional, and men do the thinking?

AL: No, not at all. That is, I believe, a real distortion of reality. I think that patriarchy has elevated the whole question of rationality to a point where it no longer has a context; and let me say this: Rationality is a tool, it is a bridge, a road. Like any road it must lead from somewhere to somewhere, or else it is just an exercise in futility. If we cannot anchor that rationality in our feelings and, on the other hand, have it lead toward a future where we can in fact survive, then rationality has no meaning; and we are now trapped in the age of rationality that has no vision at one end and has no acknowledgement of the true sources of self on the other. It would be ridiculous to believe that we can exist cut off from any part of ourselves. But there has been a false emphasis in Western European thought upon what is rational and a total rejection of what is emotional.

MK: Is that what you mean when you focus on the difference between poetry and rhetoric?

AL: Yes. That is exactly the difference. When I say that the difference between poetry and rhetoric is being ready to *kill ourselves instead of our children,* I mean, if we are really ready to put ourselves behind what we believe, then we can bring about change. Other than that, it is only empty rhetoric, and it is our children who will have to live out our destinies.

MK: In "Uses of the Erotic: The Erotic as Power" you described the erotic as one of the sources of power and knowledge in our lives.

AL: The power of the erotic, the uses of anger, we must not run from these parts as women. We have been encouraged to reject the power of the erotic, because the erotic has been used so cruelly against us, but we must be able to acknowledge all of the parts of ourselves and see how they contribute to the work we have to do in this world.

MK: You described this power of the erotic in your book *Zami* where it is also based on old African and Caribbean legends, but could you explain why you called it a biomythography?

AL: I called it a biomythography because it is not only autobiography. It also partakes of myths and history and a lot of other ways we use knowledge; and I used those myths in *Zami*, the myth of MawuLisa and her youngest daughter, Afrekete, who is changed into Eshu, the prankster because I believe that there are some very, very definite ways in which African women, women of African descent, raise their children that hold true in many different places, and that does in fact reflect the sources of our power. For example, it is the West African women of Dahomey who have the legend, who have the belief and who demonstrate this, that there is not a contradiction between the taking of lives and the giving of life and the making of war, so that you have your Dahomeyan amazons who were the fiercest warriors of the king. It is very important to have that, because, in fact, in the lives of so many Afro-American women, my mother, my mother's generation, I saw that these women were nurturing, they were cherishing, they were loving, but they were also really tough warriors, you know. So, we need to know that that is part of our tradition. This is why I think it is so necessary, I think, to weave myths into our world.

MK: Why did you choose the title *Zami: A New Spelling of My Name?*

AL: Well, in West African Systems, the question of naming is a vital one. So, their children are born, and they are not named for eight days, because this is the time that a child spends deciding whether it wants to stay in this world. Once a child decides that it is going to stay, then a name is given. And many names are given. There are some secret names, there are names of times, names of family; and throughout your life, in Yoruba traditions, when something important happens, you gain another name, or you are given another name. The American Indians have this also. So, the process of naming is a way of rebirth, of underlining rebirth. And it is something that is happening in the book. Now, *Zami* is a word that is used in Carriacou, meaning *women who work and live together,* and it is a very beautiful word. I remember my mother using this word when I was a child, meaning just friends. I didn't know what it meant, I didn't know that it meant women-identified women, women who love each other, but when I came across it, I really wanted to claim it as my own, as a Black lesbian. And, originally, it probably came from Patois, which is a combination of French and Spanish, probably from *les amies,* the friends.

MK: But in *Zami* you not only described the love between women but also the isolation of black lesbians in the 1950s; and this reminded me of Gloria Naylor's *The Women of Brewster Place,* where in one story she delineated the homophobia in the black community in the late 1960s or early 1970s. Has this climate changed in the 1980s?

AL: Well, the homophobia in the Black community was a real reality; and yes, it is changing slowly. It is changing slowly because of the work of a number of very, very brave women and also because Black lesbians, and Black gay men also, have assumed much more of a presence. We have come out of our isolation and in mending together have had a presence about which we have been able to say, "We are Black, we have always been Black, we are involved, have always been involved in our communities," and this, of course, is true.

Along with that terrible homophobia has always gone a sort of silent acknowledgment of the maiden aunt or the unmarried people in our Community. Within the Black Community, difference has been used so cruelly against us, that we tend to trigger on it and believe that Black can be defined in some kind of homogeneous way. Well, this is not true. And to the extent that the Black Community begins to recognize that, the Black Community is also touching its strength in difference; we are Black, we are different.

MK: In your essay "The Uses of Anger," you pointed out that each of us had a right to her own name, a right that often is ignored, even among white academic feminists. Do you see any development of the awareness about the importance of differences within the white feminist movement?

AL: Well, the feminist movement, the white feminist movement, has been notoriously slow to recognize that racism is a feminist concern, not one that is altruistic, but one that is part and parcel of feminist consciousness. If it is not, then the white feminist movement cannot really exist, and to a certain degree it almost floundered on this point. I think, in fact, though, that things are slowly changing and that there are white women now who recognize that in the interest of genuine coalition, they *must see* that we are not the same. Black feminism is not white feminism in Black face. It is an intricate movement coming out of the lives, aspirations, and realities of Black women. We share some things with white women, and there are other things we do not share. We must be able to come together around those things we share.

MK: Would you say that there is also a difference in the writings of black and white women—for example, as far as the use of language is concerned?

AL: I think that there is. Because Black English feeds into a lot, even in the writings of those of us who don't use it. I think that the roots of Black poetry, coming from way back, were certainly articulated in the 1960s and still exist in much of our work where there is an emphasis on music and rhythm and Black speech. Now, this shows through in a lot of Black women's work. There is also a difference, I believe, because those of us who are Black women poets are intimately involved in a kind of survival that very often white women poets do not recognize for a long time. They are also intimately involved in survival, but they have different stakes. It is easier for them not to recognize that. So, I think that there is a tradition of struggle as well as music in Black women's poetry that shows through over and over again.

MK: Is there a similar difference in the writings of black women and black men?

AL: There are certain similarities. Yes, I think that there are similarities in the work of Black men and women. I think, though, that there are again real differences in the poetry of Black women and Black men—and Black men are not really doing that much in poetry. I think that Black women on all the creative fronts are really exploding right now. As we examine our identities, as we reach for our power, we are developing and forming an art and a literature that speaks to our needs. So, it is very, very exciting. Very exciting.

MK: And that includes a different use of language?

AL: I think that we are reclaiming the language. I think we are, in fact, making the language new. And that's a difference. That's a difference, yes, and we have to do that, we have to make the language our own and use it in the ways that we need to use it. In the same way that we reclaim the word *Black*.

MK: In "The Master's Tools Will Never Dismantle the Master's House," a paper you gave at a women's conference in the United States, you made it clear that all women need these different tools, not only in fiction and poetry but also in academic discourse—if we want to bring about change.

AL: It means different tools in language, different tools in the exchange of information, it means different tools in learning. It means that we use the tools of rationality, but we do not elevate it to the point that it is no longer connected to our lives. It means that we do not require from each other the kinds of narrow and restricted interpretations of learning and the exchange of knowledge that we suffered in the universities or that we suffered in the narrow academic structures. It means that we recognize that, while we are functioning in the old power, because we must know those tools, we cannot be ignorant of them, we are also in the process of redefining a new power, which is the power of the future.

MK: When you call teaching "a survival technique," do you mean teaching how to use these different tools?

AL: I think that we teach best those things we need to learn for our own survival. So, as we learn them, we then reach back and teach, and it becomes a joint process. I think that this is what keeps us new, that we do not learn from what goes on in a book. We learn from that interaction that takes place in the spaces between what is in the book and ourselves.

MK: And that is what people could learn from your poetry and from your writing as a whole?

AL: Well, as I've said, the poetry and fiction, *Zami,* and the nonfiction, the theory, are really three different ways of presenting Audre Lorde, of presenting what I know to be so.

MK: So, who is your audience then?

AL: My audience is *every* single person who can use the work I do. Anybody who can use what I do is who I'm writing for. Now, I write out of who I am, all of the ways in which I describe myself, and so, all those people who share those aspects of me, who are Black, who are warrior women poets, lesbians . . . may find themselves closer to what I'm doing, but I write out of who I am for everyone who can use what I'm saying. And, I got letters from the strangest people saying "You know, this really was important" or "you know, I'm very different from you, but . . ." or "You know, I'm a white woman, and I'm not a lesbian, but . . ." or "I am a teacher, a white male teacher, but . . . ," and I thought "well, all right, that's good, I take my hat off, fine."

MK: Audre, let me ask you one more question—You have not only raised your voice for black women in America but also for "Third World" women, women of color, you are a member of SISA (Sisters in Support of Sisters in

South Africa), and you had the initial idea for a book about the history of black women in Germany . . .

AL: I think it is so exciting, Marion, that we are now beginning to make these kinds of contacts, set up those kinds of networks, because I think, whether we describe *Black,* meaning of African descent, part of the African diaspora, or whether we use *Black* as it is used in New Zealand, in Australia, to mean those of us who stand outside, who are people of color, who are outside the structures, and who are reclaiming our land and our lives, in other words, people who use *Black,* women who use *Black* as a symbol of resistance—we have intimate connections, our oppressions are rooted in the very same systems that have stolen our land, our heirs, our children, our men, our lives. We need to identify those oppressors and to begin to see how we can move against them. What is it then that we can learn from each other? Now, what we must learn from each other is how we are *different* and be able to stand up and look at those differences—without sentimentality and without insecurity. Because if we can recognize how we are different and how we are the same, that is to say, the similarities of our goals and the differences of the particulars of our lives, we can add to each other different ways of battling. And it is a way in which the creative use of difference will help us really move toward change, toward that future we can share.

MK: And are you hopeful as well?

AL: Yes, I'm very hopeful, I have to tell you, I'm really very hopeful. It is a hope, however, grounded in a very realistic estimation of the enormity of the forces aligned against us. Because that is the only real hope there can be if we are honest about how much it is that we have to do; and I believe we can do it, and not only that, I believe we can do it with *joy!*

Notes

1. Marion Kraft, "Kulturelle und fremdsprachliche Kompetenz im Literaturunterricht. Black Women Writers—Ein Unterrichtsbeispiel für die Sekundarstufe II," *Englisch-Amerikanische Studien* 2 (1986): 239–63.
2. Gloria T. Hull, Patricia Bell Scott, and Barbara Smith, eds., *But Some of Us Are Brave: All the Women Are White, All the Blacks Are Men: Black Women's Studies* (Old Westbury, N.Y.: Feminist Press, 1982). Audre Lorde's comment appears as a cover blurb.
3. Marion Kraft, "The Bluest Eye and Black Eyed Susans: Teaching Black Women's Literature," *Englisch-Amerikanische Studien* 1 (1987): 109–19.

4. May Opitz, Katharina Oguntoye, and Dagmar Schultz, eds., *Farbe bekennen: Afro-deutsche Frauen auf den Spuren ihrer Geschichte* (Berlin: Orlanda Frauenverlag, 1986), reprinted in English as *Showing Our Colors: Afro-German Women Speak Out,* trans. Anne V. Adams (Amherst: University of Massachusetts Press, 1992).

5. Marion Kraft, "The Creative Use of Difference," in *Conversations with Audre Lorde,* ed. Joan Wylie Hall (Jackson: University Press of Mississippi, 2004), 152. The entire interview appears later in this chapter.

6. G. S., "Nutzung der eigenen Kraft: Audre Lorde in der Uni," *Neue Osnabrücker Zeitung,* May 23, 1990, 90.

7. Kraft, "The Creative Use of Difference," 151.

8. Audre Lorde, *Die Quelle unserer Macht: Gedichte,* trans. Marion Kraft and Sigrid Markmann (Berlin: Orlanda Frauenverlag, 1994).

9. Marion Kraft, *The African Continuum and Contemporary African American Women Writers: Their Literary Presence and Ancestral Past* (New York: Peter Lang, 1995).

10. See Joanne M. Braxton and Andrée Nicola McLaughlin, eds., *Wild Women in the Whirlwind: Afra-American Culture and the Contemporary Literary Renaissance,* foreword by Audre Lorde (New Brunswick, N.J.: Rutgers University Press, 1990).

11. Marion Kraft and Rukhsana Shamim Ashraf-Khan, eds., *Schwarze Frauen der Welt: Europa und Migration* (Berlin: Orlanda Frauenverlag, 1994).

12. See chapter 1.

MARION KRAFT

4
Naming Ourselves as Black Women in Europe
An African American–German and Afro-Dutch Conversation

CASSANDRA ELLERBE-DUECK AND GLORIA WEKKER

And if you ever try to reach me
And I cannot hear you,
these words are in place
of any dead air between us.
In the hand of Afrekete,
Audre Lorde, June 23, 1986

inscribed in Gloria Wekker's copy of *Our Dead Behind Us*

This essay is based on a series of conversations, on Skype and in person, in which we discussed our personal relationship with Audre Lorde, the ways in which she was posthumously responsible for connecting us, and her catalytic role in the formation of black women's organizations in Europe. We chose the dialogue format because it seemed to flow organically from Audre's ideas about black women connecting beyond borders, which are an integral part of her legacy.[1]

ENCOUNTERING AUDRE

GLORIA WEKKER: So tell me, Cass, how did you come to Germany, and how did you two meet?

CASSANDRA ELLERBE-DUECK: I arrived in Mannheim, Germany, in 1986 after participating in a one-year student academic exchange program between Hunter College and the Université Paris 8. While in Paris, I honed not only my French language skills but also my German. Paris was quite amazing during that time. It was the era of the antiracism campaign "Touche pas à mon pote."[2] Paris 8 was known for its leftist and progressive professors and student body. Moving about in that milieu gave me the opportunity to meet many students who were involved in antiracist activities and were also feminists. My interest in feminist theory and particularly black feminist thought had been awakened after reading *Sister Outsider* during my first semester at Hunter College in 1984. I had no inkling that I would one day meet Audre Lorde.

After finishing the year in Paris, I decided in January to visit some friends in Mannheim and intensify my German. Mannheim appealed to me; and after finding out that I did not have to pay university fees, I decided to stay in Germany and continue my studies. From 1986 until 1988 I immersed myself completely in the German language in order to pass the required language proficiency exam. Because the University of Mannheim was primarily dedicated to business management and economics, I decided to apply to the Ludwig-Maximilians University in Munich. My application was accepted; and shortly after my twenty-sixth birthday in 1988, I managed to pass the arduous German language entrance exam and embarked on my studies in anthropology and American cultural history.

While strolling the halls of the American studies department in May of that year, I noticed a poster announcing a poetry reading that would feature Audre Lorde. The reading was a collaboration between ADEFRA (Black German Women and Black Women in Germany) and a white German feminist group in Munich. The poster and my intuition left me no peace. I had to meet Audre, so I contacted the women of ADEFRA and expressed my interest in attending the reading. That afternoon, I was warmly greeted by Jasmine Eding and Judy Gummich from the ADEFRA chapter and was promptly introduced to Audre. The meeting took place in Judy's home, and the occasion was Audre's first reading in Munich.

I had often seen her in the halls of Hunter College, but in 1984 she had seemed larger than life, so I had not dared to approach her. I felt very insecure about my life and my studies and was plagued with many personal questions and doubts. Because I viewed Audre as very no-nonsense, I believed that I needed to have my nonsensical self together in order to approach her or even be in her presence. On this occasion, however, I had arrived fortuitously. No black female German language interpreter was available for the reading, and Audre was adamantly insisting on one. So that evening in Munich I had the honor of simultaneously translating her poetry from English into German. Although my German was far from

Cassandra Ellerbe-Dueck and Audre Lorde, poetry reading organized by Schwarze Deutsche Frauen und Schwarze Frauen in Deutschland (ADEFRA) and Kommunikationszentrum für Frauen (KOFRA), June 1988, Munich. Photograph © Cassandra Ellerbe-Dueck.

perfect, Audre insisted that I do the translating; she refused to consider the possibility of having a white German woman interpret her words. It was an evening that I will never forget. Her kindness, her words, and her genuine interest in my person touched my heart and psyche forever.

GW: How typical of Audre to have you do that translation, right then and there! She always showed an incredible trust in the capabilities of younger black women, even when they themselves did not necessarily have that trust. For me also, being in her entourage meant that I had to chair big public meetings, lead discussions, and translate for the first time in my life.

CED: You have mentioned this before, but how did you meet her?

GW: My encounter with Audre took place in the summer of 1984, when she came to Amsterdam for a long weekend on the invitation of the black lesbian group that I had cofounded. We called ourselves Sister Outsider, after her collection of essays, and our group consisted of four black women, including myself: Tania Leon from South Africa, Tieneke Sumter (who was, like me, from Suriname), and Jose Maas.[3] Our aim was to provide a space for black and migrant women who were interested in writing and performing literature. I had written to Audre in New York, care of Kitchen Table Press, after I had read *Zami: A New Spelling of My Name*. I was totally blown away by the book; I passed it around to everybody and their mother. This was the first book by a black lesbian that I had ever read, and I wanted to share it with others. There were so many points of recognition: for instance, the episode when she describes little fat Audre with bad eyesight, wriggling between her mother's legs as the mother tries to comb the daughter's unruly hair.[4] The smells of the hair oil and the pain of that episode is so vividly evoked that I felt myself back in my own mother's lap. But I was also breathlessly reading Audre's analyses of the inevitable division of roles between black and white lesbians in intimate relationships, where, based on a racist-sexist worldview, black women were assigned the butch role because they did not stand a chance of being identified with feminine beauty. I had never read anything that was so insightful, poetic, and meaningful at the same time.[5]

So when I heard that Audre was spending the summer of 1984 teaching at the Free University of Berlin, I wrote and asked her to come and spend time with us in Amsterdam. Later she recounted that when she had received the letter, she called all of her girlfriends to tell them that, of all places, there were black dykes in Amsterdam. She came, saw, and conquered not only the four women of Sister Outsider but all lesbian and feminist Amsterdam because we had organized a whole series of meet-and-greets, readings, and a dance with her, where she met women of all hues.

CED: What do you remember about that weekend?

GW: I was very fortunate that she stayed in my home. She arrived on Friday, July 13, 1984, and all of Sister Outsider went to welcome her at Schiphol Airport. We had an elaborate lunch at my place. I had set the table with white linen and a giant bouquet of sunflowers; we had white wine, and I had baked coconut and chocolate pies. Audre was not supposed to eat rich foods, but she did anyway, displaying a naughtiness and willfulness and making it clear that she was in charge of her own life. What struck me most about her was how full of life and joy she was. Whether it was good food, smart conversations, dancing, gossiping, taking notes, as she was continually doing, she was totally present. When she encountered someone, she gave that person the feeling that she really wanted to know her, without delay, as if she were saying, "Tell me your story, there is no time to lose." She had an incredible intensity and focus. Being with her felt like basking in her light, and she made me feel beautiful and smart.

On Saturday morning she had woken up early, before I had, and had taken inventory of my bookshelves. When I woke up, she was ready to be enlightened about the history and the sociology of Suriname. I talked to her for hours while she was taking notes. I had just finished an article on the "beautiful Joanna," a light-skinned enslaved woman who had been immortalized by her lover, Scottish captain John Gabriel Stedman.[6] He had come to Suriname to defeat the Maroons, who, in the view of the colonial government and the planters, were bringing the colony to ruin. During Stedman's sojourn there (1772–77), he kept a diary that often mentions Joanna. He also made numerous sketches in which her curly locks feature prominently. Yet Joanna refused to go to Europe with him after his period of service was over. Audre was mesmerized by the story.[7]

Can you say something about Audre's impact on your life and work?

CED: Toward the end of 1988, I sent a letter to Audre in Saint Croix. My purpose was to seek her advice about the route my life might take in Germany, and her response was "You must read the work of Black women writers and activists."[8] She went on to list a number of names that have come to comprise the foundation of my political and critical theory canon. Her sociopolitical activism in Germany awakened and greatly influenced my political consciousness and ultimately inspired me to research and write about the Afro–Black German community. I use the term *community* primarily in a personal sense because, after I came to Germany, I encountered a structure that offered me a sense of belonging and a safe space even while living abroad.

Now, twenty-four years later, I have come to realize that Audre's words and legacy left an indelible imprint on the lives of so many of us who spent time with her: "But my words will be there, something . . . to bounce off of, something to incite thought, activity."[9] They came to demonstrate to me the necessity of forging links with black diasporic women not only in Germany but also across Europe. In addition to unfolding my academic development, her invisible hand prompted me to register for the 2002 Network of Interdisciplinary Women's Studies in Europe (NOISE) summer school course at Utrecht University in the Netherlands. While thumbing through my tattered copy of *Farbe bekennen,* I ran across your contribution about the Sister Outsider group in the publication.[10] This prompted me to want to meet you and attend your class. That encounter brought us together, and you became my mentor and Ph.D. coadviser. You and I have genealogical roots in various locations within the Americas, but we met and began to work together in Europe. Our political convictions were and still are greatly influenced by the legacy of Audre Lorde.

And how would you describe her impact on you, personally and professionally?

GW: During different visits, whether in Amsterdam, Berlin, Los Angeles, or New York, I have been enriched immeasurably by being close to her, exchanging poetry with her, analyzing political situations, and being a witness to the everyday political choices that she made. For instance, on one occasion our organizing committee in Amsterdam accidentally doubly booked her, so she had to choose between attending an event run by a grassroots black, migrant, and refugee women's organization in the city and a meeting of academic feminists at Utrecht University. She clearly demonstrated that her priorities were with the former group. I was in awe of her determination and sovereignty at that moment: no matter what the academics said, she would not budge. She had a clarity and consistency of vision, and it worked when it was most needed.

In addition, she encouraged me to follow my passions and do the work that I needed to do. She practiced what she preached. Not only did she urge others, in "Uses of the Erotic," to find that dark kernel in ourselves that gives us joy, but she consistently searched for that kernel in her own life too.[11] Between 1984 and 1987, when I was organizing the activities of Sister Outsider, I was also a civil servant working for the city of Amsterdam. These years were the heyday of the antiracism spirit that was also infusing bureaucracy; so with two black friends and colleagues, Mea Venster and Ellin Robles, I was successfully organizing civil servants of color to improve our position and enhance the intercultural quality of city services and facilities. In hindsight, I see that I was empowered by Audre.

Above all, she gave me the courage to do what I had dreamed of doing but had not previously had the courage to undertake: in 1987 I entered a Ph.D. program at the University of California, Los Angeles, where I focused on Afro-Surinamese women's constructions of sexuality. I could not do this work in the Netherlands, where there was no one capable of supervising me and where *race* was (and still is) not part of any discourse, feminist or otherwise. Audre was a good friend, and she did not lose sight of me after I made the move. A couple of days after I arrived in Los Angeles, I experienced my first earthquake—a 6.9-magnitude one—and the first person to contact me was Audre, telephoning from Saint Croix to make sure I had

CASSANDRA ELLERBE-DUECK AND GLORIA WEKKER

survived! In 1989, she came to do a poetry reading at the Center of African American Studies at UCLA, where I was then working as a research associate. Again she stayed with me, this time in my modest one-room apartment. I remember that she loved sushi, and we were as happy as two little girls when the nearby Japanese restaurant, by mistake, gave me double takeout portions.

Fortunately I finished my dissertation in time for Audre to read it. She was facing the end of her life then and spending the summer and early autumn of 1992 with her partner Gloria Joseph in Dagmar Schultz's home in Berlin.[12] In October my Sister Outsider friend Tania Leon and I went by train from Amsterdam to Berlin to say our farewells to her. During our visit Audre insisted on discussing the dissertation with me; she was elated about my description of Afro-Surinamese women's same-sex sexual relations, which I understood as based on West African principles.[13] However, she objected to my "postmodern language use," which she, "as a simple librarian," could not appreciate.[14] I remember that she read us the poem "Today Is Not the Day" in which she contemplates her death, while tears streamed from our eyes:

> I can't just sit here
> staring death in her face
> blinking and asking for a new name
> by which to greet her
>
> I am not afraid to say
> unembellished
> I am dying
> But I do not want to do it
> looking the other way.
>
> Today is not the day.
> It could be
> but it is not.[15]

Tania, by then, knew that she had breast cancer.[16] We were all grieving but also immensely connected, knowing how much we had meant to each other and the gifts we had given each other as black lesbian women of different generations and different transnational sensibilities. We celebrated the knowledge that we had given each other a home. I gave Audre a ritual bath, surrounding her with incense, candle, flowers, and the fragrances of rose and sandalwood to prepare her for the next part of her journey. She gave me one of her gold bracelets, with snakeheads, that she had inherited from her mother, Linda. Her motto, "When I dare to use my words in the service of my vision, then it does not matter whether I am afraid," still hangs above my desk and has empowered me at many moments in my life.

WILD WOMEN IN THE WHIRLWIND

CED: Gloria, you and M. Jacqui Alexander rightly state that Audre was anchored at the intersection of three major sociopolitical movements of the twentieth century: civil rights, feminist / black feminist, and LGBT.[17] Aspects of the three can be seen in the developments that took place in Germany. Just as black feminists in the United States found it necessary to create their own organizations, Afro–Black German activists contended with the issues of racism and marginalization in white German feminist groups.[18] The mentoring and support that Audre gave to activist Black German women was indispensable to the formation of a movement. Her influence was the wind beneath the wings of Black German women's political activism and feminism. Audre was the godmother of the movement.

GW: Yes, starting with the idea (which originated with Andrée Nicola McLaughlin) that Audre connected and embodied the three movements, let's flesh out some of the differences and similarities between the situations for black people in Germany and the Netherlands, both of which she influenced. I want us to speak of how those three movements took shape in each of our national settings. I have a hunch that Audre's role was different in Germany and in the Netherlands because the racial configurations were different. Yet in both settings it was predominantly black women who were most strongly interpellated by her. All of this points to the importance of reflecting on and writing a comparative social and political history of the black presence in Europe.

CED: When I think about the activity and excitement that occurred among black female activists in the Netherlands and Germany in the 1980s, I picture "wild women" in a cross-border "whirlwind."[19] I use *wild* here in a positive sense to describe the enthusiasm and sassiness of this period, when many black women in Germany and the Netherlands (and other European countries too) were propelled into a new and powerful sense of self. McLaughlin highlights the global nature of black women's self-empowerment during this period: "Such organized political activity on the part of self-identified

'Black women' reflects a burgeoning intercontinental Black women's consciousness movement."[20] We no longer felt like what Nirmal Puwar refers to as "Space Invaders" or "bodies out of space."[21]

GW: I know what you mean when you refer to "Space Invaders." When I think of Amsterdam in the 1970s, when I was becoming active in the women's/lesbian movement, I also remember how glad I was to meet Tania Leon. She was the first other black woman whom I met in the framework of the women's movement, and we were living in the same neighborhood. We spent a lot of time together, going shopping at the nearby market and eating together, and we eventually became family. It had been terribly lonely, actually, in the women's movement. It chafed; constant vigilance was needed. Whenever Tania and I went out together, to meetings, to birthday celebrations, or to dances, it was so reassuring to have each other because before that we had often been the sole black female in a sea of white faces. Not so much has changed in that regard, by the way; I think that a high degree of apartheid still characterizes the Netherlands socially.

One night in the late 1970s stands out in particular. Tania and I had gone to the women's center, and we were having a good time dancing exuberantly, showing each other our special moves, bumping and grinding, when suddenly we became aware that we had become the center of attention. Lots of white women around us stopped dancing and were looking at us disapprovingly, and they were discussing us. That was a painful moment; clearly we had stepped outside the bounds of white lesbian-feminist respectability. These boundaries had not been clear to us before, but now they were, and we could not escape the conclusion that something in our black female bodies was unacceptable. Only later did I make connections with the Dutch cultural archive, in which black women have been labeled as utterly carnal, as sexual beings who are deemed to be freer in their bodies than white women are. We had inadvertently underlined this label. Sisterhood, even in lesbian circles, was not unconditional.

CED: I find it important to touch on the sociohistorical context of blacks in Germany to underline the significance of Audre's contribution to the Black German movement. Before 1986, a sense of an imagined community among Black Germans was virtually nonexistent. Nor were there spaces into which black people could retreat. Even today, predominantly black residential areas or neighborhoods such as where you reside in Amsterdam are absent from the German landscape. The only thing that comes close is the yearly federal meeting of the Black Germans and Blacks in Germany Initiative, where for an entire weekend Black Germans have the chance to experience and move about in a space that they can claim entirely as their own.

That movement, galvanized by Audre, took off in the mid-1980s, and it proved to be life-changing for many Germans of African/black diasporic or dual heritage. A self-determined sense of identity emerged, as did a self-as-cribed name. By naming itself, this traditionally marginalized and partially invisible population had crossed a psychologically and historically signifi-cant milestone.[22] Black Germans began articulating their specific notions and practices of blackness while claiming German identity. Moreover, they were creating a new sociohistorical narrative, positioning themselves within the African/black diaspora, and establishing their own organiza-tions.[23] The women of ADEFRA and Initiative Schwarze in Deutschland (ISD) brought a clear feminist agenda and queer presence to the move-ment, and it is striking that women were at the forefront of black conscious-ness raising and politicized mobilization in Germany. These women found themselves situated within the three intersecting axes of power and polit-ical struggle—race, gender, and sexuality—and they initiated a discourse on issues of racism and sexism in dominant white German society and the women's movement and of heterosexism and homophobia in the Black German community.

Black German women during the period were focused on the subject of self-esteem and the need to identify with positive black female role mod-els. Think about the task of grooming our tightly or loosely coiled locks, the issue of skin color and body shape; these topics affect the self-esteem and psyche of many sisters across the globe. Audre's essay "Is Your Hair Still Political?" was a big deal for me, and her choice to wear natural locks inspired and gave me the strength to do the same.[24] She was not only a sister to us but also, for many Black Germans, a missing black maternal link.[25] Audre taught us that our matrilineal heritage is a powerful source of strength and courage. For the women of ADEFRA and ISD, she embod-ied a positive black lesbian image and inspired a sense of self-esteem that many Black German women (regardless of sexual identity) were longing for. She exuded a presence that made us all feel beautiful, regardless of hair texture, body shape, skin complexion, or sexuality. I recall that she always marveled at our diverse beauty, and she contributed immeasurably to the healing of our psyche.

CASSANDRA ELLERBE-DUECK AND GLORIA WEKKER

GW: Elaborate a bit on the presence of black people in Germany and the characteristics of the population.

CED: Contrary to the belief of many white Germans, people of African descent did not suddenly appear in Germany after 1945. As May Ayim's research has shown, blacks have been present in Germany as far back as the twelfth century.[26] However, the more recent history of this population is closely linked to Germany's colonial and fascist past.[27] The vast majority of Black Germans born in West Germany after 1945 were of dual heritage.[28] The children born to white German women were raised and socialized primarily in settings where the black male father figure or other black family members were either unknown to the children or totally absent from their lives.[29]

The year 1986 was a milestone in Black German history. It marked the publication, under Audre's impetus, of the women's anthology *Farbe bekennen,* which was inspired by Audre's personal involvement with May Ayim, Katharina Oguntoye, and Dagmar Schultz—

GW: I just want to briefly interject that Audre worked to bring together Black German and Black Dutch women, which resulted, among other things, in my contributing to *Farbe bekennen.*[30] But she was also not above mundane matters, like arranging sleeping quarters with Katharina for Tania and me when we visited Berlin.

CED: In the anthology, thirteen Black German women bared their souls by vividly recounting what it meant for a black child to grow into adulthood in a context in which a shared narrative of black identity and a sense of belonging and community were absent. I would like to focus on two important aspects that particularly concern Black German girls. They deal with the mother-daughter dyad as it relates to the formation of a racial identity and a positive sense of self. White German mothers of black female children are certainly capable of transferring their personal experiences and cultural perceptions of womanhood to their daughters.[31] However, they were and are still unable to transfer their racial status to their offspring.[32] The majority of Black German girls and women had to survive in conditions that were void of positive and nurturing black female role models.

Along with being involved in ADEFRA and ISD, I am the mother of a Black German daughter. I have come to realize that it is nearly impossible to help a black child explore and articulate blackness when you as a white person know very little about or have minimal contact with black people. This was unfortunately the case for most Black German children born between 1945 and the early 1980s: there was simply no one present who could teach those youngsters how to be black. Moreover, many were confronted with discrimination and endured racism inside their own families.[33] The topic of racism is still a very delicate subject in Germany. Some Germans believe that not discussing or acknowledging racism creates a colorblind society. Some politicians and officials have actually disputed or denied the existence of racism in Germany.

GW: In general terms I agree with you. Audre gave an incredible boost to us in the Netherlands, too, but there has been a difference in the rise of black consciousness in Germany and in the Netherlands. For a long time in the Netherlands, there was no vocabulary to speak about race. In my family, when I was growing up, we talked about being brown, a tiny brown island amid an ocean of *bakras* (whites) or of having a little "tinge of color." We never talked about being black.

After a formative year as an exchange student in the United States, I started studying law in Nijmegen in 1969. At that time there were already active black student groups in Amsterdam, Nijmegen, Groningen, Wageningen, and other university towns. Inspired by black theoreticians and activists such as Walter Rodney, Stokely Carmichael, Angela Davis, and James Baldwin, students from Suriname and the Dutch Antilles (territories that were then still part of the Dutch empire) were talking in independent study groups about the independence of these colonies. We talked about anticolonialism, about racism in the Netherlands, and we began to translate the work of Eldridge Cleaver, H. Rap Brown, and others into Dutch. But the main actors in these debating groups were men; the women had more serviceable roles.

Later, when the women's movement came into full force, white women's issues took center stage, while black women's issues were seen as marginal. It was a classic setup, of course, but we did not have the language of intersectionality at our disposal at that time. All we knew, as black women, was that we were continually getting the shaft, that our issues were put on the back burner in whatever company of allies we found ourselves. We fought constantly to get race onto the agenda of the women's movement; and the presence of black men, with whom we often co-organized, was a serious point of conflict with white feminists.

CASSANDRA ELLERBE-DUECK AND GLORIA WEKKER

I became active in the black consciousness movement in the Netherlands before I became involved in the women's movement, a sequence that was not possible in Germany. Moreover, by the early 1980s (even before Sister Outsider) a black gay and lesbian organization called SuHo (Surinamese Gays) had formed. Audre thus stepped into a situation in the Netherlands that was different from the situation in Germany. We were more than ready for her vigorous input, for her help in creating a discourse that made it possible to talk about ourselves, proudly and unapologetically, as black women. But we had already taken steps on our own to organize ourselves as blacks, and she vindicated that tremendously. One of the crucial things she did was to show us, without necessarily using the term, how intersectionality worked. She clarified that we did not have to choose among being black, being a woman, being from a particular class background, and having a sexuality. She lived intersectionality before the term was coined in the late 1980s.

CED: Tell me about the genealogy of the black presence in the Netherlands and composition of those early populations.

GW: The social histories of black populations in Europe are widely divergent. We are in dire need of a comparative approach to the black presence in Europe, one that takes into account different national narratives and histories. I suspect that particular compositions and genealogies, in connection with the national discourses that construct each population, will have consequences for that population's organizational timing and capacity. You have just outlined how the Black German population came into being, and the literature that has become available since the 1980s underlines that history.[34] It is clear to me that intense exclusion and vilification of Black Germans existed, both before and after World War II. The fact that only pejorative terms were available for self-identification was reflected in isolation and in internalized oppression and self-hatred. It seems to have been an untenable social and psychic dwelling place.

The situation of blacks in the Netherlands was different, although racism was still a considerable part of the picture. By 1919 a Surinamese organization, Vereniging Ons Suriname, composed of intellectuals, laborers, and students was already functioning in Amsterdam. Members were intent on going back to Suriname and were interested in keeping up to date on political and economic developments there. Before World War II, single

Surinamese and Antillean men and women were arriving in the Netherlands, and some got involved with white partners and had children. The most common dyad involved Afro-Surinamese and Antillean men with white Dutch women. The men included anticolonial thinker Anton de Kom, who was also active in the resistance against the Germans; jazz musician Arthur Parisius, better known as Kid Dynamite; and student Waldemar Nods.[35] These three men stayed with their families until the end of their lives, which, for de Kom and Nods, took place in German concentration camps. After World War II, entire Surinamese families began coming to the Netherlands. They did not consider themselves interlopers but lived by the motto "we are here because you were there." Simply, the "mother" country offered them more economic, educational, and artistic possibilities.

CED: Would it be fair to say that, for both Black German and Dutch women, Audre's political and creative work, wisdom, and vision helped us articulate our diverse, black/African diasporic, and female selves? She helped many of us create self-determined spaces and recognize the similarities and parallels of our lives in dominant white European contexts. She encouraged us to love and name ourselves, document our stories, develop a black/African diasporic consciousness, claim and create our own spaces, and to reach out to one another transnationally.

GW: Yes, I wholeheartedly agree. There is a before and after Audre in the Netherlands, to which the many black and migrant women's organizations and mixed men's and women's organizations that blossomed after her can attest.

BLACK WOMEN AND TRANSNATIONAL NETWORKS IN EUROPE

CED: Audre continually stressed the transnational dimensions of the black diaspora. She was adamant that blacks of both genders, particularly black women, should create cross-border connections.

GW: I want to underline that thought. It is exceptional, in the context of the time, how transnationally oriented Audre was. Having lived in the United States for considerable stretches of time, I have seen how possible it is for both white and black Americans to be oblivious to the rest of the world. Among other writers of Audre's generation, June Jordan also had a distinctly transnational outlook. It is gratifying to see how this strain of Audre's work has been taken up and further theorized by feminist schools of thought.[36]

CASSANDRA ELLERBE-DUECK AND GLORIA WEKKER

CED: It is also amazing to see how her transnational orientation directly and indirectly influenced the cross-border networking of black women in Europe, even twenty years after her passing. Since the late 1970s, black women activists in the European space have networked tirelessly and politically mobilized around social justice issues.[37] Some of those networks are now defunct, but some are still active or have inspired the formation of new networks that currently engage in cross-border alliances.

The research that I conducted between 2007 and 2009 has highlighted the extreme importance of transnational and intercontinental connections among black women in Europe.[38] I conducted ethnographic interviews in various German cities and in Vienna, Austria, with many of the organizers of and participants in the 2007 Black European Women's Congress. Vienna hosted this highly publicized event, which was organized by the city's International Center for Black Women's Perspectives (AFRA) and Amsterdam's TIYE International, the umbrella association of twenty-one national organizations of black, migrant and refugee women in the Netherlands. One of the goals of this gathering was to establish an international network for black female activists, although the delegates decided that the term *council* (rather than *congress*) would better serve and accentuate their endeavors. Thus, the organization was later renamed Black European Women's Council (BEWC).

I have already mentioned the significance of tangible space and the notion of safe space for blacks in Germany. This carries an even greater significance for blacks in Austria.[39] Networks are crucial for black women and girls in that country, who often live in isolated contexts in which access to or information about networks or black women's organizations is unavailable.[40] Therefore, the space provided by the congress cannot be overestimated. Black female delegates from sixteen European countries came together to explore and create strategies aimed at enhancing the visibility and involvement of black women on the political stage at the European Union level. This was the first time that an international event of this scale had been organized by black women in Austria. Delegates from ADEFRA attended the 2007 conference, and the registration from Germany was so massive that the congress team was forced to limit the number of participants from Germany.[41]

In 2009, during impromptu interviews with Béatrice Achaleke, current BEWC president, and Helen Felter of TIYE, I began to see glimmers of

Audre's influence in both women's political mobilization tactics. Helen and Béatrice are experts at networking and building international coalitions and believe strongly in the increased political participation of black women in their respective European countries.[42] Both spoke about their encounters over the years with members of ADEFRA. While Helen met May Ayim in the Netherlands in the 1980s, Béatrice never met either May or Audre. Nonetheless, she referred to the Black German movement and May's political and academic work numerous times during our interview. This sheds light on the flow of ideas and information across borders. In May Ayim and the Black German movement, Béatrice saw tangible role models for her own political work. My insight was that Audre's work undoubtedly served as a catalyst for the political mobilization of Black Germans and certainly influenced May's political consciousness and creative work, and this was later passed down to Béatrice. In other words, Audre's political work and influence—indirectly and posthumously—is still encouraging black women to come together, build coalitions, and create international networks. Her activism, intellect, wisdom, creativity, and love—a significant aspect that should not be forgotten—left indelible imprints on the lives of countless black women and women of color in Europe.

GW: At some point, other women will have to write their stories about what Audre accomplished in South Africa, New Zealand, and all those other places she visited, toward the end of her life.

CODA

CED: We have been fortunate to have known Audre personally and, through her, to have met and begun to work together. Her work clearly has become traveling theory and practice in Europe.

GW: The roles since played by black women in our respective countries are highly significant. We need to delve deeper into what makes the stakes for black European women so high—personally, institutionally, and organizationally—that they have been at the forefront of most of these deeply important initiatives. This is an ongoing effort, as I am sure that Audre would agree.

CASSANDRA ELLERBE-DUECK AND GLORIA WEKKER

Notes

1. Not all of these conversations were recorded, so we have tried to reconstruct and expand on our notes and memories.
2. "Touche pas à mon pote" translates as "hands off my buddy." It was the slogan of the initiative SOS Racisme, which was formed to replace more radical antiracism and pro-immigration movements and morph them into a political party. The slogan had paternalistic undertones and primarily addressed white French people. For more information, see the SOS Racism website, www.sos-racisme.org.
3. Audre Lorde, *Sister Outsider: Essays and Speeches* (Trumansburg, N.Y.: Crossing Press, 1984). For a description of the entire weekend, see Gloria Wekker, "Audre Lorde, in de hand van Afrekete," *Katijf* 3 (1984): 3–8. For an analysis of the group Sister Outsider, see Gloria Wekker, "Überlieferinnen: Porträt der Gruppe Sister Outsider," in *Farbe bekennen: Afro-deutsche Frauen auf den Spuren ihrer Geschichte*, ed. Katharina Oguntoye, May Opitz, and Dagmar Schultz (Berlin: Orlanda Frauenverlag, 1986), 239–50. Jose Maas was succeeded in Sister Outsider by Joyce Spies, who has ties to Indonesia.
4. Audre Lorde, *Zami: A New Spelling of My Name* (London: Sheba, 1982), 32–33.
5. Ibid., especially chap. 23.
6. John Gabriel Stedman, *Narrative of a Five Years' Expedition against the Revolted Negroes of Suriname*, ed. Richard Price and Sally Price (Baltimore: John Hopkins University Press, 1988).
7. Gloria Wekker, "De mooie Joanna en haar Huurling," *Oso* 3, no. 2 (1984): 193–203. See also Jenny Sharpe, *Ghosts of Slavery: A Literary Archaeology of Black Women's Lives* (Minneapolis: University of Minnesota Press, 2003); and Saidya Hartmann, "Venus in Two Acts," *Small Axe* 26 (2008): 1–14.
8. Audre Lorde, letter to Cassandra Ellerbe-Dueck, July 1988.
9. Mari Evans, "My Words Will Be There," in *Conversations with Audre Lorde*, ed. Joan Wylie Hall (Jackson: University Press of Mississippi, 2004), 71–78.
10. Wekker, "Überlieferinnen."
11. Audre Lorde, "Uses of the Erotic: The Erotic as Power," in *Sister Outsider*, 53–59.
12. For more on Dagmar Schultz, see chapter 2.
13. Gloria Wekker, "'I Am a Gold Coin (I Pass through All Hands, but I Do Not Lose My Value)': The Construction of Selves, Gender, and Sexualities in a Female, Working-Class, Afro-Surinamese Setting" (Ph.D. diss., University of California, Los Angeles, 1992). For a later and more elaborate version, see Gloria Wekker, *The Politics of Passion* (New York: Columbia University Press, 2006).
14. Audre's phrase "postmodern language use" points to the philosophical school of thought in which master narratives are rejected and analyses of power and discourse are foregrounded. She was chiding me for using language that she thought was obscure and inaccessible.
15. Audre Lorde, "Today Is Not the Day," in *The Marvelous Arithmetics of Distance: Poems, 1987–1992* (New York: Norton, 1994), 57–59.
16. Tania Leon died in 1996.
17. M. Jacqui Alexander and Gloria Wekker, "Audre Lorde," in *Encyclopedia of Feminist Theories*, ed. Lorraine Code (New York: Routledge, 2000), 312–13.
18. The terms *Afro-German* and *Black German* (often used interchangeably) are self-ascribed designations.
19. Joanne M. Braxton and Andrée Nicola McLaughlin, eds., *Wild Women in the*

Whirlwind: Afra-American Culture and the Contemporary Literary Renaissance (New Brunswick, N.J.: Rutgers University Press, 1989). The title of this section was inspired by the book.

20. Ibid., 150.
21. Nirmal Puwar, *Space Invaders: Race, Gender, and Bodies out of Place* (London: Berg, 2007).
22. While Germans of dual European and African or African/black diasporic heritage are highly visible in terms of their phenotype, people of color in Germany are still commonly perceived as not being "real" Germans and experience exclusion in daily life as well as in the nation's historical consciousness.
23. I approach the concept of African diaspora as a metaphorical and analytical framework to examine practices of blackness within the German-speaking context.
24. Audre Lorde, "Is Your Hair Still Political?" in *I Am Your Sister: Collected and Unpublished Writings of Audre Lorde,* ed. Rudolph P. Byrd, Johnnetta Betsch Cole, and Beverly Guy-Sheftall (Oxford: Oxford University Press, 2009), 224–27.
25. Chinosole, "Audre Lorde and Matrilineal Diaspora: 'Moving History beyond Nightmare into Structures for the Future . . . ,'" in Braxton and McLaughlin, *Wild Women in the Whirlwind,* 379–94.
26. Oguntoye et al., *Farbe bekennen,* 237.
27. Fatima El Tayeb, *Schwarze Deutsche, der Diskurs um "Rasse" und nationale Identität, 1890–1933* (Frankfurt am Main: Campus, 2001).
28. Tina Campt, "'Afro-German': The Convergence of Race, Sexuality, and Gender in the Formation of a German Ethnic Identity" (Ph.D. diss., Columbia University, 1996).
29. Fatima El Tayeb, "'If You Can't Pronounce My Name, You Can Call Me Pride': Afro-Germans, Activism, Gender, and Hip Hop," *Gender and History* 15, no. 3 (2003): 462.
30. Wekker, "Überlieferinnen."
31. Jayne O. Ifekwunigwe, *Scattered Belongings: Cultural Paradoxes of "Race," Nation, and Gender* (London: Routledge, 1999).
32. France Winddance Twine and Jonathan W. Warren, *Race-ing Research, Researching Race: Methodological Dilemmas in Critical Race Studies* (New York: New York University Press, 1999).
33. Sven Halfar's film *Yes I Am* (Hamburg: Filmtank, 2006) looks at the lives of four Black German hip hop artists: Adé Odukoya, D-Flame, Madamee, and Xavier Naidoo. It not only examines their careers in the music industry but also calls attention to everyday racism in Germany. D-Flame's story particularly caught my attention because he experienced racism from his own mother, who at times hurled racial slurs at him when she was angry.
34. Oguntoye et al.'s *Farbe bekennen* has been published in English as *Showing Our Colors: Afro-German Women Speak Out,* trans. Anne V. Adams (Amherst: University of Massachusetts Press, 1991). Also see Ika Hügel-Marshall, *Invisible Woman: Growing Up Black in Germany,* trans. Elizabeth Gaffney (New York: Continuum International, 2002).
35. Alice Boots and Rob Woortman, *Anton de Kom: Biografie* (Amsterdam: Uitgeverij Contact, 2009); *Kid Dynamite,* dir. Hans Hylkema (Amsterdam: Pieter Van Huystee, 2001); *Sonny Boy* [about Waldemar Nods], dir. Maria Peters (Amsterdam: Shooting Star, 2011).
36. Inderpal Grewal and Caren Kaplan, *Scattered Hegemonies: Postmodernity and Transnational Feminist Practices* (Minneapolis: University of Minnesota Press, 1994); M.

Jacqui Alexander and Chandra Talpade Mohanty, *Feminist Genealogies, Colonial Legacies, Democratic Futures* (New York: Routledge, 1997).

37. Organizations include Organisation of Women of Asian and African Descent (founded in 1978), Southall Black Sisters (founded in 1979), Zami (founded in 1991), and Sister Outsider (founded in the 1980s).

38. For more on this project, known as the European Sixth Framework Research Project Searching for Neighbours (SeFoNe), visit www.sefone.soton.ac.uk.

39. For a detailed account of the political mobilization of black Austria, see Araba Johnston-Arthur, "'Es ist Zeit, der Geschichte selbst eine Gestalt zu geben . . .': Strategien der Entkolonisierung und Entmächtigung im Kontext der modernen afrikanischen Diaspora in Österreich," in *Re/Visionen: Postkoloniale Perspektiven von People of Color auf Rassismus, Kulturpolitik und Widerstand in Deutschland*, ed. K. Nghi Ha, N. Lauré al-Samurai, and Sheila Mysorekar (Münster: Unrast, 2007), 423–44.

40. Cassandra Ellerbe-Dueck, "Networks and Safe Spaces of Black European Women in Austria and Germany," in *Negotiating Multicultural Europe: Border, Networks, Neighbourhoods,* ed. Heidi Armbruster and Ulrike Hanna Meinhof (Basingstoke, U.K.: Palgrave Macmillan, 2011), 159–84.

41. Béatrice Achaleke, personal communication with Cassandra Ellerbe-Dueck, August 1, 2009.

42. Cassandra Ellerbe-Dueck, "The Black European Women's Council: 'Thinking oneself into the new Europe,'" *African and Black Diaspora* 4, no. 2 (2011): 145–60.

5
Frontiers

An Interview with Audre Lorde

PRATIBHA PARMAR AND JACKIE KAY

PRATIBHA PARMAR: We are really glad that you're willing to do this interview even though it's transatlantic and on tape. We want to start by asking you about your stay in Berlin, before you came to London in 1984 for the First International Feminist Book Fair. Can you tell us if there was any contrast between your experiences in London and your experiences in Berlin?

AUDRE LORDE: Well, I was in Berlin for three months before I came to London, and there were some very striking differences. To begin with, visually, Berlin is a very calm city. But it is an extremely white city, and the whiteness of it encourages a certain smug assumption that is different from the United States and England. There are few Black people in Berlin, so there's little question of interaction, except on the most objectifying of levels. Being stared at, for instance, if you walk down the street, not always with hostility even, but with curiosity. Landing in London, the first difference is a visual one. So many Black people! There was so much color in the streets, it made my heart sing.

JACKIE KAY: Could you talk about the racial tension that you noticed in the streets of London, and how that in fact differed from New York?

AL: After having come into the airport and been with you all on the train and seeing so many Black people I was not prepared for the rather rude level of racism that I met in the streets of London itself. Certainly, racial tension is a reality of life in New York and can get really nasty. But this was more personal and immediate. Do you remember, Jackie, when we walked into the bakery to buy some cookies, and the woman came over and said in quite a nasty tone of voice, "Now, don't touch anything!"? As if I would touch her wares! I doubt if I were a white woman who had come into her shop that she would have reacted that way. That's one example. There's a raw frontier quality about the racial confrontations on the streets and in the subways of London that shocked me. And it should not have shocked me because the danger that we experience as Black people in New York cannot be underestimated. White Berliners are isolated from Black people, and they defend that separation. They are interested in dealing with racism in America, and in England, but are much less prepared to deal with racism in terms of their Turkish and Middle Eastern workers who are the "Black" people of Germany. That would bring racism too close to home.

PP: You came for the first ever International Feminist Book Fair that was organized in London by a mainly white women's group. First of all, in your opinion, how international was that book fair? Secondly, you were one of the very few guest black women writers who played a crucial role in actually confronting head on the type of racism that we see quite frequently in the white women's movement: the kind where there is a tokenistic gesture for including black women or, when black women are included, they are particular black women who are already quite famous or who are going to be crowd pullers. One of the problems with the organization of that book fair was that none of the black women in London was asked, and furthermore, the way in which it was organized made black women in Britain feel that it was not something that they could take part in.

You actually refused to take part in the lesbian forum because so many black women that night were being turned away from hearing you and other black women speak. Can you say what you felt about that whole experience and where you think that kind of behavior is coming from? Finally, because of your intervention and your support for the black women who were challenging their right to be able to attend that forum, they were able to participate, and it went ahead. But it did leave a very bad taste. Till this day, as far as we're concerned, nothing much has been either written or spoken about what actually happened and what black women's experiences were at that particular book fair. So, could you say something about that?

AL: You're quite right, Pratibha, this is a hard one to deal with. It was a very difficult and disheartening situation. I am much more interested in seeing what we—me, you, the Black women of London, even the white women—can learn from that situation. The white women's defensiveness that arose whenever certain questions were raised has to do with the fact that white women hide behind a guilt which does not serve us nor them. I would like to move beyond that guilt. The fact remains: The International Feminist Book Fair was a monstrosity of racism, and this racism coated, distorted, and deflected much of what was good and creative, almost visionary, about having such a fair. Now, if anything is to be learned from that whole experience, it should be so that the *next* International Women's Book Fair does not repeat these errors. And there *must* be another Feminist Book Fair. But we don't get *there* from *here* by ignoring the mud we have to plod through. If the white women's movement does not learn from its errors, it will die by them.

Now, how international was it? I was impressed with the number of Black women invited—Faith Bandler from Australia, Flora Nwapa from Nigeria, and the other African women, as well as women from the United States of America. But it seemed to me that token women had been invited to be showcased, and this always sends off a bell in my brain, even when I myself am one of those women. That awareness did not solidify until I stood up for my first reading to a packed house and saw almost no Black faces, and *that* was the kiss-off! What was going on? I didn't know, but I knew something was up, and the rest, more or less, is history. I was very angry.

I had come to London not because I loved going to book fairs but because the idea of a First International Feminist Book Fair excited me. I very much wanted to make contact with Black women in England; I thought, "Well, *this* is the ideal place to do it." I was not well at the time, but I came from Berlin to London despite the strain of travel. What made it worthwhile for me was knowing that I would make contact with a new group of Black women. We could sit down together; and I would find out who you were, listen to you, because I had never met you before. I *knew* that you existed, the Black feminists of England, and I wanted us to share space, to look into each other's faces and explore our similarities and differences, and see what we share and what we don't. That meeting was a major objective for me but to accomplish it was very difficult because it appeared that the local Black women were not involved. When I raised this question with one of the organizers, I was quite taken aback by her defensiveness. My question was not meant as an attack, certainly not at that time. It was a question which I have gotten used to having to ask in white feminist circles in the United States but which I had not expected to have to ask in London. The aggressive defensiveness that the question aroused, the really hostile and demeaning responses on the part of some white feminists here got my back up. I was accused of "brutalizing" the organizers by simply asking why Black women were so absent.

I remember some of the earliest tacky battles of the 1960s in the white women's movement in the States; a Black woman would suggest that if white women truly wished to be feminist, they would have to reexamine and alter their actions, and the whole discussion would be perceived as an attack on white women's very essence. This is so wasteful and destructive. I realize that the women who organized the International Feminist Book Fair truly believed that by inviting foreign Black women they were absolving themselves of any fault in the way they dealt with Black women. But we should all be able to learn from our errors. They totally objectified Black women by not choosing to deal with the Black women in their own communities.

Channels of communication between Black and white women must be kept open, certainly; but until white women begin to see the results of their blindness and other acts of omission and cancellation and begin to ask certain questions of themselves, there is a limited input that Black women can have into the white women's movement, not because we wish to be separatist but because trying to raise their consciousness about racism at every turn is just too costly for us. We are not machines, and we have limited sources of energy, and we must choose those areas where that energy will be most effective. Our children are *dying*. All over the world, Black women are in the process of examining who we are: What are our differences? What are the ways in which we do not see each other? How can we operate together better as a unified front? These are questions of survival, and we must expend our primary energy on these questions at the same time as we recognize that without coalition we will always be more vulnerable. However, we *must* be alone at times to build our strengths, rather than siphon off our energies into some vain attempt at connection with a group of women who are not prepared to deal with either their history or ours. Now, your history as Black women in England is a very complex one, and I certainly do not know enough to generalize. I can only react to what I see going on. But it was unfortunate that white women's defensiveness apparently kept them from hearing the questions I tried to raise because I raised them in the truest spirit of sisterhood, which does not mean without anger. The trivializing and personalizing of this dialogue was yet another attempt to come between the reality of the situation and their responsibility for those realities. The intransigent quality of the organizers' refusal to hear was most oppressive to me.

Unchallenged, racism ultimately will be the death of the women's movement in England, just as it threatens to become the death of any women's movement in those developed countries where it is not addressed. Feminism must be on the cutting edge of real social change if it is to be a true movement. In the same way, unless the German women's movement accepts the fight against anti-Semitism as crucial to the survival of that movement *it* is going to die. Whatever the core problem is for the people of a country will also be the core problem addressed by women, consciously or otherwise. We do not exist in a vacuum. We are anchored in our own place and time, and we are part of communities that interact. To pretend that we are not is ridiculous. So I felt enraged by silence and evasion, and I was determined not to have that rage turned either on myself or on other Black women. I looked at the source of it and acted to change it. If I altered any consciousness, then it was good. I reacted with anger because sometimes that is the only appropriate response to racist actions. And we all need to be reminded that anger between peers is not fatal, but sometimes silence is.

Also, I wanted to say to the Black women of London, young Black women with whom I was in contact: It is not all in your head. Don't let them muck around with your realities. You may not be able to make very much inroad, but at least you've got to stop feeling quite so crazy. Because, after a while, constantly exposed to unacknowledged racism, Black women get to feeling really crazy. And then, it's all in our heads, the white women say. They say we're being this, we're being that, but they never acknowledge there's a problem and that they are a part of it. When I questioned the social situation at the book fair, those women talked double-talk to me. They seemed terrified of Black women or at least determined not to deal with us.

Rather than keep yelling at the gates, we've really got to begin to look at ourselves in terms of what do we need most and start to give that to each other. One of the areas that has got to come under scrutiny is how we deal with each other across our own differences as Black women. In other

PRATIBHA PARMAR AND JACKIE KAY

words, how do we learn to love each other? And I feel hopeful. I even feel hopeful about the book fair because I met you all and that was important to me, really important, to look at your faces, to have questions raised, to have my coat pulled by Black women who could give *me* something to think about too, in terms of a progress and a future. I really value that.

Before we get off onto the next question I want to say, therefore, Pratibha and Jackie, the first International Feminist Book Fair is a landmark for us all. In years to come you may look back at that and see that it was at that point, that you really saw beyond revision, that it was not "all in your head," and that you had to pursue your own interests because if you waited to build a joint movement, it was not going to happen for a while. If I yelled and screamed and got dirty looks and made women cry and say all kinds of outrageous nonsense about me, nonetheless, I hope it really reinforced for other Black women here that racism in the London women's movement is not an isolated phenomenon, and it doesn't merely exist in their heads. "Hey! She's really saying it too. It's not something that I feel and have got to look away from." And that's always important. I hope a new kind of unity, or a new kind of inquiry between Black women in London will begin. We can worry about exclusion until the fences molder and rot away, and there's nothing left to be excluded from, or we can look at where we are, *who* we are, and begin to build structures and institutions of our own.

JK: You came over for the first International Feminist Book Fair, and as a result of being here, you met a lot of different black women. We'd like to know what, if any, differences you saw between the black feminists that you met here and black American feminists. Did you feel that there were any differences in the way that we survive, in the way that we confront conflicts? Did you feel that there *was* a movement here of black women that you could identify? Do you feel that the issues that black women are dealing with over here are related in any way to the issues that black women are dealing with in America?

AL: Certainly the issues are very similar. There are issues that we share, and there are particular and specific places in which our struggles differ. I felt very, very close to you and to the struggles that were going on here. I also felt the weight of the forces against you, and I thought in the light of that, that you were being wonderfully resourceful in maintaining the kinds of connections that you have with each other, the existence of Sheba [Feminist

Publishers], the way you work together, this very tape, the Brixton Women's Group, the Black women writers. You should be proud of yourselves. You should also recognize how much you've done. Like all of us, you have to ask yourselves, what do you need to become stronger, and then set about giving it to yourselves individually and as a group; these questions of how we attend the differences among us has to become a central question within groups of women of color. We are grappling with many of the same problems and conditions in some similar ways.

In other ways our solutions are different. Take the issue of how we name ourselves, for example. In the United States, *Black* means of African heritage, and we use the term *women of color* to include Native American, Latina, Asian American women. I understand that here, *Black* is a political term which includes all oppressed ethnic groups, and the term *women of color* is frowned on.

I love the ways in which you are connected with each other in day to day living; the fact that women live in houses together or share flats. It feels as if there is, in some ways, much more of a living connectedness here than in the States, and this is one of the ways that we as Black women need to develop. This does not always exist to as large a degree among Black women in the United States. There are many Black women there who are *just* beginning to call themselves feminists and who vary widely on their definition on what Black feminism *is*. I hope there will soon be some kind of international conference of Black feminists where we can begin to look at who we are because I believe that the woman who defines herself as a Black feminist living and working in the Northeastern States, as I do, is very different from the woman who lives in rural Georgia, or Kentucky, and who calls herself a Black feminist there; and we are both very different from *you*, from the woman who lives in London, or Glasgow, the Black woman who was born and bred in Berlin, or Amsterdam, and who also calls herself a Black feminist. I would like to see us get together and discuss who we are, and no doubt if we all desire it enough, it will in fact come about. I look forward to that. In the meantime, these are questions we need to be asking ourselves on a more immediate basis. I love the fact that you get together so often.

JK: We are very concerned at the moment with the right-wing turn this whole country is taking, there is a really threatening feeling in the air, and when I was in New York this summer, I felt that there as well. We're

PRATIBHA PARMAR AND JACKIE KAY

particularly concerned about the growing number of black women who are disassociating themselves from black feminism, saying the very same things that white people and black men would applaud and can use against us. What do you feel are the reasons for black women treating each other and hurting each other in this kind of way, and how do you think we can constructively do something about this?

AL: You have a right to be angry, but that anger must become articulate. Yes, there has been a very strong right-wing turn. It's not only in England. The racism, sexism, and self-hatred that simmer below the surface of any situation of oppression, have now risen to the surface and are being officially sanctioned. That threat that we feel on the streets as Black women, as Black lesbians, is real, and it does increase. As I see it, it is going to get worse before it gets better, and we *must* be able to look that fact in the eye and continue to work and to live and to love because it *will* get better—and it will get better because you and I and the woman down there across the street are going to keep on doing what we know needs being done. It may not come about in our lifetimes, but what we are doing is invaluable and necessary in the long run—pushing it along. When you say that Black women are beginning to turn away from feminism, you're missing a very important point, which is that, by and large, most Black women, at least in America, have not dealt with issues of feminism as such at all because they have been reluctant to see the connections between our oppression as Black people and our oppression as Black women.

Much of that reluctance is a result of the rampant racism in the white feminist movements. Our liberations cannot be separated. Some Black women have accepted those intersections and are beginning to say the things that need to be said, within our communities and to each other. That is what is going to have to happen. These women who bad-mouth feminism in our communities are our concern in an immediate and survival way. How do we reach these Black women who belittle and attack us? It is our responsibility, and we must do it, but it is not something that happens overnight. We have been raised to work out our pain and frustration on each other, and we do it without thinking, often, for whatever reasons we can find.

Black women mouth the enemies' words against us, Black feminists, because they do not see those words acting against themselves as well. Getting that across to them is one of our most important tasks, and we can only do it on their turf because they don't come to ours. But we share communities, and there are many places where our lives intersect as Black women, feminist and non-feminist. And those are the places where we need to make contact and coalition. It requires patience and perseverance and the determination to work and identify ourselves in often hostile territory. But all our asses are in the same sling.

How do you think I feel when I hear Alice Walker say, "Black feminism sounds like some kind of spray!"?[1] I feel really sad. It hurts me, but it hurts me for Alice too, because I hear her testifying against herself in a way that is painful, and because she does it in a way that also testifies against me. All the time Black women are surrounded by forces that attempt to make us speak out against each other, and all of us have had the experience of opening our mouth and having a frog jump out, but we also have to realize that we are responsible for our own frogs. I know Alice would not attack other Black women in a white women's forum, so I would like to presume that it was not meant as an attack. But the fact remains it was heard as an attack upon Black feminism by many, and it was a very demoralizing statement. I would, in the last analysis, fall back on my mama: her voice saying, "Well, honey, sticks and stones can break your bones, but words will never hurt you!" and well, yeah, words do hurt, but the fact remains, they don't kill, and I'm interested in getting to action. We make ourselves strong by doing the things we need to be strong for. I want to keep calling us back to a kind of centeredness. I really do like the idea of some day being able to take part in an international conference on Black feminism, a Black women's book fair, womanist, feminist, whatever you want to call it. And I am planting that vision inside of your heads, and hopefully maybe you will take it up and help make it happen.

PP: How do you feel about the need for black women internationally to make links with each other? We *are* doing that in some ways, but do you feel that what we are doing is enough, and that do we need to do more to actually make an international movement of black and "Third World" women? At the moment it seems that we all are working very much in isolation from each other in our different countries, and the need for that international dialogue between us is really crucial. How do you think we could actually strengthen these links?

AL: Pratibha, I think that an international network is absolutely essential,

PRATIBHA PARMAR AND JACKIE KAY

and I think it is in the process of being born, which is what this dialogue is all about. I feel very excited and very heartened, whenever I think about it, because I feel this is the way it's going to happen. I'm sorry that I was not in Nairobi. It happened there in one way beneath the surface: women making contact with each other over specific areas of our lives that we can fertilize and examine. This is what Black feminism is all about—articulating ourselves, our needs, and our resistances as women and as women within our particular environments. We don't exist in the abstract.

How can we do it? Ah, Pratibha, but we *are* doing it, look, we are sitting here now on both sides of the ocean strategizing. I think about the Black Australian women and their land rights struggles. I think with great excitement about the young Black women I met in Germany, Afro-German feminists. I think of Gloria Wekker in Amsterdam and the Sister Outsider Collective, Timeke and Tania and Joyce. There is a wonderful richness of Black women that I find all around the world. You need to be in touch with those women; they need to be in touch with you. Yes, we all need to see, hey, that there are aspects of our lives that are crazy-making because we are Black women and they happen no matter where we are. What does it mean? What particular ways do we combat that? We need to look at the ways in which we are invited to testify against ourselves, against our beauty, against our daughters. We need to be able to compare notes. How can we do it?

We can do it by finding out who we are and by making attempts to see or to find out who we are not, meeting when we can, and in the absence of that, sharing our work, our thoughts, our letters, our strengths. Transoceanic conversations such as this. Maori women in New Zealand. Aboriginal women in Australia. Women in Samoa and Papua and Fiji. *Charting the Journey,* that's what you mean, isn't it?[2] How do we get there from here?

What you chart is already where you've been. But where we are going, there is no chart yet. We are brave and daring, and we are looking ahead. Our Black women's vision has no horizon. I would look about me. Where are the places in which Black women are in need? Where are the places in which we can work? Where are those places in our communities? It's long and uphill work, but we *are* part of our communities, and we are there as Black feminists, and we are an inseparable and integral part of life. So what if some Black women say, "We are not feminists"? That's less important than all of you working together on a project, and out of that will come the respect that is inevitable. By their labor, Black feminists help build that dam, win that battle, save that daycare center. That's one way of doing it.

I don't think that we get very far with frontal challenges, although sometimes challenges are absolutely necessary because people have got to be kept on their toes, and sometimes you can't just stand around and take that shit without saying *something* because it's bad for the psyche. But, on the other hand, you can become so invested in what you're saying that you think talk is the only action necessary. I'm talking from a position of doing both all the time and trying to find some good balance in between. *Charting the Journey*. We are hungry for heroes. To paraphrase June Jordan, we are the women whom we want to become. We can become ourselves. I'm so impressed with Sheba, with the press, with how you work together, and with the film. I love to see Black women achieving on so many levels, and you are doing it. That's really wonderful. I would like to inject even more of that into Black women's groups everywhere where the necessity for being political is often one that's still being discussed rather than assumed. Our lives are political and our very existence as Black women. Wherever we find ourselves over the earth, a network is being born of Black feminist survival, and I applaud it. We are going to make it, no matter what. I find you very affirming. You bring a lot of joy to me and therefore a lot of strength. It won't be easy. But all of our strengths together are going to turn this whole world around.

Notes

1. Hermione Lee, "Rally Neat, Alice," *Observer,* May 5, 1985, 24.
2. Lorde is referring to the collection of essays in which this interview was originally published: Shabnam Grewal, Jackie Kay, Liliane Landor, Gail Lewis, and Pratibha Parmar, eds., *Charting the Journey: Writings by Black and Third World Women* (London: Sheba, 1988).

PRATIBHA PARMAR AND JACKIE KAY

6
Audre Lorde and Her French-Speaking Readers

❦

RINA NISSIM

I first met Audre Lorde in 1984 at the First International Women's Book Fair in London, through Dagmar Schultz, who had published us both in German. I had already read Audre's essays, and I was immediately impressed with her strength, political lucidity, determination, and courage. There in London, she blew up when she realized she had been invited as the token black woman. She was supposed to read her poems, but practically all the seats had been sold in advance, and women of color could not get into the hall. Audre certainly made herself heard; the hall was emptied and the seats redistributed according to a quota system. It took a long time and many white women stormed out. Finally, in that electric ambiance, I discovered the power of her readings. Audre did not simply read her poetry; like many African American speakers and poets, she *declaimed* it, which gave extraordinary force to her emotions and greatly moved her audience.

We met again in Amsterdam because we also had the same Dutch publisher. Audre and I were both there for book tours, but the publishing house was on the brink of bankruptcy, and our books had not been printed. Though the publisher canceled my tour without telling me, Audre's was maintained as scheduled—but with no books! A friendship developed through these encounters, but it was Dagmar who really brought us together. I had known Dagmar since 1974, when we met through our engagements in the self-help movement and later in women's health centers. She was also my

Front cover of French magazine *Lesbia*, January 1993. Reproduced with permission of Jacqueline Pasquier, formerly chief editor of *Lesbia* (published between 1982 and 2012).

mentor in publishing. Audre came to Berlin regularly; she taught poetry and did lecture tours, and Afro-German groups were created around her work.

Audre had overcome breast cancer years before, but it had metastasized to her liver, and she was in bad condition.[1] In 1984, she had started anthroposophic treatment in Berlin with mistletoe. On my advice she went to the Lukas Klinik, near Basel, for continued anthroposophic treatment. She showed courage and incredible willpower in choosing to spend a long period in Switzerland, even though she did not speak German. Much weakened, she was accompanied there by Frances Clayton, who shared her life at the time and saw her every day. I also went for support. Not all of the staff members understood her case; some were even overtly racist. For example, the dietician thought Audre ate raw food "like all the barbarians in Africa"! But she had an incredible ability to take what was useful to her and ignore the rest, and she got a great deal out of her stay. From 1987 on, she received treatment and good advice from the naturopath Manfred Kuno. She lived with her metastases for nine years, which is exceptional, and during that time she continued to write, travel, read her poetry, and teach.

AUDRE LORDE IN FRENCH: A COPUBLISHING VENTURE

I was too young to fully understand the importance of the 1960s Black Revolution in the United States. I was sixteen in 1968, which did not stop me from singing and playing my guitar against the bourgeois order on the Place du Bourg de Four in the center of Geneva. But Dagmar Schultz was way ahead of me: in 1983 she had already published *Macht und Sinnlichkeit* (*Power and Sensuality*), a collection of essays by Audre Lorde and Adrienne Rich.[2] At that time, my publishing house, Les Editions Mamamélis, was just getting started. I had published my first book, *Mamamélis* (*Natural Healing in Gynecology*), with the Geneva Women's Health Center. Although I had received requests for translations into different languages, starting with German, I did not yet know that the book would be a bestseller and able to sustain my publishing house for many years.[3]

I am first and foremost a health worker, a naturopath, and my book ideas were about women's health and autonomy. So the next ones I published were translations of books about medicinal plants to use during pregnancy (Susun Weed's *Wise Woman Herbal for the Childbearing Year*), yoga for women (Adelheid Ohlig's *Luna Yoga*), and others. In 1992, after spending five years in India researching medicinal plants and women's health and enduring a big professional upheaval, I once more took charge of the publishing house. A new bestseller came out in 1994, my book *La ménopause: réflexions et alternatives aux hormones de substitution.* Now Les Editions Mamamélis was on firm ground, and my publications on women and health were never out of print. I finally had the funds to publish books that might not sell well, and I was particularly committed to presenting Audre's work to French-speaking women. I wanted to expand publishing on political subjects, especially on relationships of power.

Les Editions Mamamélis had a wide distribution in Europe (Switzerland, France, and Belgium), but for Audre I also wanted to reach French-speaking Canada; and after some research I met Anne-Marie Alonzo and Les Editions Trois. Anne-Marie was born in Egypt and I in Jerusalem one year later; her family immigrated to Canada and mine to Switzerland. The parallel ends there. After a serious accident at age fourteen she became almost quadriplegic, which did not keep her from studying and being awarded a Ph.D. She wrote twenty books and won numerous prizes. A poet, playwright, translator, and literary critic, Anne-Marie was also cofounder of the magazine and publishing house Trois. After a lengthy correspondence, we finally met when I traveled to Quebec. For the publication of Audre Lorde's books, we started with *Le journal du cancer* (*The Cancer Journals*) and *Un souffle de lumière* (*A Burst of Light*) in one volume, published in Geneva, and *Zami: une nouvelle façon d'écrire mon nom* (*Zami: A New Spelling of My Name*), published in Montreal. The two books came out simultaneously in the summer of 1998. The copublishing adventure worked out very well. Les Editions Mamamélis paid for foreign rights and translations, and we shared the printing costs. *Zami* was printed in Canada, *The Cancer Journal* in Switzerland. We sold the two books in our regions, and Les Editions Trois also distributed my other books in Quebec. I did not expect extraordinary sales, and this turned out to be true—a few hundred copies. Luckily that was not a problem for my publishing house, thanks to the women's health books that sold very well. What mattered most was that Audre Lorde's work was available in French in public libraries and universities, where it would encourage further thinking. In 2003 I published *Sister Outsider: essais et propos d'Audre Lorde* (*Sister Outsider: Essays and Speeches*) in Switzerland, still as part of the copublishing venture with Les Editions Trois. Unfortunately, Anne-Marie died in 2005, and her publishing house folded a year later.

In 2010, I engaged in a copublishing venture with the magazine *Nouvelles Questions Féministes,* each of us hoping to discover a new audience through the other. I felt very proud to have published the U.S. feminist authors who had inspired and moved me most.[4] Of course, I would have liked to have published Audre's poetry, but, sadly, poetry is very risky for a publisher. Not only are audiences small, but translation costs are high and it is difficult to find a style in French that honors the original work. The same was true for Adrienne Rich's work: I ultimately chose to publish a collection of her essays rather than her poetry.

AUDRE LORDE'S RECEPTION IN FRENCH-SPEAKING EUROPE

To promote Audre's books in France, I toured with Ada Gay Griffin and Michelle Parkerson's film *A Litany for Survival: The Life and Work of Audre Lorde* (1995). At the time it was not subtitled, so I had to read aloud the French translation with a tiny lamp on my knees, but I had practiced a lot and it worked out well. I was accustomed to packed halls during my lecture-debates on women's health, but I quickly realized that Audre was not really recognized in France. Among the reasons was intellectually dominant French-style universalism, which countered attempts to broach inequality head on. In addition, Eurocentrism created a lack of curiosity about other cultures, even in feminist circles.

After the film, at the Paris Women's Center, some women started shouting at each other, wanting to know why so few people were present, thereby causing the few women who were not part of their group to flee. At Bagdam Cafée in Toulouse I could not keep the women's attention for more than twenty minutes; they preferred to talk among themselves and sip their drinks. Movie houses were better venues, even for lesbian and feminist circles. In Marseille (at the Centre Evolutif Lilith) and at the Lesbian Film Festival in Paris (Cineffable), the film and Audre's work were better received. But more interesting than the numbers was the reaction. Viewers found this black woman—a lesbian and a warrior who emphasized that she was also a mother and who did not hide the fact that she had been battling cancer—a bit frightening. By the end of the twentieth century, many women had published testimonies on breast cancer, often within a framework of self-treatment. But in the late 1990s, the off-putting effect of the word *cancer* in the title of a book was very clear. Nonetheless, Audre's experience with the disease, her confrontation with the medical establishment and with fear—but also with strength and *joie de vivre*—were a true inspiration.

Racism was a parallel problem in France. Were we ready to ask ourselves about what separates us in issues of race, class, and power, even within the women's movement? The 1999 French Coordination Lesbienne meeting was the scene of a major conflict over racism. After a screening of *A Litany for Survival*, viewers clashed about the place, or lack thereof, given to women of color in the lesbian movement and its organizations. Reactions were very defensive, even violent. Many white women tried to block the debate with arguments such as "I can't be a racist because I supported the struggle of Algerian women." Filmmaker Dalila Kadri from Marseille met strong resistance when she and other women wanted to discuss her film project, *Ombres Solaires* (1999). The French lesbian movement split, not over skin color but over the place allotted to discriminations other than lesbophobia, such as racism or class discrimination. The situation was an eye opener, and "Zami" groups, inspired by Audre Lorde, were created among North African, African, and African American women (in Lyon and

Marseille) to work on their multiple identities as women of color and lesbians and tackle issues of oppression.

In Marseille, Dalila Kadri continued making films that explored questions of overlapping systems of discrimination: *Lucioles,* 2004; *Marseille, le panier des songes,* 2008; and *Le chant des amazones,* 2010. In the meantime, reactions to Audre's work were playing out as they had in the United States in the 1980s, when white women were reading and listening to her lectures. Audre had the ability to link racism, sexism, and class inequality; more importantly, she had the lucidity, finesse of language, and courage to extract a sense of what cannot be heard, of what no one wants to admit or confront. Through conflicts, progress was slowly made. Her multifaceted personality and her complexity, delivered in one blow, both seduced and raised hackles. Moreover, she never assumed the position of the victim; no one could feel sorry for her or co-opt her to satisfy a conscience. In other words, Audre shook things up, and that was a good thing—except when it came to selling books. The pioneers, the lesbians of color in France who spoke in the 1990s and tried to question the lesbian feminist movement about racism and inequality, were rather broken in the fray, according to the accounts I have heard. The lesbian feminist movement remained largely white and unrepresentative of the multiplicity of French society. Women of color joined other struggles or completely abandoned that kind of activism, trying to live their differences and combat inequality in alternative ways.

Audre's writings, particularly her essays, continue to interest francophone academics and women interested in feminist theory. For instance, "The Transformation of Silence into Language and Action" was reprinted in 2008 in *Black feminism: anthologie du féminisme africain-américain, 1975–2000.*[5] The editor, Elsa Dorlin, places Audre at the forefront of both the third wave of African American feminism and the queer movement because of her radical politicization of the erotic.[6] After a 2010 colloquium at Lausanne University on anger, courage, and political creation, Marie-Claire Caloz-Tschopp reissued excerpts from Audre's "The Uses of Anger: Women Responding to Racism" and "Eye to Eye: Black Women, Hatred, and Anger" to open the third volume (*La colère, une passion politique?*) of a five-volume set of the proceedings. My contribution, whose title translates as "Women, Collective Anger?," was also included in this subgroup.[7] Maybe now there is a place for women of color in academic circles, at least at the student level, to research and publish ideas that will move our thinking forward in the "Old World." I am sure the photocopiers have been working overtime to print out pirated copies of Audre Lorde's work.

After publishing the French translation of *Sister Outsider* in 2003, I went on tour again. This time I read aloud particularly powerful passages on poetry, eroticism, racism, and sexism, which I followed with question-and-answer periods; and I found the young Parisian squats (that is, people who reappropriated housing without paying rent) to be quite open to Audre's work. More recently I discovered a copy of her "The Uses of Anger" at an Info Kiosk (the library of the squat movement) in Haute Savoie, France. I contacted one of the young women involved with the project and explained that the problem is not losing royalties because I ask nothing for reproductions. Rather, not mentioning the source prevents readers from discovering other Audre Lorde texts. This was the first of many such conversations. As a result, in 2012 two of Audre's essays, "The Uses of Anger" and "Age, Race, Class, and Sex: Women Redefining Difference," appeared on infokiosques. net. So it is clear that Audre has broken into alternative, anarchist circles, and I'm delighted!

Black feminisms are alive and well in the United States, but what exists in French-speaking Europe? As a former colonial power that still has overseas departments and territories, France has trouble questioning itself about its history, as does Belgium.[8] In response to the groundbreaking writings of Frantz Fanon, the 1970s French women's liberation movement took up the slogan "Femmes, décolonisons-nous!" (women, we must decolonize ourselves!). The women's health movement, with its international outlook, understood that women in "Third World" countries (and women of color here in Europe) were undergoing forced sterilization while white women were having trouble getting abortions; and we rebelled against these two facets of the same attempt to control us. But other than that issue, there was not much visible action to take on racism until the rise of the alter-globalist movement, the World March of Women, the neighborhood-marching "Ni putes, ni soumises" (neither sluts nor submissive), the Feminist Collective against Racism, the Lesbian Collective against Fascism and Racism, and the Indigenous Women's Collective.

What is left today? We have the Lesbians of Color Space (www.espace -locs.fr), organizing events and giving support. This group considers itself to be the heir of Audre Lorde, especially in making connections among race, class, and sex. The Groupe du 6 Novembre, founded in 1999, has brought together lesbian descendants of colonialism, slavery, and postcolonial immigration. On November 6, 2010, it sent out an appeal in support of abortion rights for indigenous, undocumented, and Roma women. While some "Zamis" still exist among women from the Antilles, there is no longer much of a visible organization or any publishing connection.

It is true that women of color have not lived on the French mainland as long as they have in the Americas; and if each community counts itself separately, their numbers may feel very small. Migrant and second-generation immigrant women have sometimes hoped to escape racism through conformity—especially because there have been no struggles against slavery in continental France. But why is there so little feedback from white women? The deafening silence is worrisome. As Audre Lorde told her students, "One of the lessons I think the [19]60s need to teach us is that liberation is not the private problem of any particular group, that Black people are not a big basket of homogenized chocolate milk. We are particular people and we have differences that we can use, that we can recognize, identify, and use for our common goals, in our common struggles. I don't need to be you in order to work with you, I don't need to be you to honor your blackness."[9]

Racism concerns us all.[10]

Notes

1. Lorde's struggle is documented in Audre Lorde, *The Cancer Journals* (Argyle, N.Y.: Spinsters, 1980); and Audre Lorde, *A Burst of Light* (London: Sheba, 1988).
2. Dagmar Schultz, ed., *Macht und Sinnlichkeit: Audre Lorde und Adrienne Rich; Ausgewählte Texte*, trans. Renate Stendhal (Berlin: Orlanda Frauenverlag, 1983).
3. Rina Nissim, *Mamamélis: manuel de gynécologie naturopathique à l'usage des femmes* (Geneva: Editions Dispensaire des Femmes, 1984), published in English as *Natural Healing in Gynecology: A Manual for Women*, trans. Roxanne Claire (New York: Pandora, 1986).
4. The press also published Adrienne Rich, *La contrainte à l'hétérosexualité et autres essais*, trans. Françoise Armengaud, Christine Delphy, Lisette Girouard et Emmanuèle Lesseps (Genève-Lausanne: Mamamélis-Nouvelles Questions Féministes, 2010).
5. Audre Lorde, "Transformer le silence en paroles et en actes," in *Black feminism: Anthologie du féminisme africain-américain, 1975–2000*, ed. Elsa Dorlin (Paris: L'Harmattan, 2008), 75–80.
6. See also Laura Alexandra Harris, "Féminisme noir-queer, le principe du plaisir," in Dorlin, *Black feminism*, 177–219.

7. Audre Lorde, "Racisme, haine et colère [extracts from *Sister Outsider*]," in *La colère, une passion politique?, vol 3., Colère, courage et création politique,* ed. Marie-Claire Caloz-Tschopp (Paris: L'Harmattan, 2011), 5–6; Rina Nissim, "Femmes: colère collective?," in Caloz-Tschopp, *La colère,* 87–100.

8. Switzerland, with its four languages, is a special case. The country's German-speaking majority is more focused on Germany, and Audre gave readings in Zurich. Although Switzerland had no colonies, its citizens did amass great fortunes (in Neuchatel, among other cities) by chartering boats to transport slaves. In Geneva, because of the United Nations presence, the intercultural mix is significant: in one elementary school in the Jonction neighborhood, 121 nationalities are represented. But inequality is deep, and it is also racial. Current important struggles concern the well-being of undocumented immigrants, who include many women in domestic service.

9. The quotation is from *A Litany for Survival: The Life and Work of Audre Lorde,* dir. Ada Gay Griffin and Michelle Parkerson (New York: Third World Newsreel, 1995).

10. Jennifer Gay translated this essay from the French. I would also like to acknowledge the help of Paola Bacchetta, Magali Cecchet, Grazia Gonik, Aldridge Hansberry, and Suzette Robichon.

7
Finding My Sisters
Audre Lorde and Black Women in Switzerland

ZEEDAH MEIERHOFER-MANGELI

Audre Lorde not only inspired and mentored the work of black women in Switzerland but also challenged my own growth and development around issues of race, feminism, and the sisterhood of black women in the diaspora. I met Audre at a series of events in 1986 and 1988 that only made sense to me later. I recall two women meeting across a lecture room—a skeptical listener from the mother continent, who, while fighting to keep the identity she knew, found and embraced new ones; a mentor from across the Atlantic seeking treatment for her illness, who, with her soft poetry full of words as powerful as rocks against which waves formed, started a flood.

In formal and informal settings we developed banter, a way of friendly arguing because, to my ignorant and unexposed young self, Audre's attitudes, thoughts, and philosophies seemed radical and militant and unnecessary. I often felt irritated by her points and reacted defensively when she said things such as "the true feminist deals out of a lesbian consciousness whether or not she ever sleeps with women."[1] Only many, many years later did I understand why a certain militancy and an unconditional love of sisterhood were necessary in the fight for the self, voice, and space of black women. Remembering Audre and her insistent ways today brings a smile to my face. She signed her books for me and called me her sister. She talked of revolution, of resistance, and of a health culture that refused to find gentleness for women's bodies. But at the beginning, I didn't understand her or her vision for black women.

As a young black African activist living as a minority in lily-white Switzerland, I was often the only person of color in the political spaces to which my activism took me. I met Audre in 1986 at the Paulus Academy in Zurich, a cantonal think tank of the Catholic church. After our initial introduction and greeting, Audre asked me, "Where are the other Black women?" I explained that many of us were not politically aware or interested in issues of liberation, feminism, and the political participation of migrants in this environment that we now called our adopted home. She ignored my response; and in 1988, at another meeting at the same academy, where she was scheduled to read essays and poems from *Macht und Sinnlichkeit,* she asked me, in her slow deep voice, "Hello again, Zeedah, where are the Black women?"[2] I tried to answer, but again she ignored me. This question-answer continued during her next two visits to Zurich. The third time she asked me, "Where are the sisters?" I answered that I didn't know but pointed out that, at this workshop, two black women were present. Audre called the two of us together and told us that we had to link up and look for the other black sisters in Switzerland. This was a daunting task for me. At that time, in my eager early twenties, I was the mother of two children, balancing various domestic affairs and fighting to stay sane in a hostile foreign country. I didn't have the energy or the interest to look for anyone.

In the 1980s many black women in Switzerland were isolated because our numbers were so few. Unlike the United Kingdom, France, Italy, and other former colonial countries, Switzerland has not typically drawn African migrants. For many of them, language barriers, different educational systems, the high cost of living, and very bureaucratic visa application processes make it geographically and socially unattractive. I imagined that, like me, many black women in Switzerland were challenged to get through a regular day, which more often than not included racial abuse, institutional and social exclusion of all sorts, physical violence, various economic difficulties, and homesickness (often accentuated by acutely romanticized images of the homelands we had left). So coming to a poetry reading by a self-styled "black, lesbian, mother, warrior, poet" was far down on our agenda of realities. Audre, however, helped contextualize some of the dichotomies that I and other women were dealing with.

I was born in Kenya—a Mkamba by tribe, an African, a beloved daughter, and a cherished sister. I was a spoiled and pampered grandchild, a trusted friend, and the niece of powerfully feisty women. My mother was a hardworking government officer and my late father had been a teacher, which enabled me to gain a semblance of middle-class access to education. This background, a rich part of my identity, was a respectable profile, or so I thought as I settled into middle-class Switzerland. But I realized very soon that I had become just a color, one that bore all sorts of connotations of oppression, inferiority, stereotyping, and judgment. Audre made me understand this, judge it, and want to fight against it; she helped me to stop making excuses for my blackness and the fears of others. Audre said it was right to stand up to those who chose to be racist rather than confront my knowledge, power, story, passion, and zeal. She made me understand that I was not only part of a struggle but also carried an epistemology of the African people.

Audre's lectures were full of anecdotes about black women's relentless fight for acknowledgment, be it in their struggle against patriarchy or their place in science, history, and literature. It was new at this time to talk about the theory of difference. The need for harmony among women and the belief that there is strength in numbers had marred some of that analysis, at least in Switzerland's feminist communities, where migrant women were whispers. We were few in number, seldom recognized, seldom invited, and rarely heard, no matter how clearly we spoke German. White deafness to our words seemed to be selective. Yet during a clear and intimate conversation, Audre told Carmel Fröhlicher (a Haitian woman whom I'd met at Audre's 1986 lecture, where she had translated Audre's spoken introduction to *Macht und Sinnlichkeit* from English to German) and me that we needed to stop accusing white women because they will always find a reason not to hear us. We needed to get ourselves organized and raise our voices and visibility. She emphasized that as blacks we were a group, not isolated individuals, and that there was a need for an organized collective rather than just Kenyan cookouts, Nigerian clubs, and Caribbean parties. She said that we needed to raise the community's consciousness and develop a common agenda in Switzerland and in Europe. We learned new words such as *solidarity* and *diaspora* and realized that Audre was right: there were many black women out there!

I admit to being skeptical about much of what Audre said. For example, she talked about lesbian communities in Africa, where women officially practiced and lived a lesbian life. I come from an ethnic group in which it is socially acceptable for women to marry women; however, such marriages are for the purposes of surrogacy and do not involve sexual relations. Yet Audre insisted on her knowledge and experience, citing similar communities in southern Africa, and I thought, "How typical, another f—— American who thinks she knows Africans better than we know ourselves!" Our interaction prompted what became part of my oral herstory research about women's relationships. At the first opportunity, I sought out my grandmother and other women in my family for clarification. Indeed, my grandmother said, some women did "warm each other's back!" which is to say, in "grandma speak," that women may occasionally have had physical relations, but this was rare because the surrogacy relationship was that of mother and daughter as opposed to lover and lover. I never told Audre about my findings. I know a part of me was irritated that she might be right, but I didn't, and still don't, call all women who live with women and love women lesbians.

Audre inspired the consciousness that in 1988 led to the formation of the Women of Black Heritage (WBH) group and in 1993 to the founding of the Meeting Place and Resource Center for Black Women. I took part in both of these developments. After our 1986 meeting with Audre, Carmel Fröhlicher and I stayed in touch and developed a friendship. Together, we approached different women and shared our vision with them, inviting them to join us in creating WBH. Our group soon included black women from all corners of the globe: New Orleans, Haiti, New York, Kenya, Mali, Martinique, South Africa, Cameroon, the Bahamas, South Carolina, and Zurich. Our differences were huge, but we managed to bond over them; our identity as black women in Switzerland became our common foundation.

This was new territory for several of us. Audre had talked about power and privilege, race, gender, class, skin color, health, age, and even hair type. We could, as black women, reclaim our identity. We were more than just a color, and our identity was so multifaceted that we ourselves were overwhelmed. We discussed these issues in meetings and hundreds of phone calls. (The members of WBH lived far apart, so the telephone took on a new level of importance.) We were asking questions and debating about who we were. A sister from Martinique said she was raised as French and felt, acted, and was treated as French, while another sister, also from the Caribbean, said she was American, without a pretext. Fired up by my newfound Audre–inspired militancy, I could not understand why any black woman would want to be associated or identified with her former "masters." I was

African and black, and I loved being identified with my continent and my skin color. This arrogance arose from naïveté and my excitement about the possibility of choosing my identity. Of course, such expressions led to intense discussions that were sometimes painful or embarrassing. For example, during an event about the role of Columbus in the history of colonial slavery, a sister from the Caribbean publicly accused Africans of selling her people. Another black sister left the group because we did not allow non-black women to join.

The narratives of women from Haiti, Africa, America, and New Zealand took our dialogue to new horizons, and with that came new arguments, discourses, and divisions. The intersections were dynamic: some black women felt African, while others insisted that Europe was their new home and they wanted to adopt that identity. The term *Afro-Deutsche* was also coined at about this time, crystallizing new thoughts and visions for black women in Germany, including the articulation of Second World War legacies, long ignored or conveniently forgotten. Audre often talked about the multiple identities of African, black, Caribbean, and lesbian women and the importance of embracing them. We were learning by doing, and it was hard. Moreover, in these years Audre was very ill, so we didn't get many opportunities to sound off or reflect with her. Instead, we read and read and argued, sulked, reconciled, discussed, cooked, ate, met, and grew. We bonded.

Audre talked about the importance of accepting and using one's anger. At her 1988 lecture at the Paulus Academy, she chastised us for being slow in our revolution because we were waiting for things to be perfect. As she wrote in "The Uses of Anger," "every woman has a well-stocked arsenal of anger potentially useful against those oppressions, personal and institutional, which brought that anger into being. Focused with precision it can become a powerful source of energy serving progress and change."[3] She told black women that it was all right to fail at some things, that it was all right to contradict oneself in the process of growing. Names could be changed, as could identities, sexualities, and norms. This was a very radical notion at a time when being black and proud was already a progressive stance. Suddenly black women were talking about being black, Afro-German, and bisexual; suddenly we were interrogating the cultural identities we had held onto so tightly. Now that we'd left "the motherland," being African was not enough anymore, so we became black women, sisters, part of a larger community. The first seed of the urgency and need for solidarity and sisterhood among black women was sown in my mind.

Audre's militancy was motivating, and I became passionate about creating a space to which only black women had access. Her theories of difference made so much sense, and I found the courage to publicly challenge and confront white feminists, whose blind spots mirrored patriarchal tendencies. Audre's title "The Master's Tools Will Never Dismantle the Master's House" became a personal mantra.[4] The WBH group was the basis and foundation for the growth of many black women's awareness, including mine. It was my launching pad. Audre had challenged me, and I examined my questions about my own power and privilege. I learnt to locate the "us" and the "them" but also the "me" in "us"—not as an antagonistic dislocation but as proof that the whole functions out of the individuals and that there are necessary intersections. From hearing and meeting Audre and reading her writings, I learned that it was all right to be different, that learning from mistakes can increase courage, and that wanting social change can make a person unpopular and lonely.

It was not easy for African or black women to live in Switzerland during the 1980s and 1990s. Learning how to construct our own reality and situate our own lives and work within a European perspective was a continuous challenge but one that Audre had also addressed. Moreover, the subject of how to face the second generation was imminent. Audre spoke and wrote about her daughter and the confrontations of a racist environment. I learned early that my own daughters would constantly shuttle between battling patriarchy and forcing white sisters to understand their role in the systems and norms that oppress black people, particularly black women. Audre introduced the critique of white feminism, and together we discovered black women's cultures, fell in love with bell hooks and May Ayim, and rediscovered Angela Davis. Audre told me to start writing a journal because I had so many ideas about the space that could be created.

In 1991, Barbara Scheffer-Zbinden, a university lecturer in Zurich and a mentor of mine, hosted a networking brunch for Audre and the Dutch feminist Anja Meulenbelt. Barbara also invited several non-black women who have been a critical part of this journey and who are friends and allies. Audre listened to my thoughts and was very generous and patient. I was enthusiastic and excited and ready to leave my suburban life and go out and challenge the world. She told me to write down my thoughts and visions.

But I never wrote anything until I decided to write this essay in memory of her.

Audre's persistence in asking why I had come to an event without my sisters had irritated me but also led me to wonder, How could I be my sisters' keeper when I could barely muster enough energy to come to terms with my own challenges? This self-questioning taught me, and others like me, that our survival was interdependent, even as we went our separate ways. Herein lay the secret of our survival: a racial slur in Geneva would raise waves in Basel and Zurich! My sister would be my keeper as I would be hers! This simple cliché was tangible enough to function as a foundation for the Meeting Place and Resource Center for Black Women, a pioneering project that created a unique and safe space for African and black women. By the 1990s a new generation and community of black migrant women was arriving in Switzerland, and they faced multifaceted challenges. People were still tending to fall back on colonial-era stereotypes about the black community, but the Resource Center was our own space. This was both a strategic and a political move. In the 1990s, *tolerance* was understood to mean that all opinions could be voiced, and the voices against foreigners were loud and uncensored. Racism and exclusion isolated many black women, so a space for self-articulation was timely. The center enabled dialogue and hosted relevant workshops on a regular basis. Members were involved in outreach, advocacy, and capacity building. We prioritized the positive representation of black women, especially to themselves. We offered frontline services, such as counseling and translations; and a monthly networking lunch helped us mobilize resources. All of this work was done by a small group of committed women, and it was usually voluntary.

Society was calling for assimilation, but the Resource Center promoted integration and encouraged participation and inclusion in the communities in which black women lived. During this time I ran for a seat in the Swiss parliament, the first black African woman to do so. My center colleagues and I confronted stereotypes and led workshops about the difficulty of changing mindsets. Remembering Audre's words about commonalities and difference, we understood that we had to define ourselves, recognizing that we are not homogeneous as black women but that we could survive only with solidarity and a spirit of sisterhood. The dominant models that society (including black women) had formed about black women were and

ZEEDAH MEIERHOFER-MANGELI

are so strong and set that much of our work has involved dismantling and rewriting them, especially as they concern issues of identity and self-worth.

Our project is now twenty years old; and as the needs of black women in Switzerland have changed, so has our work. We now mainly focus on events and have a virtual portal for exchange and networking (www.black-womencenter.ch). We have written a history of the Resource Center, which acknowledges Audre's mentoring role. The book, launched in December 2013, focuses on the core work of the center, its aims and objectives, and the lessons we have learned.[5] It addresses the histories of black women in Europe and the diaspora and contains intergenerational interviews. Because succession plans are part of our vision, the book also highlights the Youth Forum of the Resource Center, which was initiated in 2001.

We were, and still are, pioneers, and I think Audre would have approved.

Notes

1. Karla Hammond, "An Interview with Audre Lorde," *American Poetry Review* 9 (March–April 1980): 21.
2. Dagmar Schultz, ed., *Macht und Sinnlichkeit: Audre Lorde und Adrienne Rich; Ausgewählte Texte*, trans. Renate Stendhal (Berlin: Orlanda Frauenverlag, 1991).
3. Audre Lorde, "The Uses of Anger: Women Responding to Racism," in *The Audre Lorde Compendium: Essays, Speeches, and Journals* (London: Pandora, 1996), 175.
4. Audre Lorde, "The Master's Tools Will Never Dismantle the Master's House," in *Sister Outsider: Essays and Speeches* (Trumansburg, N.Y.: Crossing Press, 1984), 110–14.
5. Shelley Berlowitz, Elisabeth Joris, and Zeedah Meierhofer-Mangeli, eds., *Terra Incognita? Der Treffpunkt Schwarzer Frauen in Zürich* (Zurich: Limmat, 2013).

8
Audre Lorde's Relationship
and
Connections with
South African Women

GLORIA I. JOSEPH

Audre Lorde frequently described herself as a "Black, lesbian, feminist, mother, poet, warrior." The definition belies the full magnitude of her talents and gifts. She should be fully recognized as a black woman whose philosophical visions, humanitarian values, and Afrocentric religiosity, as demonstrated in her poems, writings, and essays, relegate her to a status equal to renowned male figures such as Martin Luther King, Jr., Mahatma Gandhi, the Dalai Lama, and Malcolm X. These leaders had common goals: to fight injustices, struggle for freedom, and bring about equality for all. Audre also was committed to fight for these goals, and she delivered the goods with strong messages that resonated beyond geographic and political boundaries.

Much of Audre's poetry vividly expresses her African ancestral values as well as her empathy with and sensitivity to the plight of the oppressed peoples of South Africa. "The Winds of Orisha," "From the House of Yemanjá," "Sisters in Arms," "Party Time," "Prism" (for Joyce Seroke, a South African activist), "The Evening News," and "Call" are outstanding expressions of her concerns and of her identification with and love for her South African sisters and their families.[1] In "A Burst of Light: Living with Cancer," she writes, "Battling racism and battling heterosexism and battling apartheid share the same agency inside me as battling cancer. None of these struggles are ever easy, and even the smallest victory is never to be taken for granted. Each victory must be applauded because it is so easy not to battle at all."[2] In Audre's battles against oppressions, commitment was a central component, along with the belief that spirituality and politics nourish one another. Her commitment to the struggle to end apartheid and to the development of an empathetic sisterhood with the women of South Africa were ideals central to her attraction to the organization Sisterhood in Support of Sisters in South Africa (SISA).

A 1981 South African film, *Awake from Mourning,* produced by Betty Wolpert, a deeply committed English filmmaker, features South African women who met in Soweto in 1978, after the bloody Soweto Uprising of 1976.[3] The uprising was sparked by courageous children who refused to continue to accept substandard Bantu education taught in the alien Afrikaans tongue. They were cut down by the South African police, with the support of the government—a horrendous, brutal assault in which many young people were jailed, tortured, maimed, and killed, while others had to flee their country. The group of South African women who met in Soweto two years later resolved to take actions to assure a better life for the impoverished and oppressed peoples of South Africa. With the memories of their children's blood still fresh in their minds, they determined to "awake from mourning" and keep their children's spirits alive. Through self-help groups, they chose to develop themselves and their collective power as women.

I was a professor at Hampshire College in Amherst, Massachusetts, when I first viewed *Awake from Mourning.* The film had a powerful emotional impact on me; it was a call to action. I became involved in the founding of SISA, an acronym that translates as "mercy" in Xhosa. I convened a cadre of black women who were committed to offering support and showing solidarity with the women of South Africa. These women, who were to be the founding mothers, the core of the organization, were Zala Chandler, Johnnetta Cole, Audre Lorde, Andrée McLaughlin, and Barbara Riley. Their loyalty, political integrity, and professionalism had long been proven.

SISA's purpose was to link hands and resources with our sisters in South Africa on the basis of the everyday necessities and needs of their lives. A major objective was channeling some of the rich resources available to North American women directly to our South African sisters. SISA's major activities were fundraising and communication with the South African women. The two groups that became SISA's recipients were the Maggie Magaba Trust and the Zamani Soweto Sisters Council. Betty Wolpert was instrumental in establishing the Maggie Magaba Trust, whose purpose was to promote self-help groups, provide educational bursaries, and give aid to penniless families and pensioners. The group of women who met in Soweto in 1978 developed into the Zamani Soweto Sisters Council, a nonprofit organization engaged in teaching women dressmaking, patchwork, quilting, and knitting skills and offering a literacy program. The women envisioned a permanent space, a building that would house all of their activities. A campaign was launched for the construction of a multipurpose building. Their valiant efforts were rewarded, and the building was completed in 1987.

The founding of SISA marked the beginning of Audre's direct interactions with her South African sisters via words and deeds. SISA became a major platform for her to raise funds, fulfill her deep commitment to the support of projects, and show solidarity with the women of South Africa. SISA's fundraising has come largely through donations and contributions from audiences at film showings, musical concerts, lectures, and poetry readings. Audre gave major benefit poetry readings around the United States and gained generous funds. She was undoubtedly SISA's major individual fundraiser. After a reading she would address the audience, deliver messages about SISA's needs, and request donations. Audiences gave willingly and generously. Adrienne Rich, Sonia Sanchez, Johnnetta Cole, and other founding mothers were also proficient fundraisers. These donations contributed to the needs of the ongoing self-help activities as well as to the building of the center. Audre's communications with the South African sisters included business and friendly letters as well as a lively exchange of holiday sentiments.

In June 1986, members of the Maggie Magaba Trust and the Zamani Soweto Sisters Council traveled to London to display and sell their works, mainly quilts, at the Brixton Art Gallery. Three members of SISA—Audre, Andrée, and I—traveled from the United States to meet the group. For Audre, this exhilarating and heartwarming experience was a once-in-a-lifetime moment. She was meeting her South African sisters, coming face to face with women who had previously been only images, women whose names and words had evoked deep emotional and spiritual connections. Their voices, expressions, laughter became an actuality; Audre often said that this meeting had become permanently etched in her consciousness.

On the evening of June 15, a special memorial gathering of the women was held in a beautiful outdoor garden in London, and Audre's reading from her work was the main attraction. It was an inspirational reading that aroused emotions and created an atmosphere of connection and solidarity between Audre and her South African sisters. The women were composed, attentive, filled with thoughts of home and admiration for the women of SISA. Among those present was Ellen Kuzwayo, the mentor, spirit, and initiator of the organizations. She was known as Ma K, the mayor of Soweto. Audre's vision had truly become a reality, and she was ecstatic. It was not often that that she could so readily experience such a treasure.

After the events in London, the South African women traveled to southern France for a brief respite and vacation before returning to their homes, where their lives were ruled by horrific apartheid laws. Andrée had to return to the United States, but Audre and I had the privilege of accompanying the women to Les Quelles in Bonnieux. Les Quelles, owned by Betty Wolpert, was a beautiful old reclaimed silk factory restored to a grand old villa. The grounds were so very beautiful with majestic stone buildings amid a stone yard. The scent of lime trees mingled with the lovely fragrance of other blooms, and the swimming pool sparkled.

Our time with the women at Les Quelles was exquisite and enjoyable and soul wrenching. There was a feeling of shared deep friendship. The days were spent in relaxation with no evidence of stress or pressure. We derived intense pleasure from our interactions. Our daily activities consisted of collectively preparing and sharing meals, taking walks around the surrounding grounds of the villa, and discussing quilting, hair styles, marriage, and raising children. Yet one incident revealed an underlying anxiety. During one of our walks outside the villa, we came upon cherry trees loaded with luscious fruit. Audre and I started to pick a few from the low-hanging branches, and the South African women were immediately stricken with fear! They worried that we could all be severely punished, sent to jail, and held in detention. Such were the realities of life in South Africa. This incident markedly affected Audre, and she offered them detailed explanations about differences in behaviors and interpretations of laws in various countries. However, we refrained from picking those delicious cherries.

I think the most stressful moment occurred when we were all in the swimming pool. The South African women had observed me swimming and were eager to follow suit, though they had no experience or skills. All in all, the scene was quite humorous: the women struggled to stay afloat, Audre and I vainly tried to support their bodies in the water, and Betty panicked at the thought of having them survive South Africa's apartheid only to drown in her pool.

The evenings were exceptional. We had our meals outdoors under a wide spreading lime tree, with the sweet scent of blossoms perfuming the air. Here we were, two African American women, learning a few words in Xhosa and Zulu as we shared the stories of the fifteen women of the Zamani Soweto Sisters Council and the Maggie Magaba Trust. They told us their stories in the evenings, and at night in her room Audre wrote and wrote. There was uniqueness to each tale yet an underlying similarity in terms of suffering, a commitment to struggle, and an appreciation for accomplishments and the strength of unity. As Audre and I discussed the stories we had heard, her emotions alternated between melancholy and an unwavering anger against the devastating effects of apartheid.

Song and dance seemed to be a part of the joys of struggle among the women. Meals were usually followed by spontaneous singing with such expert harmonizing that Audre and I asked if they sang together in a choir or chorus. They were amused at our question but appreciated our compliments. Dancing was more or less spontaneous but usually had a specific meaning. For example, words to a song led to animated dance movements, the entire group participating with jokes and laughter. Or when telling a story about the Comrades (a group of young rebels), the women demonstrated the high-stepping spirited rendition of their machine gun dance. The most memorable dancing moment occurred when two lines were formed and singly each woman danced down the row to the clapping and cheering of the others. When it was Audre's turn, she danced as if propelled by an inner spirit. She was captivating, and the sisters' rousing responses told me that they had witnessed an extraordinary Audre.

Audre and I left Les Quelles a few days before the others did. Our farewells were sweet and compassionate with the strong feeling that this was not goodbye but a look forward to future reunions and continued sisterhood.

Notes

1. Audre Lorde, *The Collected Poems of Audre Lorde* (New York: Norton, 1997).
2. Audre Lorde, "A Burst of Light: Living with Cancer," in *The Audre Lorde Compendium: Essays, Speeches, and Journals* (London: Pandora, 1996), 321.
3. *Awake from Mourning*, dir. Chris Austin (Gays Mills, Wisc.: Worldwise, 1982).

GLORIA I. JOSEPH

II
CONNECTIONS

9
Sisterhood as Performance in Audre Lorde's
Public Advocacy

LESTER C. OLSON

"There is a pretense to a homogeneity of experience covered by the word *sisterhood* that does not in fact exist," Audre Lorde declared in a 1980 speech in Amherst, Massachusetts.[1] Yet in a 1985 speech to black women at Medgar Evers College in New York, she emphasized, "I *am* your sister."[2] I believe that Lorde's references to sisterhood were not a performative contradiction in her public advocacy but reflected her tactical negotiation of the double binds facing black women and lesbians. During the last decade of her life, as she critically examined differences among women during her international sojourns, she developed an evolving stance on sisterhood. There was a seismic shift in her primary audiences during the mid- to late 1980s, especially after 1984, when she moved from New York to the Virgin Islands and Germany. She focused increasingly on black women's diverse communities (which encompassed the black women of Australia and New Zealand, who were not of African descent), while engaging the ramifications of the African diaspora in numerous international forums around the globe.

For two decades, I have been systematically studying Lorde's public advocacy. My essays usually have presented a rhetorical criticism of a major speech or offered an overview of her public address, which consists of numerous poems, speeches, essays, open letters, pamphlets, and books. Here, however, with the goal of capturing Lorde's standpoint on sisterhood, I examine several public speeches, which she delivered in international settings.[3]

That stance moved beyond demographic categories, geographic locations, and ethnic heritage, even though each of those factors remained salient in her sensibility and activism. Instead, Lorde featured sisterhood fundamentally as a performance, action, or deed enacting solidarity among women. Lorde evoked sisterhood to instill a communal commitment among women activists to strengthening the life-enhancing possibilities of "the erotic" for women (as she defined it) and to intervening collectively to transform oppressive relationships of power, privilege, and resourcefulness.[4] Sisterhood was not so much a term for naming a general relationship than it was a performed way of life enacted by a certain subset of women. For Lorde, being a sister was more than simply being a woman.

At Harvard University in 1982, Lorde asked, "Can any one of us here still afford to believe that efforts to reclaim the future can be private or individual? Can any one here still afford to believe that the pursuit of liberation can be the sole and particular province of any one particular race, or sex, or age, or religion, or sexuality, or class?"[5] As her incisive questions suggest, focusing exclusively on sisterhood might have the problematic result of deflecting attention from other, often overlapping, oppressions across social differences such as race, economic class, and sexuality. One obvious limitation of emphasizing sisterhood was Lorde's willingness to enter into coalition with black men and gay men of any race, even though she viewed white gay men, such as myself, with healthy skepticism.[6] Her openness to working in coalition with gay men such as Essex Hemphill and Joseph Beam deepened after her experiences as a keynote speaker at the "Third World Lesbian and Gay Conference" in 1979.[7]

After first commenting on Lorde's references to herself as "sister outsider," I will consider some options for characterizing her standpoint on sisterhood, such as cosmopolitan, diasporic, transatlantic, and transnational sisterhood, because each of these ways of modifying sisterhood has value for recognizing salient features of Lorde's advocacy, while nonetheless deflecting attention from other consequential features of it, or possibly having entailments that could misrepresent her advocacy. Noting such entailments will help to refine a precise sense of sisterhood for Lorde. That these categories are not analytically distinct is consistent with Lorde's sensibility inasmuch as she regularly used multiple names for her identity to explore how the terms interacted with one another and could obfuscate or distort by reduction to one or another of them.[8]

LESTER C. OLSON

Lorde dealt regularly with being a part of communities that were generally oppressed, even by otherwise oppressed groups to which she also belonged. As a black, lesbian, feminist, socialist, poet, and mother, she experienced chasms in already marginalized black communities across differences of sex and sexuality.[9] When she spoke to predominantly black audiences, she regularly addressed the ways in which sexism and heterosexism damaged solidarity in black communities. This pattern in her advocacy is exemplified by such essays as "Scratching the Surface: Some Notes on Barriers to Women and Loving," "Sexism: An American Disease in Blackface," and "Eye to Eye: Black Women, Hatred, and Anger."[10] It recurs in her speeches, especially "I Am Your Sister" at Medgar Evers College in 1985 and her two public speeches at the "I Am Your Sister" conference in Boston in 1990, where most of the participants were "women of Color," an expression she at first used to name a coalition among diverse women from various racial minorities within U.S. culture and, after the early 1980s, across international boundaries.[11]

Likewise, in the United States, when Lorde addressed feminist audiences, which usually consisted primarily of white heterosexual women, she would press her concerns about the ways in which racism and heterosexism harmed solidarity among women in the interest of realizing political, economic, and social change for women. For example, in her 1981 keynote speech to the National Women's Studies Association in Storrs, Connecticut, she highlighted how racial conflict fractures and weakens women as a group: "What woman here is so enamoured of her own oppression that she cannot see her heelprint upon another woman's face?"[12] In the aftermath of several sustained confrontations with white heterosexual women during the late 1970s and early 1980s, she came to believe that she needed to make difficult decisions about how to use her limited life's energy, as her health crisis deepened. On June 21, 1984, in Berlin she wrote, "Rather than siphoning off energies in vain attempts to connect with women who refuse to deal with their own history or ours, Black women need to choose the areas where that energy can be most effective."[13]

As a way to name her own recurring life situation, she coined the expression "Sister Outsider," which became the title of both her 1984 book and a poem.[14] A motif in her advocacy, the phrase emphasizes the stark alternative between being an isolated individual and an active participant in a community; and her writing around the issue was typified by concerns that a retreat from community would leave her vulnerable, oppressed, and less able to survive. In one of her best-known speeches, "The Master's Tools Will Never Dismantle the Master's House," she affirmed, "Without community there is no liberation, only the most vulnerable and temporary armistice between an individual and her oppression. But community must not mean a shedding of our differences, nor the pathetic pretense that these differences do not exist."[15] The speech reiterated comments she had written in her journals a month earlier on October 3, 1979, although there she had featured her own life predicament.[16] *Sisterhood* was one of her sometimes hazardous expressions for entering into community with others, dangerous when it served as a "pretense to a homogeneity of experience."[17]

COSMOPOLITAN SISTERHOOD

Lorde's view of solidarity among women might be characterized as an embrace of cosmopolitan sisterhood inasmuch as she considered herself a citizen of the world with political responsibilities to look beyond U.S. boundaries. *Sister Outsider* (1984) featured her trips to Russia and Grenada, and *A Burst of Light* (1988) focused on apartheid in South Africa and chronicled her travels to Germany, Switzerland, Australia, Saint Croix, and elsewhere.[18] According to Kwame Anthony Appiah, "there are two strands that entwine in the notion of cosmopolitanism. One is the idea that we have obligations to others, obligations that stretch beyond those to whom we are related by the ties of kith and kin, or even the more formal ties of a shared citizenship. The other is that we take seriously the value not just of human life but of particular human lives, which means taking an interest in the practices and beliefs that lend them significance."[19]

These qualities aptly characterize Lorde's sensibility in her advocacy. For instance, in an October 25, 1985, journal entry written in East Lansing, Michigan, she noted, "For me as an African-American woman writer, sisterhood and survival means it's not enough to say I believe in peace when my sister's children are dying in the streets of Soweto and New Caledonia in the South Pacific."[20] She sought, moreover, to cultivate her audience's commitment to responsibility in the world, as she recorded in a February 18, 1984, journal entry written in Ohio: "Last night I gave a talk to the Black students at the University about coming to see ourselves as part of an international community of people of Color, how we must train ourselves to question what our Blackness—our Africanness—can mean on the world stage. And how as members of that international community, we must assume responsibility for our actions, or lack of action, as americans."[21]

Yet there is a notable problem: when the literature on cosmopolitanism is invested in human rights, it may at times minimize human differences because it universalizes western cultures in ways that could colonize non-western cultures.[22] As Arabella Lyon and I have noted elsewhere, human rights rhetoric can be used for advocacy from a range of political positions, including the position of severely oppressed people.[23] Yet Lorde regarded the language of human rights as a tool that elites usually mobilize harmfully. By selectively using that language, they could either deflect attention from oppressive mistreatment or dominate and control already oppressed populations—which, in the case of South Africa, was a majority of the citizens.[24] In a 1982 speech at Harvard University, she commented, "Our papers are filled with supposed concern for human rights in white communist Poland while we sanction by acceptance and military supply the systematic genocide of apartheid in South Africa, of murder and torture in Haiti and El Salvador."[25] In *Apartheid U.S.A.* she regularly mentioned South Africa to emphasize how human rights rhetoric worked to the disadvantage of already oppressed people.[26] The problem with characterizing Lorde's standpoint as cosmopolitan sisterhood is that we may associate her with an uncritical embrace of human rights when in fact she scrutinized human rights rhetoric, distrusting its integrity and its general tendency to universalize British, European, and American principles across other cultures.[27]

DIASPORIC SISTERHOOD

After 1984 Lorde became especially focused on diasporic sisterhood with women of African descent, as exemplified in her incisive naming of "Afro-Germans," "Afro-French," "Afro-Dutch," and more generally "Afro-European[s]," whom she saw as "a growing force for international change."[28] During her stay in Berlin, she asked in a May 23, 1984, journal entry, "Who are they, the German women of the Diaspora? Where do our paths intersect as women of Color—beyond the details of our particular oppressions, although certainly not outside the reference of those details? And where do our paths diverge? Most important, what can we learn from our connected differences that will be useful to us both, Afro-German and

Afro-American?"[29] The term *diaspora* refers to the dispersal of a people who lack compelling claim to or control over a homeland, which might be a factor in Lorde's recurring use of the lowercased word *american*. She remarked in an October 10, 1984, journal entry written in New York, "As an African-American woman, I feel the tragedy of being an oppressed hyphenated person in America, of having no land to be our primary teacher. And this distorts us in so many ways. Yet there is a vital part that we play as Black people in the liberation consciousness of every freedom-seeking people upon this globe."[30] When she continued, "as Afro-Americans we must recognize the promise we represent for some new social synthesis the world has not yet experienced," she risked presenting "Afro-Americans" as role models for other nations, thus positioning one portion of the black diaspora as emblematic for the rest.[31] But in her essay (and in her pamphlet with the same title) "Apartheid U.S.A.," she added, "The connections between Africans and African-Americans, African-Europeans, African-Asians, is real, however dimly seen at times, and we all need to examine without sentimentality or stereotype what the injection of Africanness into the socio-political consciousness of the world could mean."[32]

The 1984 edition of *Sister Outsider* makes no references to diaspora or cosmopolitanism and few to either civil or human rights. For Lorde the notion of diaspora began to resonate after her relocation to Saint Croix and Germany, and she mentions it in her 1985 speech in East Lansing, Michigan, at the "Black Woman Writer and the Diaspora Conference."[33] In an April 2, 1986, journal entry referring to "Ties That Bind," a conference in Saint Croix that her partner Gloria Joseph had planned with the Sojourner Sisters, Lorde exulted, "In addition to being a tremendous high, these days are such a thrilling example to me of the real power of a small group of Black women of the Diaspora in action."[34] Her work as a founding member of Sisterhood in Support of Sisters in South Africa (SISA), an organization that Joseph had founded, continued to fire her interest in both diasporic and transatlantic sisterhood (which I will discuss in the next section).[35]

Yet Lorde criticized the idea of diaspora or geographic dispersal in connection with the term *black:* "There is the reality of defining Black as a geographical fact of culture and heritage emanating from the continent of Africa—Black meaning Africans and other members of a Diaspora, with or without color."[36] She continued: "Then there is a quite different reality of defining Black as a political position, acknowledging that color is the bottom line the world over, no matter how many other issues exist alongside it." She saw "certain pitfalls" with that approach to defining *black*, notably that "it takes the cultural identity of a widespread but definite group and makes it a generic identity for many culturally diverse peoples, all on the basis of a shared oppression," which in her view "runs the risk of providing a convenient blanket of apparent similarity under which our actual and unaccepted differences can be distorted or misused."[37]

Further, Lorde knew that *black* does not imply African descent in either New Zealand or Australia.[38] In Australia the word refers to indigenous aboriginal peoples such as the Wurundjeri, while in New Zealand it refers to the Maori. In an October 10, 1984, journal entry, she observed,

> When an African-American woman says she is Black, she is speaking of her cultural reality, no matter how modified it may be by time, place, or circumstances of removal. Yet even the Maori women of New Zealand and the Aboriginal women of Australia call themselves Black. There must be a way for us to deal with this, if only on the level of language. For example, those of us for whom Black is our cultural reality, relinquishing the word in favor of some other designation of the African Diaspora, perhaps simply *African*."[39]

Such reflections suggest that, while diasporic sisterhood mattered profoundly to Lorde, her vision of sisterhood extended beyond an African heritage to encompass the "Black" women of New Zealand and Australia who were not of African descent.

The term *diasporic sisterhood* can be problematic because it tacitly sets up priorities among oppressions by giving race central attention, despite Lorde's conviction that there is no hierarchy of oppressions. Many of her speeches addressed to black women as sisters pressed intersecting and overlapping concerns about sexuality, heterosexism, and homophobia among these women. Perhaps the best example of this pattern in Lorde's advocacy is her 1985 speech "I Am Your Sister," whose conclusion affirmed, "I am a Black Lesbian, and I *am* your sister," precisely because she wanted to be recognized and treated as such by other black women—a way of creating solidarity in dealing effectively with intersecting oppressions.[40] Her concern about same-sexuality as a chasm among black women also surfaced in her 1985 speech "Sisterhood and Survival" at the East Lansing conference.[41] And as she had already noted in her earlier essay "Scratching the Surface," sexuality divided black women as "heartless competitors for the scarce male."[42]

In short, to name Lorde's views of sisterhood *diasporic* may occlude her abiding concerns about other forms of bias, which often intersected with race to further oppress women, as well as various distinguishable strands of racism. In her 1985 keynote speech in Melbourne, she explained, "When I say I am Black, I mean I am of African descent. When I say I am a woman of Color, I mean I recognize common cause with American Indian, Chicana, Latina, and Asian-American sisters of North America [as well as] . . . Black South African women [and] . . . my Black sisters of Australia."[43] As a term, *diasporic sisterhood* does not capture her abiding commitment to common cause with women of diverse races or her recognition of the varying meanings of *black*.

TRANSATLANTIC SISTERHOOD

After 1984 much of Lorde's work took place in the Virgin Islands and Germany as she regularly crossed the Atlantic Ocean for medical treatments and public activism. Thus, *transatlantic sisterhood* is a useful term to encompass her advocacy in the Caribbean, Europe, Britain, and the eastern United States, especially New York and Massachusetts. Yet the term remains imperfect because, like *diasporic*, it may deflect attention from her advocacy elsewhere around the globe. Her work in support of SISA and her recurring concerns about South Africa as well as her advocacy in New Zealand and Australia underscore the international character of her activism.

In an interview, Lorde alluded to "trans-oceanic conversations" among women.[44] Nonetheless, while *transoceanic sisterhood* would include her appearances in the South Pacific, it is less useful than *transatlantic* for identifying the predominant forums for her activism and advocacy. Moreover, using either geographic term could implicitly deracialize and desexualize her activism by foregrounding the locations of her advocacy at the expense of race, sex, and sexuality. For instance, Lorde observed that Berliners "are interested in dealing with racism in America, and in England, but are much less prepared to deal with racism in terms of their Turkish and Middle Eastern workers who are the 'Black' people of Germany."[45]

TRANSNATIONAL SISTERHOOD

Transnational sisterhood might be the most valuable term to use when thinking geographically about Lorde's advocacy. As Donald E. Pease has explained, "the transnational is not a discourse so much as it is itself a

LESTER C. OLSON

volatile transfer point that inhabits things, people, and places with surplus connectivities that dismantle their sense of a coherent, bounded identity. Drawing upon an interstitial dynamic that it advances, this complex figuration bears the traces of the violent sociohistorical processes to which it alludes." He notes, "The transnational mobilizes plural, often competing discourses that generate contradictions, new truths, and ruptures." Unlike globalization and international studies, it "names an undecidable economic, political, or social formation that is neither in nor out of the nation-state. Inherently relational, the transnational involves a double move: to the inside, to core constituents of a given nation, and to an outside, whatever forces introduce a new configuration."[46] These statements aptly encapsulate Lorde's international activism in that she sought to build coalitions within national boundaries to transform their oppressive practices while cultivating international solidarity.

In my opinion, Pease's tidy distinctions do not capture the diversity of international studies at the time of Lorde's advocacy. She used the term *international* rather than *transnational* because the distinction was not then available, but she used it so seldom that it would be risky to attempt to encapsulate her sense of the term from those few instances.[47] I do believe that Pease's sense of *transnational* works accurately for describing her activism in Australia. In Lorde's 1985 keynote speech there, she enacted sisterhood with black aboriginal women to counter their experiences of erasure, nonrecognition, and disengagement from the relatively privileged women who were attending the conference. In considering this speech, I find it useful to remember Lorde's earlier disappointment with the 1984 International Feminist Book Fair in London, which she considered "a monstrosity of racism" that "distorted much of what was good, creative, and visionary about such a fair." She explained, "I think the organizers of the Bookfair really believed that by inviting foreign Black women they were absolving themselves of any fault in ignoring input from local Black women . . . They totally objectified *all* Black women by not dealing with the Black women of the London community."[48] To her, the organizer's decision to feature token accomplished black women from abroad evaded the more difficult, necessary work of examining racial conflicts within the local community.[49]

When Lorde delivered her keynote in Melbourne, she began by acknowledging her difficulty in finding ideas to share that would have mutual use for her audience: "I have struggled for many weeks to find your part in me, to see what we could share that would have meaning for us all." Minutes later, she reiterated this difficulty: "I find my tongue weighted down by the blood of my Aboriginal sisters that has been shed upon this earth." She amplified, "For the true language of difference is yet to be spoken in this place. Here that language must be spoken by my Aboriginal sisters, the daughters of those indigenous peoples of Australia with whom each one of you shares a destiny, but whose voices and language most of you have never heard." She affirmed that "where we sit now today, Wurundjeri women once dreamed and laughed and sang . . . Where are these women?" Her speech sought to enact solidarity with the absent black women of Australia, although she was careful to underscore that the term did not have the same meaning in Australia as it did in the United States. She concluded, "I will move on. But it is the language of the Black Aboriginal women of this country that you must learn to hear and to feel."[50]

Lorde firmly declined to play the role of a token black woman from abroad, whose presence would provide a relatively safe, evasive, and distant engagement with "difference." At the same time, she was confronting an audience of predominantly white women with the necessity of dealing with black aboriginal women. We might view her speech as a performative contradiction because she claimed to decline becoming a token black even as she assumed a keynote role nonetheless. Yet it would be more accurate to observe that she negotiated a double bind by using her role as speaker to stress a crucial absence that otherwise would have gone unnoticed. This combination of tactical moves in her advocacy allowed her to enact transnational sisterhood in ways that neither transatlantic nor diasporic sisterhood captures. The tactical moves illustrate the way in which she moved across national boundaries as she built coalitions within and across international spaces to transform local relationships of power, privilege, and resourcefulness. Like the other geographic names for sisterhood, the term *transnational sisterhood* may implicitly deracialize and desexualize Lorde's activism by foregrounding the locations of her advocacy at the expense of particular overlapping biases. Even so, the transnational has to do with disrupting oppressive relationships within and between nations, and the ambiguities here could apply to sexuality, sex, age, race, or whatever biases needed to be confronted and changed to advance social justice.[51]

LESTER C. OLSON

CONCLUSION: CONCERNING SISTERHOOD UNMODIFIED

For Lorde, sisterhood is not simply demographic (*women*), geographic, or even relational (*oppression*). Rather, sisterhood is contingent, and it is enacted in ways that demonstrate a communal commitment to doing something about transforming oppression while encouraging oppressed women to embrace each other within and across national boundaries. Sisterhood among women is contingent inasmuch as relationships of power, privilege, and resourcefulness can vary significantly with location, position, and social identities across various cultures, as Lorde regularly stressed. Sisterhood is a deed or a performance.

Lorde habitually drew connections among apparently disparate concerns: "Battling racism and battling heterosexism and battling apartheid share the same urgency inside me as battling cancer. None of these struggles are ever easy, and even the smallest victory is never to be taken for granted."[52] On November 8, 1986, she affirmed, "I have always known I learn my most lasting lessons about difference by closely attending [to] the ways in which the differences inside me lie down together."[53] Even so, after 1984 she centered emphatically on black women and the African diaspora, while welcoming other, often overlapping, groups of oppressed people to also use her words.

Notes

1. Audre Lorde, "Age, Race, Class, and Sex: Women Redefining Difference," in *Sister Outsider: Essays and Speeches by Audre Lorde* (Freedom, Calif.: Crossing Press, 1984), 116. For commentary on this speech, Lester C. Olson, "Liabilities of Language: Audre Lorde Reclaiming Difference," *Quarterly Journal of Speech* 84 (1998): 448–70.
2. Audre Lorde, *A Burst of Light: Essays* (Ithaca, N.Y.: Firebrand, 1988), 26.
3. I thank Dagmar Schultz for sharing thirty-two audio cassettes of Lorde's poetry readings, discussions, and public speeches, most of which were delivered in Europe. I have also secured numerous recordings from other sources. For an orientation to Lorde's advocacy as a public speaker, see Lester C. Olson, "Audre Geraldine Lorde (1934–1992), Professor of English, Poet, Black Lesbian, and Socialist," in *American Voices: An Encyclopedia of Contemporary Orators*, ed. Bernard K. Duffy and Richard W. Leeman (Westport, Conn.: Greenwood, 2005), 285–92; and Lester C. Olson, "Audre Lorde (1934–1992)," in *The Literary Encyclopedia*, posted March 14, 2011, www.litencyc.com.
4. Audre Lorde, "Uses of the Erotic: The Erotic as Power," in *Sister Outsider*, 53–60. For commentary, see Lester C. Olson, "Traumatic Styles in Public Address: Audre Lorde's Discourse as Exemplar," in *Queering Public Address: Sexualities in American*

Historical Discourse, ed. Charles E. Morris III (Columbia: University of South Carolina Press, 2007), 249–82.

5. Lorde, *Sister Outsider,* 140.
6. For example, see ibid., 139; and Lorde, *Burst of Light,* 16.
7. Alexis De Veaux, *Warrior Poet: A Biography of Audre Lorde* (New York: Norton, 2004), 254–56.
8. For example, see *Sister Outsider,* 120–21.
9. For example, see Audre Lorde, "Between Ourselves," in *The Collected Poems of Audre Lorde* (New York: Norton, 1997), 223.
10. Lorde, *Sister Outsider,* 45–52, 60–65, 145–75.
11. Lorde, *Burst of Light,* 19–26.
12. Lorde, *Sister Outsider,* 132. For commentary on this speech, see Lester C. Olson "Anger among Allies: Audre Lorde's 1981 Keynote Admonishing the National Women's Studies Association," *Quarterly Journal of Speech* 97 (2011): 283–308.
13. Lorde, *Burst of Light,* 64–65.
14. Lorde, "Sister Outsider," in *Collected Poems,* 317.
15. Lorde, *Sister Outsider,* 112. For commentary on this speech, see Lester C. Olson, "The Personal, the Political, and Others: Audre Lorde Denouncing 'The *Second Sex* Conference,'" *Philosophy and Rhetoric* 33 (2000): 259–85.
16. Audre Lorde, *The Cancer Journals* (San Francisco: Aunt Lute Books, 1980), 12–13. For commentary, see Lester C. Olson, "Audre Lorde's Embodied Invention," in *The Responsibilities of Rhetoric,* ed. Michelle Smith and Barbara Warnick (Long Grove, Ill.: Waveland, 2010), 80–95.
17. Lorde, *Sister Outsider,* 116.
18. Ibid., 13–35, 176–90; Lorde, *Burst of Light,* 27–39, 56–64, 69–72, 131–34.
19. Kwame Anthony Appiah, *Cosmopolitanism: Ethics in a World of Strangers* (New York: Norton, 2006), xv.
20. Lorde, *Burst of Light,* 74.
21. Ibid., 53.
22. Appiah, *Cosmopolitanism,* esp. 59, 82–84, 162–66.
23. Arabella Lyon and Lester C. Olson, "Human Rights Rhetoric: Traditions of Testifying and Witnessing," in *Human Rights Rhetoric: Traditions of Testifying and Witnessing,* ed. Arabella Lyon and Lester C. Olson (London: Routledge, 2012), 1–11, esp. 4–5.
24. For example, see Lorde, *Burst of Light,* 28, 32, 36–37.
25. Lorde, *Sister Outsider,* 140.
26. Audre Lorde, *Apartheid U.S.A.* (New York: Kitchen Table: Women of Color Press, 1986), reprinted in *Burst of Light.*
27. See Susan Koshy, "Minority Cosmopolitanism," *Proceedings of the Modern Language Association* 126 (2011): 592–609, esp. 594.
28. Lorde, *Burst of Light,* 57.
29. Ibid., 56–57.
30. Ibid., 66.
31. Ibid.
32. Ibid., 37–38.
33. Ibid., 72.
34. Ibid., 97.
35. Ibid., 61, 78, 101, 107, 119.
36. Ibid., 66.
37. Ibid., 67.
38. Ibid., 69–72.

LESTER C. OLSON

39. Ibid., 67.
40. Ibid., 26.
41. Ibid., 73.
42. Lorde, *Sister Outsider*, 50.
43. Lorde, *Burst of Light*, 70.
44. See chapter 5.
45. Ibid.
46. Donald E. Pease, "Introduction: Re-Mapping the Transnational Turn," in *Re-Framing the Transnational Turn in American Studies*, ed. Winfried Fluck, Donald E. Pease, and John Carlos Rowe (Hanover, N.H.: Dartmouth College Press, 2011), 4, 5, 5–6.
47. For example, see Lorde, *Sister Outsider*, 16, 19, 35, 181, 187; and Lorde, *A Burst of Light*, 36.
48. Lorde, *Burst of Light*, 63.
49. See chapter 5.
50. Lorde, *Burst of Light*, 70, 71.
51. See chapter 10 for an exploration of transracial alliances in Lorde's work.
52. For example, see Lorde, *Burst of Light*, 116–17; and Lorde, *Sister Outsider*, 139.
53. Lorde, *Burst of Light*, 117–18. A similar passage appears in Lorde, *Sister Outsider*, 120–21.

10
Transracial Feminist Alliances?
Audre Lorde and West German Women

KATHARINA GERUND

The West German reception of Audre Lorde's literary, cultural, and activist work has not only been fundamental to the Afro-German movement but also provided a significant intervention into West German discourses on diverse yet related topics such as race, national identity, heteronormativity, gender and feminism, and breast cancer. From the beginning, Lorde's writings were marketed in Germany as women's literature. Most of her works were published by Orlanda Frauenverlag, which perpetuated Lorde's focus on black women as well as her activism. In 1987, for example, Orlanda hired its first Afro-German staff member, and its leadership has since become an integrated team.[1] The first German edition of Lorde's *The Cancer Journals* opened up a venue for discussing breast cancer and included a contribution by a German woman, Waltraut Ruf, who suffered from the disease. She confirmed that this book was relevant for every woman, regardless of nationality, sexuality, or ethnicity.[2] Several of Lorde's books were published by the German press Fischer, which is larger than Orlanda, but they, too, explicitly targeted a female audience. For example, Fischer's edition of *Zami: A New Spelling of My Name,* changed the subtitle to *Ein Leben unter Frauen,* which translates as *A Life among Women,* emphasizing women's communities over the writer's personal account.[3]

Lorde's role in the Afro-German movement has been well established: Ria Cheatom calls her the "mother of the movement," and Stefanie Kron credits her as one of its major initiators.[4] With Black German women, Lorde coined the term *Afro-German,* a reference to *Afro-American* reflecting the "central role that US activism had for Afro-Germans."[5] In this context, her presence in West Germany was crucial, and many Afro-German women describe meeting her as an extraordinary, even life-altering experience.[6] She inspired Afro-German women such as Ika Hügel-Marshall, Helga Emde, and May Ayim to become writers, and her poetics "shaped the content and form chosen by Afro-German writers."[7] Moreover, she encouraged Afro-German women to recognize each other. Cheatom recalled a reading in Stuttgart at which some black women sat scattered among a predominantly white female audience. After the reading, Lorde asked the white women to leave the room. Cheatom said, "Suddenly I *saw* the other Black women, even those, whom I would not have recognized at first sight . . . Audre encouraged us to approach one another . . . This was a phenomenal moment in my life."[8]

Lorde's lectures, readings, and meetings with German audiences were vital to her lasting influence, which also affected white feminists and white women. She was first introduced to German audiences alongside a white poet, Adrienne Rich, linked as lesbian writers in a volume edited by a white woman, Dagmar Schultz. This 1983 book, *Macht und Sinnlichkeit,* was a selection and collection of Rich's and Lorde's work; and according to Schultz, it was intended to instigate discussions about racism and anti-Semitism in the women's movement.[9] In other words, while Lorde's works may speak primarily to black women, they also have the potential to promote sisterhood across the color line and embrace differences among women. Her interactions, connections, and coalitions with black and white German women offer a model for transracial feminist alliances.

AUDRE LORDE'S WORK AND ITS IMPLIED AUDIENCES

Several aspects of Lorde's work lend themselves readily to forging connections across national, racial, and gender divides. Above all, her writings and speeches interpellate her readers and listeners as active and potentially activist subjects endowed with a certain degree of power. While she has often been regarded as separatist because of her emphasis on women's communities and relationships, her complex work is far more than the manifestation of an "angry black woman" (though anger is certainly central to it).[10]

Her work emerges as challenging rather than separatist, which increases its relevance beyond one specific group (for instance, white women, black women, or lesbians) and enables it to resonate in different places, contexts, and discourses.

Lorde explained that she thought "of [her] responsibility in terms of women because there are many voices for men."[11] She did not address women as a passive audience but encouraged them to raise their voices. Moreover, she frequently "asked members of the dominant communities to assume a responsibility for active listening" and for working to overcome differences that might separate the audience from the speaker.[12] With its inclusive approach, its activist stance, and its interactive openness, as well as its merging of art, life, and activism, her radical poetics enabled exchange and critical dialogue with her readers and listeners, particularly with women and people of the black diaspora.

For Lorde, life, art, and social activism were inextricably intertwined. She claimed that "the question of social protest and art is inseparable for [her]."[13] Elsewhere she wrote, "I write my living and I live my work."[14] She adhered to the feminist dictum that "the personal is political"; one might even say that, for her, "the political is not only personal, it is lyrical."[15] For women particularly, "poetry is not a luxury" her well-known aphorism states. Her poetry worked to debunk the hegemony of white European knowledge production, and it emerged as liberatory practice: "The white fathers told us: I think, therefore I am. The Black mother within each one of us—the poet—whispers in our dreams: I feel, therefore I can be free."[16] Lorde countered patriarchy and rational Enlightenment thinking with a matrilineal black tradition that claims emotion as a revolutionary tool. She conceived of poetry as an "agent for combining feeling and thinking."[17] Her poetics and her idea of the erotic took tacit knowledge—or, in Alexis Shotwell's terminology, "implicit understanding"—seriously and used its potential for "personal and political transformation."[18]

Lorde's proto-intersectional approach facilitated her significance for women from different backgrounds. She held that "there is no hierarchy of oppression."[19] That thesis paved the way for "the emergence, some years later, of Deborah King's theory of multiple jeopardy and Kimberlé Crenshaw's theory of intersectionality."[20] It also made it possible for Lorde to relate directly to other oppressed people. Her theory of difference did not deny real differences in terms of race, age, sex, or class but proclaimed that

KATHARINA GERUND

they need not simply be "tolerated, but seen as a fund of necessary polarities between which . . . creativity can spark like a dialectic."[21] The "house of . . . difference" that she envisioned stood in contrast to the "master's house," which, as the title of one of her speeches reveals, will never be dismantled by the master's tools.[22] She called on women to realize a radical social transformation, shifting from "conquer and divide" to "define and empower": "If I, Audre Lorde, do not define myself, the outer world certainly will, and . . . probably will define each one of us to our detriment, singly or in groups."[23]

Lorde's vision of global sisterhood is inclusive, not only because it encompasses women from different backgrounds and the multiple facets of every woman's identity but also because it covers numerous topics and agendas: "There is no single-issue struggle because we don't live single-issue lives."[24] Along with her radical critique of racism, white feminist complicity in patriarchal and racist power structures, and homophobia, she extended an invitation to those whom she criticized: "We welcome all women who can meet us, face to face, beyond objectification and beyond guilt."[25] Aimee Carrillo Rowe holds that the "critique of white feminism . . . is compulsory" and "arises not from a space of separation from, but from an impetus towards connection. That is, the absence of such critiques signals a process of subalternization, whereas their presence is a function of alliance."[26] Lorde's openness to interracial dialogue and even alliance is reflected in the Afro-German movement, which was shaped primarily by Afro-German women but, from the start, also involved white women. Although she has been criticized for "not writing in a voice that specifically marks her discourse as African American," this very quality might have made her work relevant to readers of different nationalities, sexes, sexualities, ethnicities, and ages and contributed to her international influence as a writer, activist, and theorist.[27]

For Lorde, "gender [became] the location of unity capable of bridging differences: shattering the silence surrounding gender oppression and naming the means by which women are kept divided becomes the strategy for building that bridge."[28] Her connections with Afro-German and white German women help us envision how gender and feminist solidarity across the color line might be enacted in other scenarios. The exchange among African America, Afro-Germany, and white Germany not only made space for a necessary reconceptualization of Germany as a diasporic place and a reinvestigation of the gendered African/black diaspora but today also offers insights into the possibilities and limits of transnational and transracial feminism.

AFRO-GERMAN AND WHITE WOMEN: THE POSSIBILITIES OF TRANSRACIAL FEMINISM

In addition to her globalized consciousness of women, oppression, and solidarity, Lorde "proved herself a perceptive and outspoken commentator on events in Germany."[29] For example, in 1988, she described Berlin as a "very calm" and "extremely white city"; she observed that the whiteness of Berlin "encourage[d] a certain smug assumption." Because there were few black people, there was "little question of interaction," and blacks were often stared at with hostility or mere curiosity; she argued that Berlin was, in fact, a segregated city.[30] White Berliners, she said, "are interested in dealing with racism in America, and in England, but are much less prepared to deal with racism in terms of their Turkish and Middle Eastern workers who are the 'Black people' of Germany. That would bring racism too close to home."[31] The connections and interactions between Lorde and Afro-German women are addressed in essays throughout this book; Lorde positioned these women in an "international community of people of color" and recognized their connections as a prerequisite for her vision of a global feminism.[32]

In her preface to *Die Quelle unserer Macht: Gedichte,* Marion Kraft hoped that blacks, white women, and men would use Lorde's oeuvre to better understand themselves, their life conditions, and the power of language.[33] Nonetheless, in West Germany, Lorde's works mainly (though not exclusively) circulated among feminist and black audiences. Lorde described her German audiences at a reading in Dresden as mainly "white women, and young Afro-German men and women."[34] For many white women, Lorde and her work was challenging and guilt-inducing. In the Swiss women's magazine *Emanzipation,* for example, Liliane Studer reflected on a 1989 meeting with the poet and addressed her own discomfort and anxiety. As a white, middle-class, heterosexual woman living in one of the world's wealthiest nations, she experienced a strange feeling of guilt. Realizing that this initial reaction was unnecessary and nonsensical, she pointed out the need for all women to "think, reflect, act."[35] Likewise, in a 1989 article on Lorde's reading in Hamburg, Mechthild Bausch and Marlies Rademacher responded to Lorde's challenge to the audience: "What is your work?" They pointed out that Lorde was less known in West Germany than other African American women writers were, and they regarded her writings as "sometimes banal . . . though pointed." Bausch and Rademacher described the reading: "It is as if a witch would recite a Shakespeare drama in person. Even though Audre Lorde might like neither witches nor Shakespeare's dramas."[36] Here, Lorde's difference was contained by the white western tradition of a Shakespeare drama, but the witch comparison still marked her as other. This problematic but telling simile exposed the authors' struggle to find an adequate language to describe their experience at Lorde's reading and to share that atmosphere with their readers. Their article attests to the challenging character of Lorde's work and reveals some listeners' and readers' inability to deal with her writings, her performance, and her presence. White women often demonstrated not only a lack of understanding but also an unwillingness to confront their whiteness.

Despite the problems of transracial solidarity and understanding, possibilities for collaboration did arise. Lorde's activism and the project *Farbe bekennen,* a milestone in Afro-German history, triggered a continuing legacy in German discourses about ethnicity, race, and gender. The book's heterogeneous group of editors, which included a white woman (Dagmar Schultz), productively complicated its implications and attested to the necessity for and possibilities of creating a group of women to work together across the color line to achieve political goals and exercise agency. This is not an easy task and may come at the cost of painful revisions for white feminists, as Schultz's account of encounters between white women and Afro-Germans at readings of *Farbe bekennen* has made clear: "They feel offended, burst into tears, and often hurriedly receive consolation from a whole group of *white* women. The escape into victimhood apparently constitutes the easier way out."[37] The women here resorted to their status as victims rather than confronted their complicity in racism, oppression, and epistemic violence. Their reaction evaded the potential to deal critically with whiteness as a "location of structural advantage, of race privilege," a "standpoint," and a "set of cultural practices that are usually unmarked and unnamed."[38] According to Rowe, "feminist efforts to build inclusive and transformative alliances [often] . . . fail": "When it becomes easier to turn away than to touch the blemished interface between us, isolation and anger, pain and defensiveness keep us from our own healing."[39]

Farbe bekennen, first published in 1986, opened the possibility of a critical dialogue among all women about whiteness, feminism, and racism. Later the editors discussed the influence of their project. Although both May Opitz and Katharina Oguntoye pointed out that it did contribute to changes in German social conditions, they also noted that Afro-Germans must continue to strive for self-articulation and agency.[40] While Afro-Germans have developed networks and gained visibility in German society, open and subtle forms of racism continue, and social recognition and integration are still major problems. Nevertheless, according to Dagmar Schultz, the confrontation between Afro-German women and their white sisters has initiated dialogues across racial boundaries and put racism onto the feminist agenda. She emphasized the importance of Lorde's lectures and readings, which gave white women an opportunity to meet an African American author.[41] In 2005, Schultz again evaluated the legacy of the 1980s and 1990s: "The coalition politics black and white women fought for in the 1980s and 1990s are only rudimentarily realized on an organizational level in Germany. An increasing number of white women [have], however, understood that white is not the norm. This insight can hopefully contribute to a development of an international intercultural women's movement on a global and local level."[42]

Lorde's contributions enriched the lives and thinking of many white and Afro-German women and were essential to the Afro-German movement. Equally important were Afro-German women's own initiative and the general zeitgeist. As Eleonore Wiedenroth-Coulibaly has explained, almost simultaneously in different places throughout the Federal Republic of Germany, Black Germans were creating new spaces to meet and connect with each other.[43] In 1973, Karin Thimm and Du Rell Echols published *Schwarze in Deutschland: Protokolle.* In 1984 (the year of Lorde's first visit to Germany), Gisela Fremgen published . . . *Und wenn du dazu noch schwarz bist: Berichte schwarzer Frauen in der Bundesrepublik.*[44] An emerging black consciousness and growing feminist concerns were significant preconditions for Lorde's influential role in West Germany. According to Fatima El-Tayeb, Lorde's interest in reaching out to Afro-Germans "is indicative of the important role of women and feminist issues in the first decade of Afro-German activism."[45] For her part, Schultz regards the encounter with Lorde and the Afro-Germans as a step toward a critical awareness that "whiteness cannot remain invisible . . . and whites are required to consider

KATHARINA GERUND

how they might use the power and privileges they enjoy because of the color of their skin."[46] In other words, she believes that Lorde directed attention to what Adrienne Rich called "white solipsism" to describe the presumed universality of a white perspective and the impossibility of color-blindness. To Rich, "white solipsism" meant "to think, imagine, and speak as if whiteness described the world"—"tunnel vision" rather than a "consciously held *belief*."[47] She urged women to overcome guilt, which leads to paralysis, and to confront racism not as a monolithic entity but in its multifaceted forms: "We cannot hope to define a feminist culture, a gynecentric vision, on racist terms, because a part of ourselves will remain forever unknown to us."[48]

Assuming that race and racism rely on a "racialized common sense," I perceive several implications for possible feminist alliances between black and white women as well as the confrontation of prejudices and racism. Shotwell argues that "having an articulation of race as implicit knowledge helps to describe the mechanism of 'race' in its continued creation and development in this world" and that it "provides an account of how consent to hegemonic reproduction of . . . [racial and gender formations] is itself materially but not necessarily discursively propagated." She adds that such an articulation of race is necessary to affect positive transformations.[49] Negative affect—"feeling bad"—might be useful in the processes of changing racialized common sense and of producing "meaningful solidarity across difference." Shame in particular can bring implicit meanings to the surface, "make unspeakable things viscerally present."[50] Lorde's emphasis on forms of knowledge other than propositional/explicit knowledge (such as the erotic or feeling) might be helpful as we confront racism and facilitate solidarity among feminists. According to Shotwell, whites should confront feelings of unease and discomfort rather than try to escape them.[51] She partially recuperates the potential of white guilt—albeit with modifications: "First, white people need to do more than become aware of what we do individually to support taken-for-granted racist customs and practices; we need to take action. Second, we need to have a way of working with the negative affect that awareness of racism rightly carries. Third, we need to open routes for deep political transformation on both personal and systemic levels."[52] Shame, as she explains with reference to Eve Sedgwick, is different from white guilt as "it expresses a sense of connection that has been variously termed 'empathy,' 'sympathy,' and 'feeling-with,'" and this aspect might help to "produce political solidarities." It can disrupt "conceptual habits" and facilitate transformations of the implicit understandings that shape racial formations.[53] In line with Lorde's thinking, she argues that difference needs to be respected to produce a solidarity that is *not* based on "an expanded sense of 'us'" and potentially reifies the "primacy of whiteness."[54]

Rowe believes that "transracial feminist alliances are expansive. They provide the basis for shared experience and meaning from which we are excluded if we stay within our own racial ranks," yet "transnational feminist alliances are not automatic. Solidarity cannot be assumed, but must be fought for."[55] In the German context, transracial dialogue has required and continues to call for white feminists' critical engagement with whiteness and racism. Schultz explains that, in her encounter with Lorde, she learned that her conscious and critical confrontation with her whiteness was a precondition for their mutual trust and friendship.[56] Critical awareness of whiteness as usually unnamed marker of a yet equally racialized identity is an indispensable prerequisite for transracial feminist solidarity and for addressing racism as a mode of oppression inherent to white feminism. Ruth Frankenberg says that when white people "look at racism, we tend to view it as an issue that people of color face and have to struggle with, but not as an issue that generally involves or implicates us . . . With this view, white women can see antiracist work as an act of compassion for an 'other,' an optional, extra project, but not one intimately and organically linked to our own lives. Racism can, in short, be conceived as something external to us rather than as a system that shapes our daily experiences and sense of self."[57]

Rowe accents this point when she contends that "we must understand whiteness as a mode of belonging in order to dismantle the force of its privileging and marginalizing tendencies."[58] She proposes a *"politics of relation"* in which we create selves "as a function of where we place our bodies and with whom we build our affective ties" and strive toward "a relational notion of the subject, a coalitional subject." This politics of relation moves toward a theorization of "experience and agency as *collective processes*."[59] It "offers a frame to foreground the conditions under which our affective investment emerge, as well as the fissures and fault lines that constitute feminist difference. For such a frame to render visible, or otherwise tangible, the relational *practices* conducive of transracial feminist alliance, it

KATHARINA GERUND

must provide a relational approach to the politics of speaking and listening."[60] In this approach, whom we love is not only political but also "who we are becoming."[61] What Rowe calls "differential belonging" highlights "the multiple paths we may travel in our circle of belonging," and it "is not to be bound by the regulatory practices of any particular group nor by the need to remain consistent or pure, but rather to take a risk and move in the direction of multiple others. As in becoming other."[62]

CONCLUSION: SOLIDARITY AND TRANSRACIAL FEMINISM

Lorde, among other black feminists, prefigured theoretical ruminations about the possibilities of transracial feminist alliances and the interconnections between race and feminism that are crucial to Frankenberg's and Rowe's empirical scholarship. She called for and to some degree brought about a critical reflection of whiteness in the feminist movement at a time when Frankenberg's seminal study of whiteness as social construct was initially taking shape. Frankenberg's 1993 book "emerged out of the 1980s" when "white feminist women like [herself] could no longer fail to notice the critique of white feminist racism by feminist/radical women of color."[63] Lorde's theory countered a male genealogy with a matrilineal tradition and emphasized feeling as a liberating force, and Rowe's approach to the politics of love and the centrality of affective ties and (be)longings is reminiscent of this notion.

Lorde's theoretical and activist practice had the potential to cross color lines. Rowe and Shotwell point out the role of feelings and affect in creating solidarity; similarly, transracial feminism requires the confrontation of implicit understandings of race and gender, of racialized and gendered common sense. Critical whiteness studies has increased the awareness of racist structures within feminism. Lorde's approach to feelings draws attention to a form of tacit or implicit understanding, which Shotwell calls "sensuous knowledge."[64] This knowledge has to be examined and confronted to facilitate feminist alliances across difference. Lorde's interactions with white and Afro-German women reveal that transracial feminist alliances may be uncomfortable for white women but are essential for both feminist and antiracist activism. These interactions expose the main problems in collaborations between white and Afro-German women—such as white guilt, racism, and white superiority—but also indicate their possibilities, productivity, and creativity.

Angela Davis has written, "Through her life, [Lorde] galvanized alliances among individuals and groups who were not expected to discover points of convergence. Thus her legacy is claimed by poets, writers, scholars and activists, by working-class people and women and men of all racial backgrounds."[65] In Germany, her legacy is primarily claimed by Afro-Germans and feminists. However, the potential of transracial alliances requires us to consider not only the preconditions and possibilities of coalitions between black and white women but also the relations among different diasporic or immigrant groups in Germany. Thus, feminist solidarity in and beyond Germany must continue to develop methods and strategies for working together—and, in line with Lorde's vision, not despite but because of difference.

Notes

1. Dagmar Schultz, "Witnessing Whiteness—Ein persönliches Zeugnis," in *Mythen, Masken und Subjekte: Kritische Weißseinsforschung in Deutschland,* ed. Maureen Maisha Eggers, Grada Kilomba, Peggy Piesche, and Susan Arndt (Münster: Unrast, 2005), 524.
2. Waltraut Ruf, "13 Jahre nach einer Brustkrebsoperation," in *Auf Leben und Tod: Krebstagebuch,* by Audre Lorde (Berlin: sub rosa, 1984), 103.
3. Audre Lorde, *Zami: Ein Leben unter Frauen,* trans. Karen Nölle-Fischer (Frankfurt am Main: Fischer, 1993).
4. Nicola Lauré al-Samarai, Katja Kinder, Ria Cheatom, and Ekpenyong Ani, " 'Es ist noch immer ein Aufbruch, aber mit neuer Startposition': Zwanzig Jahre *ADEFRA* and Schwarze Frauen / Bewegung in Deutschland," in *Re/Visionen: Postkoloniale Perspektiven von People of Color auf Rassismus, Kulturpolitik und Widerstand in Deutschland,* ed. Kien Nghi Ha, Nicola Lauré al-Samarai, and Sheila Mysorekar (Münster: Unrast, 2007), 351; Stefanie Kron, *Fürchte dich nicht, Bleichgesicht! Perspektivenwechsel zur Literatur Afro-Deutscher Frauen* (Münster: Unrast, 1996), 114.
5. Fatima El-Tayeb, " 'If You Can't Pronounce My Name, You Can Call Me Pride': Afro-German Activism, Gender, and Hip Hop," in *Dialogues of Dispersal: Gender, Sexuality, and African Diasporas,* ed. Sandra Gunning, Tera W. Hunter, and Michele Mitchell (Oxford: Blackwell, 2004), 66.
6. Dagmar Schultz, preface, *Auf Leben und Tod: Krebstagebuch,* by Audre Lorde (Frankfurt am Main: Fischer, 2000), 8.
7. Jennifer E. Michaels, "The Impact of Audre Lorde's Politics and Poetics on Afro-German Women Writers," *German Studies Review* 29 (2006): 21, 30.
8. Lauré al-Samarai et al., "Aufbruch," 351. The translation is mine.
9. Schultz, "Witnessing," 522.
10. Barbara Christian, "The Truth That Never Hurts: Black Lesbians in Fiction in the 1980s," in *Feminism: An Anthology of Literary Theory and Criticism,* ed. Robyn R. Warhol and Diane Price Herndl (New Brunswick, N.J.: Rutgers University Press, 1997), 789.

KATHARINA GERUND

11. Claudia Tate, ed., *Black Women Writers at Work* (New York: Continuum, 1985), 104.

12. Lester C. Olson, "Liabilities of Language: Audre Lorde Reclaiming Difference," *Quarterly Journal of Speech* 84 (1998): 448.

13. Audre Lorde, "My Words Will Be There," in *I Am Your Sister: Collected and Unpublished Writings of Audre Lorde,* ed. Rudolph P. Byrd, Johnnetta Betsch Cole, and Beverly Guy-Sheftall (Oxford: Oxford University Press, 2009), 164.

14. Audre Lorde, "Self-Definition and My Poetry," in Byrd et al., *I Am Your Sister,* 156.

15. Lori L. Walk, "Audre Lorde's Life-Writing: The Politics of Location," *Women's Studies* 32, no.7 (2003): 828.

16. Audre Lorde, *Sister Outsider: Essays and Speeches* (Berkeley, Calif.: Crossing Press, 1984), 38.

17. Alexis Shotwell, *Knowing Otherwise: Race, Gender, and Implicit Understanding* (University Park: Pennsylvania State University Press, 2011), 26.

18. Ibid., ix.

19. Audre Lorde, "There Is No Hierarchy of Oppression," in Byrd et al., *I Am Your Sister,* 220.

20. Rudolph P. Byrd, introduction, in Byrd et al., *I Am Your Sister,* 29.

21. Lorde, *Sister Outsider,* 111. Despite the significance of her theoretical texts for black feminist thinking, Lorde said "that [as a poet] she doesn't write theory" (7). She destabilized the assumed opposition between poetry (or, more generally, literature and art) and theory (or, more generally, scholarship, science, and knowledge).

22. Lorde, "Difference," 203.

23. Lorde, *Sister Outsider,* 112; Lorde, "Self-Definition," 156.

24. Lorde, *Sister Outsider,* 138.

25. Ibid., 133.

26. Aimee Carrillo Rowe, *Power Lines: On the Subject of Feminist Alliances* (Durham: Duke University Press, 2008), 177.

27. Maureen C. Heacock, "The 'Sharpened Edge' of Audre Lorde: Visions and Re-Visions of Community, Power, and Language," in *Sharpened Edge: Women of Color, Resistance, and Writing,* ed. Stephanie Athey (Westport, Conn.: Praeger, 2003), 171.

28. Tina Richardson, "Changing Landscapes: Mapping Breast Cancer as an Environmental Justice Issue in Audre Lorde's *The Cancer Journals,*" in *Restoring the Connection to the Natural World: Essays on the African American Environmental Imagination,* ed. Sylvia Mayer (Münster: LIT, 2003), 140.

29. Michaels, "Audre Lorde's Politics and Poetics," 22.

30. Hall, *Conversations,* 171.

31. Ibid., 172.

32. Audre Lorde, "Showing Our True Colors," *Callaloo* 14, no. 1 (1991): 69–71.

33. Marion Kraft, preface, *Die Quelle unserer Macht: Gedichte,* by Audre Lorde (Berlin: Orlanda Frauenverlag, 1994), 13.

34. Lorde, "Showing," 70.

35. Liliane Studer, "Auf Leben und Tod: Eine Begegnung mit Audre Lorde," *Emanzipation* 11 (1989): 8.

36. Mechthild Bausch and Marlies Rademacher, "Schwarze Göttin in New York," *Hamburger Rundschau,* July 20, 1989. The translation is mine.

37. Schultz, "Witnessing," 524. The translation is mine.

38. Ruth Frankenberg, *The Social Construction of Whiteness: White Women, Race Matters* (Minneapolis: University of Minnesota Press, 1993), 1.

39. Rowe, *Power Lines,* 2.

40. Katharina Oguntoye, May Opitz, and Dagmar Schultz, eds., *Farbe bekennen: Afro-deutsche Frauen auf den Spuren ihrer Geschichte* (Frankfurt am Main.: Fischer, 1992), 10–12.
41. Ibid., 14.
42. Schultz, "Witnessing," 526. The translation is mine.
43. Eleonore Wiedenroth-Coulibaly, "Zwanzig Jahre Schwarzer Widerstand in bewegten Räumen: Was sich im Kleinen abspielt und aus dem Verborgenen erwächst," in Ha et al., *Re/Visionen*, 404.
44. Gisela Fremgen, . . . *Und wenn du dazu noch schwarz bist: Berichte schwarzer Frauen in der Bundesrepublik* (Bremen: Edition CON, 1984); Karin Thimm and Du Rell Echols, *Schwarze in Deutschland: Protokolle* (Munich: Piper, 1973).
45. El-Tayeb, "Pronounce My Name," 66.
46. Schultz, "Witnessing," 524. The translation is mine.
47. Adrienne Rich, "Disloyal to Civilization: Feminism, Racism, Gynephobia," in *On Lies, Secrets, and Silence: Selected Prose, 1966–1978* (New York: Norton, 1979), 299.
48. Ibid., 306, 308.
49. Shotwell, *Knowing Otherwise*, 44–46.
50. Ibid., 73, 77.
51. Ibid., 80.
52. Ibid., 84.
53. Ibid., 86, 90.
54. Ibid., 104.
55. Rowe, *Power Lines*, 4.
56. Schultz, "Witnessing," 523.
57. Frankenberg, *Social Construction*, 6.
58. Rowe, *Power Lines*, 38.
59. Ibid., 3, 10.
60. Ibid., 11–12.
61. Ibid., 3.
62. Ibid., 44.
63. Frankenberg, *Social Construction*, 2.
64. Shotwell, *Knowing Otherwise*, 48.
65. Beverly Guy-Sheftall, epilogue, in Byrd et al., *I Am Your Sister*, 256.

II
Emotional Connections
Audre Lorde and Black German Women

TIFFANY N. FLORVIL

In a 1986 letter to Audre Lorde, Marion Kraft, who is of African American and German descent, wrote, "Our experiences might be very different, indeed but more important for me was to recognize the commonalities, the discrimination and oppression black women are facing all over the world, but also their strength, their creativity in various fields—and their dedication to life!" She continued, "Why is it then, that sometimes we *fear* these commonalities? On the train back from Berlin I reread 'Eye to Eye,' and found some of the answers to that question and I was very moved."[1] In the letter, Kraft discussed Lorde's books *Sister Outsider* and *Zami* as well as the Afro-German anthology *Farbe bekennen* (later translated as *Showing Our Colors*), her recent interview with Lorde, and a *Frankfurter Rundschau* article on Black Germans.[2] She concluded, "How glad I am to have made your acquaintance, and how important your work is to me. With love and respect, Marion."[3]

Women across the African diaspora share affinities stemming from their struggles with discrimination. As Kraft's correspondence reveals, Audre Lorde inspired many Black German women to develop new projects based on the belief that, as Black Germans, they were entitled to be a part of both the African diaspora and majority-white Germany. Their interactions with Lorde also helped them embrace their own internal differences. Afro-Germans are heterogeneous, with diverse historical, social, and cultural backgrounds. Moreover, some have lacked sustained contact with their relatives of African descent, instead growing up with foster parents or white German family members or in orphanages. After World War II, Black Germans, unlike some other Afro-diasporic minorities, were scattered across Germany instead of being concentrated in urban neighborhoods. Before Lorde's visit in the 1980s, most lacked a positive sense of identity or community. Thus, she served as a linchpin for the Afro-German movement, allowing Black Germans to fill a void and engender connections through their writing and emotions. In particular, the affective encounters between Lorde and Afro-German women, which took place from 1984 until her death in 1992, enabled these women to feel less isolated and to manifest respect, hope, longing, and frustration. Their correspondence reveals that emotional practices, even when tense, motivated Afro-German women to mobilize, seek and retain recognition, and forge solidarity.[4]

FEELING AND CONNECTING

By way of her publications, seminars, interviews, and readings in Germany, Lorde became a mentor to many Afro-German women.[5] They were particularly drawn to her ideas about the interconnections among poetry, emotions, the erotic, identity, and female kinship. For Lorde, all women were potential poets: "each one of us holds an incredible reserve of creativity and power, of unexamined and unrecorded emotion and feeling" that is "neither white nor surface" but "dark," "ancient," and "deep."[6] She stressed that women could use this reservoir to deal with sexism, racism, and homophobia. Viewing poetry as a habitual act of survival, resistance, communication, and community building, Lorde declared that it could turn women's "hopes and fears" into positive acts that reflected and reconstituted individual lives, affirmed multiple emotions, and "transform[ed] the silences."[7] According to Fatima El-Tayeb, "[she] claimed poetry as a radical, feminist form of expression exactly because of its association with qualities disvalued within Western intellectual tradition—emotion, intuition, collectivity, nonlinearity, and the oral—qualities that had also been attributed to women and people of color."[8]

Lorde described the erotic as "a resource within each of us that lies in a deeply female and spiritual plane, firmly rooted in the power of our unexpressed or unrecognized feeling."[9] She held that it had been debased and neglected in Western society, where it had become synonymous with women's inferiority, denying their promise and agency.[10] She also cautioned women not to confuse the erotic with pornography, as the latter was "a direct denial of the power of the erotic, for it represents the suppression of true feeling."[11] Lorde believed that, by valuing the erotic, women could cultivate a stronger sense of self-worth—an idea that empowered Black German women as they confronted a white German society that defined blackness negatively and equated it with foreignness. She also maintained that, "anger is a very healthy emotion. It helps tell us something, it also helps move us in to action for change."[12] She embraced anger as a "liberating and strengthening act of clarification" that helped her describe her vision of society and could also help Afro-German women dismantle racism in Germany.[13]

During readings in Germany, Lorde frequently introduced herself as a "black, lesbian, feminist, warrior, poet, mother, and African Caribbean American woman," using these monikers to show the inextricable bond among her identities, activism, and writing.[14] During Dagmar Schultz's "Racism and Sexism" seminar, Lorde remarked, "As I say as a 49 year old black feminist lesbian socialist mother of two, one including a boy, there is always something wrong with me, there is always some group of people who define me as wrong. It is very encouraging, I learn a lot about myself and my identities that way."[15] She valued her multiple identities and the ability to define herself on her own terms. In turn, Afro-Germans imbibed her ideas about self-identification, creating the designations *Black German* and *Afro-German* to counteract pervasive derogatory terms such as *darky* (*Bimbo*) and *mixed-breed children* (*Mischlingskinder*). For several of these women, the term *Black German* functioned as an inclusive designation, much as *Black British* did.

Lorde shared affective knowledge and reflective practices about writing and the African diaspora that were new to many Afro-German women. She did not see poetry as a performance because "it is something that we share and hopefully we each take from this place something that makes us more [of] who we wish to be."[16] Yet her readings and seminars did, in one sense, operate as performances, which, according to Diana Taylor, "function as vital acts of transfer, transmitting social knowledge, memory, and a sense of identity."[17] Lorde's appearances were public events as well as practices that brought people together across their differences, and they elicited love, warmth, courage, and solidarity. During a reading at the Schokofabrik (Chocolate Factory) in Berlin, for example, she imbued emotions with corporeal qualities: "I think we need to deal with our feelings and to put them out there to arm them, to give them teeth and hands to work."[18] Similarly, in Hannover, she claimed that it was our responsibility as individuals to "use our power in the service of what we believe" and eradicate injustice in society.[19] As they connected to Lorde, Black German women gained an empowering rhetoric about self-awareness that inspired them to coordinate events that challenged conventional understandings of Germany as white.

Lorde believed that poetry should be written, read, and spoken as well as valued, felt, and applied in ways that trigger love, respect, warmth, and courage. In her speech "The Dream of Europe," she declared, "I am an African-American poet and believe in the power of poetry. Poetry, like all art, has a function: to bring us closer to who we wish to be: to help us vision a future which has not yet been: and to help us survive the lack of that future."[20] Her emphasis on writing impressed many Afro-German women, motivating them to construct an alternative emotional archive that they used for collaborative projects aimed at dismantling the racism that was persisting in Germany after the Second World War.[21]

Lorde also emphasized women's bonds in her writings and public engagements, explaining at a reading of *Zami* in Berlin, "I wanted to make a lot of connections in this book, connections between women, connections between—it has been the love of women that has kept me alive for so long, and in the really hard times in my life it has served to reexamine the ways in which this worked." She stressed that no matter how these female relationships progressed—whether they were "loving," "bitter," "transient," or "painful"—they were beneficial.[22] She encouraged Afro-German women to seek fellowship with her and each other and develop affective skills that would motivate them to combat racism in Germany and to affirm their cultural autonomy by documenting their histories.

AFFECTIVE VALUE: FROM *FARBE BEKENNEN* TO PERSONAL ATTACHMENTS

Several Afro-German women—including May Opitz (later Ayim), Marion Kraft, Katharina Oguntoye, Helga Emde, Erika Hügel (later Hügel-Marshall), and Eleonore Wiedenroth (later Wiedenroth-Coulibaly)—incorporated Lorde's ideas into their lives and activism. Much of this influence manifests

TIFFANY N. FLORVIL

in the 1986 volume *Farbe bekennen*, edited by Ayim, Oguntoye, and Dagmar Schultz. Lorde was critical to the genesis of the anthology, which included poetry, autobiographical texts, interviews with Afro-German women, and Ayim's master's thesis from the University of Regensburg. Afro-Germans' relationships with Lorde, their burgeoning diasporic outlook, and their connection with other people of color made it possible for them to no longer deal "with our background and our identity in isolation."[23] In the volume's twentieth-anniversary edition, Oguntoye, who is of Nigerian and East German descent, said, "Audre Lorde invited us to make our existence and experiences known to the world" and added in a later interview that Lorde has expressly prioritized a Black German publication above her own writing.[24] On one occasion, when Afro-German women were finding it difficult to work on the anthology, Lorde met with them. She laid down her pen and said to the intergenerational group, "I will not write anymore, until I hear and read something from the black women in Germany."[25]

At the volume's heart were narratives that expressed fragmentation, confusion, isolation, and disorientation and gave voice to a longing for someone to confide in. Emde, who is of African American and German descent, recalled, "I felt degraded and discriminated against. As before, I had no contact with other Blacks, mostly because I would have preferred to deny my blackness. It wasn't enough that I belonged to a minority; I also felt lonely and isolated."[26] Reflecting a predicament that several other women in the anthology also discussed, she yearned for connections with other Afro-Germans. Yet the narratives were by no means identical. For example, while Emde was the "only Black person in [her] family," Astrid Berger lived with her devoted Cameroonian father and Jewish German stepmother in Berlin.[27]

In the anthology, the women expressed aggravation and unhappiness about being black in Germany, where their white compatriots made them feel different, ugly, and unwanted. Everyday encounters with family, friends, and strangers exacerbated their discomfort. For some, this led to self-loathing and a desire to be white or light-skinned. Ayim, of Ghanaian and German heritage, dreamed of whiteness that was unattainable "because of [her] parents' unwillingness and the weak cleaning power of soap."[28] Abena Adomako, a dark-skinned woman of Ghanaian and German descent, described her envy of light-skinned Afro-Germans.[29]

Several women wrote of the burden of being meant to feel non-German and confronted the presumption that blackness and Germanness were contradictory. In an interview published in the volume, Laura Baum, Oguntoye, and Ayim commented on oscillating between feeling excluded and a partial sense of belonging.[30] White Germans imposed labels and constructed boundaries that denied Afro-Germans an equal place in the nation. Instead of German, they were considered African American, Afro-Cuban, Afro-Brazilian—what Michelle M. Wright has called the "external African Other."[31] Despite Black Germans' diverse backgrounds, white Germans saw these compatriots as homogeneously foreign.

Farbe bekennen, along with other Afro-German publications, contributed to an emergent Afro-German literary tradition that emphasized respect and the open expression of feelings to transform them into action. Through their writing, Afro-Germans embraced their perceived otherness and resignified their collective identity. Blending their memories and creativity into autobiographical forms, these women used their experiences as discursive and affective tools for self-definition and community building. Following Lorde's advice to connect across their differences, they cultivated ties throughout the African diaspora. Kraft once remarked, "Through Audre I met not only other African German women, but also many sisters involved in the global networking of Black women."[32] By participating in international conferences, book fairs, and workshops and campaigning against racism globally, Afro-German women became invested in transnational networks.[33] In so doing, they shaped their understanding of belonging and reflected their desire for acceptance and recognition.

Forging community through their correspondence with Lorde, Afro-German women also affirmed the significance of bonds with her and other women of color. These friendships helped them survive in a German society that inaccurately imagined itself to be exclusively white. In their correspondence, we witness what Lisa McGill, in her analysis of *Zami*, has called a "covenant of women-bonding": Lorde staged "*Zami*'s community of women by first locating the ways in which she, her lovers, friends, foremothers, and Afrekete form a covenant of women-bonding."[34] Using both typewriters and pen and paper, Afro-German women wrote letters to Lorde that conveyed their love and respect, thus illustrating how important she remained in their lives long after she had left Germany. Writing to her took courage because of her prominence in feminist and Afro-diasporic circles and because correspondents needed to write in English. (Lorde did not read German.)

Black German women conveyed their attachment through sisterly and motherly metaphors that were common to the period's black and Euro-American feminist writings but that took on heightened meaning due to the writers' years of isolation and alienation.[35] These metaphors reflected Lorde's emphasis on how female kinship could transcend boundaries, which she had stressed repeatedly while in Germany. For instance, Nicola Lauré al-Samarai, of Arab and East German descent, referred to Lorde as "my dearest and so near Audre": "Thinking of you, of your warm smile gives me the strength and the power I need to overcome my doubtfulness. So, my dear mothersisterfriend, I want to send you lot of greetings and good wishes to you."[36] Kraft wrote, "You are the 'big sister' I have always longed for, and beyond all possible differences we both must learn to live with and accept, this sisterhood is real."[37] Ayim wrote, "It was on the November 9 demonstrations where I recited three poems. I was wearing your warm embracing jacket Audre and I felt as one of your daughters." She continued, "Poetry becomes a more and more powerful part in my life."[38] These examples illustrate how Black German women expressed a symbolic filial connection. Given Afro-Germans' heterogeneity, Lorde's ideas about diaspora and kinship served as a model for their movement, one that embraced difference yet recognized commonality through marginalization and sought bonds with communities of color in similar predicaments. Nonetheless, while Afro-German women gained insight from Lorde's mantra of "connected differences," several also privileged some differences over others, leading to conflict about sexuality, skin color, and authenticity.

In letters, Afro-German women expressed their connections to Lorde by showering her with affectionate phrases. Using the salutation "Dearest Audre," Ayim sent her "love and kisses and I wish you can feel it as much as I always feel you in my tough times": "Audre, I embrace you and kiss you all over."[39] The women openly conveyed their feelings, often ending their letters with "I send my love to you," "In sisterhood with love," or "You are with us, Audre, I embrace you Love."[40] As Tina Campt has pointed out, whereas other African diasporic communities have common ancestries that revolved around histories of forced, voluntary, or collective migration, Afro-Germans, because of their diversity, did not possess common narratives of home, belonging, or community.[41] Correspondence with Lorde gave these women opportunities to develop bonds that shaped them and their movement.[42] Yet their exchanges could also reflect and reproduce essentialized notions of racial and gender identities. In this way, Afro-German women variously assumed, negotiated, and performed hierarchies of blackness that reified categories of belonging, solidarity, and the diaspora.[43]

Black German women's letters underscored how Lorde had inspired their affection and optimism. Lauré al-Samarai wrote, "Dear Audre, all of us miss you and when we are together we always remember you."[44] Kraft wrote, "Your engagement in the question of Afro-German women was really very important, and personally it means a lot for me to have dealt with your writings and to have made your acquaintance!"[45] Reflecting on the 1990 conference "I Am Your Sister," held in Boston to honor Lorde, Oguntoye wrote, "It was so exciting to see all the women telling about their lives and how you and your work gave them courage." She shared her gratitude for Lorde's assistance in the Afro-German and German women's movements and said that she hoped to emulate her compassion and zeal for human rights.[46] In a letter, another Afro-German, Hella Schültheiß, remarked, "I am very happy that you have been here—a wish of my heart was fulfilled. You know, you have taught me a lot through your books, your way of reading and your way of being there and I am very grateful to you." She was "very glad [that she] got acquainted with [Lorde]" and regarded her literature, public readings, and personality as "gifts of love" that had made a difference in her life and the larger Black German community in Stuttgart.[47] In a birthday greeting, Hügel wrote, "All my knowledge from your works [is] in me and came out of me. Audre you can be very proud . . . Have a very nice birthday."[48]

In letters, Afro-German women emphasized their excitement at connecting with other Afro-diasporic women. Oguntoye wrote, "It is quite a motivation to hurry up a bit, that I can meet Jean and other black women in America and Briten [sic] again. There are so many other women I want to meet." These connections with other women of color were motivating Oguntoye to continue her social activism in the Afro-German, women's, and lesbian movements in Germany.[49] Kraft also highlighted the significance of transnational ties: "For me and Helga [Emde] it was a great pleasure to share our ideas and emotions with so many Black women from all over the world! Helga and I have become very close friends (smile), and I think we've only just begun to realize how much we need each other."[50] Later, Kraft wrote to an ailing Lorde, "And I want you to discover your own strength, rediscover it for yourself, because to us women around the world, women of the African diaspora, you have given so much, words cannot describe."[51]

Letters from Afro-German women also addressed problems that emerged among women. Recalling a reading of *Farbe bekennen* that Ayim and Oguntoye had given at the secular Jewish Lesbian Feminist Sabbath Circle (*Lesbisch-Feministische Schabbeskreis*) in West Berlin, Oguntoye said that "problems of understanding and the will . . . of understanding became visibil [*sic*]" during a discussion about anti-Semitism and racism. Sadly, "endless fighting including reproaches and selfdefences [*sic*]" occurred, making it difficult for her not to become involved.[52] Similarly, Kraft told Lorde, "Unfortunately, there have been some misunderstandings and quarrels at the latest Afro-German women's meetings. And here again, I think we must learn to understand and accept differences, and that we need one another."[53] Writing about the tensions within the Afro-German community, Oguntoye said, "I had some fights within the afro-german women's group. The conflict with Helga [Emde] and with Marion [Kraft] exploded. But really sorry I feel for the argument I had with Domenica (one of the twins), because I like her very much."[54]

Interestingly, in their letters Kraft and Oguntoye discussed hostilities that existed in meetings of ADEFRA, an Afro-German women's organization strongly influenced by Lorde.[55] While ADEFRA helped women find a degree of social cohesion, its female composition did not free it from internal strife. Although the letters did not specify the nature of the conflicts, other sources document concerns about skin color, homosexual and heterosexual alliances, generational differences about sexuality, and the collective goals of a variety of women.[56] On the one hand, Kraft saw these disputes as an opportunity to "learn to understand and accept differences." On the other hand, Oguntoye believed that "anyway I got out of that all that I have to look for my own feelings and needs. I am afraid I forgot about that in the last two years."[57] Sara Ahmed's assessments about feelings could resonate with those Black Germans: "It is not just that we feel for the collective (such as in discourses of fraternity or patriotism), but how we feel about others is what aligns us with a collective, which paradoxically 'takes shape' only as an effect of such alignments."[58] Afro-Germans' emotional exchanges and bonds were mutually constitutive elements for them personally and collectively. Despite points of disagreement, ADEFRA, along with Afro-German female ties more generally, supported a nascent Black German community in ways that much of white German society did not.

How should we read the experiences and emotions recorded in Afro-German women's correspondence with Lorde? What kinds of historical knowledge do their letters provide? These emotional missives are integral to understanding the history of community and cohesion among Afro-Germans, and they demonstrate how Lorde moved the women in profound ways. Aligning themselves through their respect, solace, and frustration, Afro-German women created an affective and diasporic community and performed cultural and political work that sought to change what constituted Germanness and to claim a space in the larger African diaspora. Writing letters, poetry, and autobiography (especially in the context of *Farbe bekennen*) helped them navigate and profess their feelings and produce a new emotional archive. Yet as their personal letters also show, the process of community building was not free from fissures and tensions. So how does this historical moment in the 1980s represent global changes in multiculturalism and transnationalism? How do the dynamics among Afro-German women and Lorde reflect similar or dissimilar patterns with African diasporic groups in Europe, the United States, and the Caribbean? Finally, how do these emotional expressions of disappointment, acrimony, progress, and solidarity line up with narratives of kinship elsewhere?

Notes

1. Audre Lorde, "Eye to Eye: Black Women, Hatred, and Anger," in *Sister Outsider: Essays and Speeches* (Berkeley, Calif.: Crossing Press, 2007), 145–75.
2. Audre Lorde, *Zami: A New Spelling of My Name* (London: Sheba, 1982); Katharina Oguntoye, May Opitz, and Dagmar Schultz, eds., *Farbe bekennen: Afro-deutsche Frauen auf den Spuren ihrer Geschichte* (Berlin: Orlanda Frauenverlag, 1986). For Lorde's interview with Kraft, see chapter 3 in this book.
3. Marion Kraft, letter to Audre Lorde, July 12, 1986, box 3, Audre Lorde Papers, Spelman College Archives (hereafter cited as Lorde Papers). In this essay, I use *Afro-German* and *Black German* interchangeably, with a few notable exceptions.
4. Monique Scheer, "Are Emotions a Kind of Practice (and Is That What Makes Them Have a History)? A Bourdieuian Approach to Understanding Emotion," *History and Theory* 51 (May 2012): 193–220.
5. Lorde was in turn influenced by Afro-Germans: see Audre Lorde, *A Burst of Light: Essays* (Ithaca, N.Y.: Firebrand, 1988). For many Afro-German women, meeting her was their first interaction with a prominent black woman.

TIFFANY N. FLORVIL

6. Lorde, "Poetry Is Not a Luxury," in *Sister Outsider*, 36–37.

7. Ibid., 37; Audre Lorde, "The Transformation of Silence into Language and Action," in *Sister Outsider*, 40–44.

8. Fatima El-Tayeb, *European Others: Queering Ethnicity in Postnational Europe* (Minneapolis: University of Minnesota Press, 2011), 47.

9. Audre Lorde, "The Uses of the Erotic: The Erotic as Power," in *Sister Outsider*, 53.

10. Ibid., 53–54.

11. Ibid., 54.

12. "Reading and Discussion in Dagmar Schultz'[s] Seminar 'Racism and Sexism' at the JFK Institute of North American Studies at the Free University of Berlin," July 7, 1984, vol. 6, p. 5, Audre Lorde Archive, Free University of Berlin (hereafter cited as Lorde Archive).

13. Audre Lorde, "The Uses of Anger: Women Responding to Racism," in *Sister Outsider*, 127.

14. See Audre Lorde, "Lesung in der Schokofabrik," November 20, 1987, vol. 12a, p. 2, Lorde Archive.

15. "Reading and Discussion," 7.

16. "Lesung in der Schokofabrik," 3.

17. Diana Taylor, "Acts of Transfer," in *The Archive and the Repertoire: Performing Cultural Memory in the Americas,* ed. Diana Taylor (Durham, N.C.: Duke University Press, 2003), 2–3.

18. "Lesung in der Schokofabrik," 7. Founded in the 1980s, the Schokofabrik was a women's center in Kreuzberg and was located in a former chocolate factory.

19. Audre Lorde, "Reading in Hannover," May 16, 1988, vol. 15, p. 1, Lorde Archive.

20. Audre Lorde, "The Dream of Europe," undated, box 17, Lorde Papers. A version of the speech is reprinted in chapter 1 of this book.

21. Ann Cvetkovich, *An Archive of Feelings: Trauma, Sexuality, and Lesbian Public Cultures* (Durham, N.C.: Duke University Press, 2003), 7–8.

22. Audre Lorde, "Reading in Berlin 'Araquin,'" July 1, 1987, vol. 8a, p. 2, Lorde Archive.

23. Katharina Oguntoye and May Opitz, "Editors' Introduction," in *Showing Our Colors: Afro-German Women Speak Out,* ed. May Opitz, Katharina Oguntoye, and Dagmar Schultz, trans. Anne V. Adams (Amherst: University of Massachusetts Press, 1992), xxi; Katharina Oguntoye and May Ayim, "Vorwort der Herausgeberinnen," in Opitz et al., *Farbe bekennen,* 17.

24. Katharina Oguntoye, "Vorwort zur Neuauflage 2006," in Opitz et al., *Farbe bekennen,* 5; Katharina Oguntoye, "Rückblenden und Vorschauen: 20 Jahre Schwarze Frauenbewegung," in *"Euer Schweigen schützt euch nicht": Audre Lorde und die Schwarze Frauenbewegung in Deutschland,* ed. Peggy Piesche (Berlin: Orlanda Frauenverlag, 2012), 24.

25. Nicola Lauré al-Samarai in conversation with Katja Kinder, Ria Cheatom, and Ekpenyong Ani, "'Es ist noch immer ein Aufbruch, aber mit neuer Startposition': Zwanzig Jahre ADEFRA und Schwarze Frauen / Bewegungen in Deutschland," in *Re/Visonen: Postkoloniale Perspektiven von People of Color auf Rassismus, Kulturpolitik und Widerstand in Deutschland,* ed. Kien Nghi Ha, Nicola Lauré al-Samarai, and Sheila Mysorekar (Münster: Unrast, 2007), 353.

26. Helga Emde, "An 'Occupation Baby' in Postwar Germany," in Opitz et al., *Showing Our Colors,* 104.

27. Ibid., 101; Astrid Berger, "'Aren't you glad you can stay here?,'" in Opitz et al., *Showing Our Colors,* 114–15.

28. May Opitz, "The Break," in Opitz et al., *Showing Our Colors,* 207.

29. Abena Adomako, "Mother: Afro-German / Father: Ghanaian," in Opitz et al., *Showing Our Colors*, 199–200.

30. Laura Baum, Katharina Oguntoye, and May Opitz, "Three Afro-German Women in Conversation with Dagmar Schultz: The First Exchange for This Book," in Opitz et al., *Showing Our Colors*, 145–64.

31. Michelle M. Wright, "Others-from-Within from Without: Afro-German Subject Formation and the Challenge of a Counter-Discourse," in "Reading the Black German Experience," ed. Tina Campt and Michelle Wright, special issue, *Callaloo* 26, no. 2 (2003): 297.

32. Marion Kraft, "For My Friend and Sister Audre Lorde," in *Transcending Silence: The Life and Poetic Legacy of Audre Lorde*, ed. Gale Louison and Mora J. Byrd (New York: African Diaspora Institute, Franklin H. Williams Caribbean Cultural Center, 1994), 7.

33. Katharina Oguntoye and May Opitz, "Preface to the English Language Edition," in Opitz et al., *Showing Our Colors*, xvi.

34. Lisa G. McGill, *Constructing Black Selves: Caribbean American Narratives and the Second Generation* (New York: New York University Press, 2005), 150.

35. Madhu Dubey, "Gayl Jones and the Matrilineal Metaphor of Tradition," *Signs* 20, no. 2 (Winter 1995): 245–67.

36. Nicola Lauré al-Samarai, letter to Audre Lorde, August 2, 1990, box 3, Lorde Papers.

37. Marion Kraft, letter to Audre Lorde, October 17, 1988, box 3, Lorde Papers.

38. May Ayim, letter to Audre Lorde, November 14, 1991, box 3, Lorde Papers. The November 9 demonstrations, which took place in both East and West Germany, were peaceful and helped to bring down the Berlin Wall.

39. May Ayim, card to Audre Lorde, May 10, 1991, box 3, Lorde Papers.

40. Katharina Oguntoye, letter to Audre Lorde, November 12, 1986, box 3, Lorde Papers; Marion Kraft, letter to Audre Lorde, March 6, 1988, box 3, Lorde Papers; Nicola Lauré Al-Samarai, letter to Audre Lorde, December 4, 1990, box 3, Lorde Papers.

41. Tina Campt, "The Crowded Space of Diaspora: Intercultural Address and the Tensions of Diasporic Relation," in "Citizenship, National Identity, Race, and Diaspora in Contemporary Europe," ed. Ian Christopher Fletcher, special issue, *Radical History Review* 83 (Spring 2002): 101–2.

42. For instance, at a national meeting of ADEFRA, a group of Afro-German women took time to write a letter that professed their love and solidarity for Lorde: ADEFRA, letter to Audre Lorde, undated, box 5, Lorde Papers. For more about ADEFRA, see note 55.

43. Michelle M. Wright, "Pale by Comparison: Black Liberal Humanism and the Postwar Era in the African Diaspora," in *Black Europe and the African Diaspora*, ed. Darlene Clark Hine, Trica Danielle Keaton, and Stephen Small (Chicago: University of Illinois Press, 2009), 260–77, esp. 269–71. Lorde also acknowledged her position as African American during several readings in Germany.

44. Lauré al-Samarai, letter, December 4, 1990.

45. Marion Kraft, letter to Audre Lorde, December 20, 1986, box 3, Lorde Papers.

46. Katharina Oguntoye, letter to Audre Lorde, October 18 and 22, 1990, box 3, Lorde Papers.

47. Hella Schültheiß, letter to Audre Lorde, August 8, 1990, box 5, Lorde Papers.

48. Ika Hügel, fax to Audre Lorde, February 18, 1992, box 5, Lorde Papers.

49. Oguntoye, letter, October 18 and 22, 1990.

50. Kraft, letter, October 17, 1988.

TIFFANY N. FLORVIL

51. Marion Kraft, card to Audre Lorde, December 9, 1991, box 3, Lorde Papers.
52. Katharina Oguntoye, letter to Audre Lorde, August 4, 1986, box 3, Lorde Papers. (Ben) Maria Baader, Jessica Jacoby, and Gotlinde Magiriba Lwanga organized the *Lesbisch-Feministische Schabbeskreis* (Lesbian Feminist Sabbath Circle), which was active in Berlin between 1984 and 1989.
53. Kraft, letter, October 17, 1988. Later in the letter, Kraft referred to "envy, a competitive attitude, misunderstandings and self-hatred that broke out at the latest meeting of Afro-German women."
54. Katharina Oguntoye, letter to Audre Lorde, October 26, 1988, box 3, Lorde Papers.
55. ADEFRA stood for Afro-German Women (*Afro-deutsche Frauen*). It was also called Afro-German and Black Women in Germany (*Afro-deutsche und Schwarze Frauen in Deutschland*) and is now known as Black women/transwomen in Germany (*Schwarze Frauen/Transfrauen in Deutschland*).
56. See, for example, Eva von Pirch, "Black Magic Woman: Erstes Bundestreffen Afro-Deutscher Frauen im Januar 1988," *Afrekete* 1, no. 1 (1988): 7.
57. Oguntoye, letter to Lorde, October 26, 1988.
58. Sara Ahmed, "Collective Feelings: Or, the Impressions Left by Others," *Theory, Culture, and Society* 21, no. 2 (2004): 27.

12
"I Cross Her Borders at Midnight"
Audre Lorde's Berlin Revisions

PAUL M. FARBER

> I went to Berlin with strong reservations and found of
> course much there . . . Most of all I found a certain amount
> of room to be.
>
> Audre Lorde, unpublished journal entry, 1984

Audre Lorde explored crisscrossings throughout her life. Scholars and enthusiasts recall her string of formative identities, her interdisciplinary writing, and the geographic spaces of Afro-diasporic longing and belonging she located on her travels around the world. Since her death in 1992, selections from her published oeuvre have gained crossover appeal, if not canonical status, throughout the fields of cultural studies. This is especially the case with her essays, which have gained prominence, in part, among a new generation of Lorde devotees, who have used her concise phrasings in public dialogues and Internet memes. In her lifetime Lorde both sought and skewed such seemingly transparent access to her writing.

In addition to her cultural theories on identification, Lorde produced a large body of work dwelling on her own estrangement and ambivalence. Her public modes of literary production display her self-revealing style, even as her poems teem with private references, intricate metaphors, imagined locations, subtle shifts in syntax, and the fodder of her dreams. One way in which she balanced her assured visions and significant fears was through the act of revision, a significant yet understudied aspect of her interdisciplinary poetic output. Revision, for Lorde, was a matter of refining her poems line by line but also stood for her greater conceptualization of poetry itself. Her archives offer glimpses into a process she once referred to as "alignment," which points to her practice of making slight but significant changes to poetic imagery as well as spacing and word placement.[1] For a traveling cultural worker aware of her own mortality, especially during bouts of illness, such attention to revision also demonstrated her spiritual commitment to practices of reflection and revisitation.[2]

Among Lorde's most essential sites of revision, a place where she worked toward proper poetic alignment, was the divided city of Berlin. Her revisions in and of the city allow us to delve into her evolving creative process. Berlin functioned as a site and signifier for her broader political project of working across lines of difference and division as well as her connected personal project of healing and transformation. This essay seeks to contextualize Lorde as a significant figure in the tradition of transnational exchange among American artists and writers across the years of a divided Berlin. I have considered revised and published works, including close readings of multiple drafts of her 1984 unpublished poem "First Impressions"; revisions from journal entries that became the poems "Berlin Is Hard on Colored Girls" and "This Urn Contains Earth from German Concentration Camps" (included in her book *Our Dead Behind Us*); and the historical revisions alluded to in her poem "East Berlin" (from *The Marvelous Arithmetics of Distance*) that span the historical divide of 1989. In each case I animate her publicly circulating work with readings of revised poems and journal entries from her archives to highlight connections within her Berlin-based poetry. A divided Berlin offered Lorde a space of creativity to continue working across lines of division and an urban locale from which to explore her own modes of identification and estrangement.

"FIRST IMPRESSIONS": TOWARD CRITICAL DISTANCE

The unpublished free verse poem "First Impressions"—which Lorde began as a journal entry on May 2, 1984, a month into her first trip to Berlin, and then typed out and revised in three iterations on May 15—exemplifies how the city's historically traumatized urban spaces served as poetic points of reflection for Lorde. In the poem, she captures her observations of life in the city through a series of pairings in which she addresses the concepts of home, health, and longing. Her observations are not centered here on Berlin's sprawling layout or central divides but its confined spaces. She opens with the lines "The toilet paper is stiff as a 20 Mark note / The stall doors are long and solid / but the latch always works / in reverse."[3] Lorde conjures Berlin as a space of intimacy as well as a strained refuge. She uses a simile to reform the idea of West Germany's economic currency (a marker of Germany's internal division) and a "latch" to counter an enclosure behind which she herself goes. As American photographer Nan Goldin did in her own contemporaneous Berlin-based work—for instance, her portraits of women in bathrooms in *The Ballad of Sexual Dependency*—Lorde locates herself in a bathroom in Berlin as a way to achieve a critical distance, albeit in momentary isolation.[4] She uses the practice of enjambment, pushing "works" and "in reverse" into separate lines to spatially convey a sense of her own tenuous safety. The poem continues:

> Houses are intimidatingly clean
> but laundries are few and expensive
> the mail comes early
> and meals quite late
> in Berlin
> a health-food store is called
> A Reform House.

Through imagery and form, Lorde conjures Berlin as a bewildering home space within which she experiences both estrangement and comfort. She uses the word "in" repeatedly to emphasize location and enclosure and to bridge and blur distinct thoughts between the lines. The phrases "in reverse" and "in Berlin" appear after line breaks, which also stand out formally in isolation, thus allowing her curiosity and suspicions about the city to coexist. The refrain functions as what Amitai F. Avi-Ram calls, in relation to Lorde's work, an "apo koinou"—that is, a word or phrase that, through enjambment, shares meaning between two lines.[5] As she bridges her lines, Lorde conjures Berlin as a whole city, not limited to just East or West. As "First Impressions" ends, she writes, "the women are small-boned and wiry also / but surprising / each one I approach / becomes some other place / to hide in Berlin." Even against the backdrop of Lorde's professorial or writerly project in Berlin, the speaker does not seek out the women in this scene for simple solidarity or generative dialogue. The poet repeats the phrase "in Berlin" but removes the line break to reaffirm that the city is a place where she experiences both self-imposed separation and refuge.

While writing this poem, Lorde experimented with the placement of "in

PAUL M. FARBER

Berlin" in her drafts. For example, the phrase does not appear as the ending line of her untitled journal version, which provided the initial lines for this poem. She added the phrase two weeks later to the final line when she first typed up the work. This first typed draft includes "in Berlin" on its own line at the end of the poem, only to be crossed out in a handwritten edit. The next draft and the final unmarked version of "First Impressions" retain the phrase, though she removes the line break and joins the final two lines as "to hide in Berlin." It is not clear if the handwritten edits on the typed drafts are Lorde's or another reader's; nonetheless, the poet's concern with how to deal with being "in Berlin" stands out. She mined the physical and cultural makeup of the divided city as a surface of reflection and turned to poetry as an outlet to consider such observations. The fact that this poem remained unpublished while much of her other writing about Berlin was prominently revised and published reemphasizes the productive tension between her site-specific productivity and "hiding" in the divided city.

MIDNIGHT'S REVISIONS AND MAPPING DIVIDED MEMORY

From the poems and journal entries written during her 1984 trip, a portrait of Lorde emerges. Berlin offered her an archive of poetic imagery and ideas as well as geopolitical challenges. She drew from her relationship to the city's physical environment in her writing about her experiences in the city. But such engagement was not merely marked by transcendence; Lorde was taken in and taken aback by Berlin, a city that led her to new paths of recovery and immense productivity as well as confrontations with historical haunts that were organic to Germany and to her own circumstances. She was aware of how her multiple intersecting identities (black, lesbian, poet, American, among other distinctions) marked her as an outsider in Berlin but also compelled her to work across difference on both sides of the city's internal divide. The Berlin Wall functioned as a key site and symbol of her poetic practice. But even as she treated the wall as a formidable structure, she highlighted the border system as part of the multiple forms of division that she encountered in Berlin.

According to her archive, Lorde began drafting her poem "Berlin Is Hard on Colored Girls," in her journal on May 8 and 9, 1984, while teaching in Berlin. The typed drafts that survive are dated February 11, March 31, and April 1, 1985.[6] At each stage, Lorde tended to choices of language and line spacing. The poem weaves recognizable symbols and sites from both sides of Berlin with private images and memories that transcend the divided city's limits.

Scholars have suggested that the poem represents the plight of Afro-German women. Melba Boyd, a poet who attended Lorde's Berlin reading at the Amerika House, contends that it "embodies [her] identification with the plight of Afro-Germans and women of color in Berlin, as 'woman' is coded as the city, with forbidden borders and American influences."[7] The "American influences" could also be read to include Lorde's own experiences in Berlin. To be sure, her poetic rendering of Berlin as a "strange woman" frames the poem around notions of identity and estrangement, not only as regards her observations of the city but, importantly, also about herself. The title of the poem is a way to signal the Afro-German community's strained relationship with the city but employs the word "colored" to convey a potential connection with U.S. racial discourse. In this and other ways throughout the poem, Lorde opens herself up as an additional, if not central, subject of the poem.[8]

Lorde locates her poem in the time space of a dream but also in the geopolitical reality of divided Berlin.[9] The poem opens:

> Perhaps a strange woman
> walks down from the corner
> into my bedroom
> wasps nest behind her ears
> she is eating a half-ripe banana
> with brown flecks in the shape of a lizard
> kittiwakes in her hair
> perhaps
> she is speaking my tongue
> in a different tempo
> the rhythm of gray whales praying
> dark as a granite bowl
> perhaps
> she is a stone.[10]

Berlin is introduced through a matrix of diasporic sites. The symbols in the first stanza—kittiwake birds, the lizard, gray whales—conjure the island tropics and connect readers to Lorde's non-U.S. home spaces in Grenada and Saint Croix. The poem works as an encoded diasporic map, and the possessive "my" stages an interaction that implies a feeling of intrusion before ceding to acts of movement and translation.

PAUL M. FARBER

The internal border of the Berlin Wall marks the spatial divide between the poem's two stanzas, the introduction of the narrative "I," and the division between the end of one day and the beginning of the next.[11] By the second stanza, the speaker traverses the woman's/city's internal border at the Berlin Wall, and the narrative perspective changes to the first person:

> I cross her borders at midnight
> the guards confused by a dream
> Mother Christopher's warm bread
> an end to war   perhaps
> she is selling a season's ticket to the Berlin Opera[12]

Without mentioning the Berlin Wall, Lorde conjures a scene of border crossing. In addition to resisting its monumental nomenclature, she finds several ways to locate and then transgress the poem's alluded boundary. She accounts for the wall not through direct naming or images of concrete architecture but through the language of "borders," "guards," and temporal trickery.

Midnight as a time of liminality is crucial to this poem. Night offers a charged temporal space, allowing for uncertainty and ambivalence and signaling intimacy between women. In geopolitical time, midnight is significant: it is a clear reference to actual East German policy during the time of Lorde's visit, which required all daily visitors from West to East Berlin to leave before midnight. By invoking travel after midnight, the poem suggests that border control ultimately fails to keep the city's division intact. In the dream and poem, crossing borders after midnight goes against protocol, and the image gestures to other ways in which the Berlin Wall is porous in the poem. For example, when Lorde writes, "she is selling a season's ticket to the Berlin Opera," in a city with two opera houses—East Berlin's *Deutsche Staatsoper* and West Berlin's *Deutsche Oper Berlin*—she envisions the East as a site of habitual ("season") yet elusive return or the West as a disavowed place, altogether with a confused geography.[13] Ultimately, in this dream elaborated on within the poem, she undermines the normalcy and logic of division.

Lorde's use of "perhaps" throughout the poem accentuates its liminal contexts and her own ambivalence about living in the city. Given its free verse style, the poem's structure comes not from meter or rhyme per se but from the rhythm created through line breaks, stanzas, and spacing. The poem begins with "perhaps," which then reappears six times, either by itself after a line break or with extra white space separating it from other words on the line. Mimicking the actual zigzagged path of the wall, the word snakes through the poem, acting as an unsteady refrain and offering a sense of structure. In this way, Lorde undermines polemic division and singular political meaning at the Berlin Wall while making sure the actions she explores in the poetic dream are both purposeful and conditional.

The poet's attention to extremes of tactility and texture is also important in the first several stanzas. These extremes are expressed through a litany of images that suggests "a tender forgiveness of contrasts." They include an interplay between the "hard" of "a granite bowl," "a stone," and "metal" and the soft, "half-ripe banana," "Mother Christopher's warm bread," "silken thighs," and the "american flag."[14] These contrasts ground the dream and the poem in the city's material conditions—such as U.S. military occupation and fortified borders—even as they summon ethereality and a forgiveness akin to letting go. Among these "contrasts," Lorde's rendering of "america" without an uppercase A offers an implicit critique of her national belonging and fits with Alexis De Veaux's formulation that Lorde selectively dropped the upper case when critically engaging the United States or while traveling abroad.[15]

In the final lines, Lorde writes:

> perhaps
> A nightingale waits in the alley
> next to the yellow phone booth
> under my pillow
> a banana skin is wilting.[16]

Lorde's imagined nighttime border crossing undermines the systems of border control at the Berlin Wall, and her dreamed excursion that culminates in a moment of potential flight. After spatializing and grounding her poem with mentions of a street "corner" and "the hair-bouncing step / of a jaunty flower-bandit" (an opaque reference to Dagmar Schultz), she introduces a nightingale, which pauses for her in the alley and symbolizes escape and restraint.[17] The nightingale, an important poetic symbol since antiquity, has traditionally embodied and negotiated divisions such as expression and silence, masculinity and femininity, and life and death.[18] In "Ode to a Nightingale," John Keats offers the bird, like a poem, as a way to transgress the in-between of these dualities.[19] Lorde revisits Keats's symbol, borrowing from the codes of canonical poetry to place her nightingale in the context of her experiences in divided Berlin. In her Berlin poems, the city's hard

PAUL M. FARBER

edges—of history, of the wall—make stone and concrete important material referents, as is the potential for soothing, softness, comfort, and flight from that urban topography.

Lorde's complex and haunted relationship with Berlin was also connected to the public memory of the Holocaust, and she extended her exploration of the divided city in another poem, "This Urn Contains Earth from German Concentration Camps: Plotzensee [*sic*] Memorial, West Berlin, 1984." Located on a lake in the northwestern outer reaches of West Berlin, Plötzensee was a former Nazi prison and execution house. In 1952 it was dedicated as a memorial to those persecuted by the Third Reich.[20] During Lorde's 1984 trip, it was West Berlin's most prominent Holocaust memorial. As her poem's title suggests, a large inscribed urn at the site holds earth from each of the German concentration camps. Lorde presumably visited the site, and she retained copies of the memorial's pamphlet in her records.[21] Toward the end of her first trip to Berlin, she began drafting her reflections as a journal entry while considering her own comforts and reservations about the city. On July 29, 1984, she wrote, "But you have to forget Plotzensee's bland lack of assuming responsibility, the obscure circumlocutions that protect Germany's children from their history and humanity. An urn of earth from concentration camps. Not ashes of Jews."[22] Lorde's identification with Jewish victims of Nazi tyranny was linked to her concerns about contemporary racism in Germany: "Nothing can come to the point of feeling what they are saying, so they can never move on. So a Germany committed to this kind of thinking only is a Germany of the past, committed to repeating the same mistakes who will it be this time? The turks? or the newly emergent Afri-German [*sic*] people?"[23] Inspired by her earlier journal entry, Lorde typed out poem drafts on February 2 and February 19, 1985, and continued to revisit and edit the poem.[24] In so doing, she connected her reflections on the history and memory of the Holocaust in Berlin to her Afro-diasporic consciousness.

In the poem, Lorde marks the memorial as a site of contradiction rather than resolution. Like Claude Lanzmann's film *Shoah* (1985), she places her vision of the site of memory around the "overgrowth" of nature and amnesiac cultures over sites of Holocaust trauma.[25] She reads physical space as a way to contend with an off-kilter feeling of historical time. Lorde's earliest drafts are titled "Plotenzee Memorial to the Resistance: Berlin 1984" and "Plotensee Memorial Berlin 1984." By the final draft in her archive, she has made two key changes. The primary title is a translation of the actual plaque inscription at the memorial ("Die Urne enthält Erde aus deutschen Konzentrationslagern"), which she had cited in the body of an early draft, and the geopolitical descriptive "West" is added to Berlin in the title. In the latter case, she recalls the specific location of the site as well as how Germany's post-1945 division created spaces of historic estrangement and sublimated traumas of the recent Nazi past. Through all iterations, her use of the year reminds readers of the influence of her first trip but also resembles the inscriptive timestamp often found on historical or memorial markers.

The poem opens with a tension staged between remembrance and erasure. Lorde uses the memorial's actual inscription to convey the gaps between what is claimed and what is rendered silent in this historical display.

> Dark gray
> the stone wall hangs
> self-conscious wreaths
> the heavy breath of gaudy Berlin roses
> "The Vice Chancellor Remembers
> The Heroic Generals of the Resistance"
> and before a well-trimmed hedge
> unpolished granite
> tall as my daughter and twice around
> Neatness
> wiping memories   payment
> from the air.[26]

Lorde's reference to "stone wall" and "self-conscious wreaths" conjure the Berlin Wall and anticipate the May 1985 controversy over President Ronald Reagan's visit to Bitburg cemetery within the context of the problematics of place-based Holocaust memory.[27] "The heavy breath of gaudy Berlin roses" suggests the empty expressive gestures of beauty in a misremembered history. Lorde uses extra space within lines ("neatness / wiping memories [*space*] payment / from the air") to convey rhythmic structure and to suggest gaps and silences in the imposed rhythms of history and memorial reparation. Rather than creating "Neatness," spacing and content form a vision that is out of sync. Society rushes to move on rather than heal or talk about its losses.

The poem goes on to describe a picnic in the lakeside park around the memorial. The eerie scene features several juxtaposed images of birth and destruction. For instance, "beneath my rump / in a hollow root of the dead elm / a rabbit kindles" conveys both a litter of baby rabbits and the birth of

PAUL M. FARBER

fire.[28] Though the picnic ends, the haunting does not cease. The interruption of a "writhing waterbug," a roach flicked but split open in her food, symbolizes degradation and a deterred potential for survival.

> The picnic is over
> reluctantly
> I stand   pick up my blanket
> and flip into the bowl of still-warm corn
> a writhing waterbug
> cracked open   her pale eggs oozing
> quiet
> from the smash.[29]

The line breaks and extra spaces build an unsteady rhythm, and the caesuras in "I stand [*space*] pick up my blanket" and "cracked open [space] her pale eggs oozing" double as physical descriptions of stepping away and breaking open. The pairing of "quiet" and "the smash" suggests the gap between silence and expression at this site.

In the poem's final stanza, Lorde marks and pushes the limits of memorial practice, both at the site and in her own poetry. Here, she distinguishes between "earth" and "ash" of human remains and reminds her readers of commemoration's inability to fully stand in for the loss of human life.[30] She highlights how the site's appeal to nature as a form of rebirth doubles as a funereal absence and hinders critical dialogue about violence and history.

> Earth
> not the unremarkable ash
> of fussy thin-boned infants
> and adolescent Jewish girls
> liming the Ravensbruck potatoes
> careful and monsterless
> this urn makes nothing
> easy to say.[31]

Themes of speech and silence coexist in these lines, as does Lorde's clear ambivalence about such sites of memory. Her gendering of the murdered Jews is carried out again in her reference to Ravensbrück, which was a predominately female concentration camp outside of Berlin. In relation to her work with German feminists, this critical addressing of their pasts serves as a call to identification. The final lines, "careful and monsterless / this urn makes nothing / easy to say," respond to the urn at Plötzensee and perhaps also to the limitations of her own poem in finding the appropriate utterances for encountering such a violent history. Like her nightingale reference in "Berlin Is Hard on Colored Girls," these lines conjure another classical symbol of poetry, the urn, and Keats's canonical "Ode on a Grecian Urn." His poem also mediates the gaps between speech and silence but owes its culminating lines to a lesson "spoken" by an urn and conveyed in quotation marks: "'Beauty is truth, truth beauty,' —that is all / Ye know on earth, and all ye need to know."[32] Lorde's ending links to and challenges Keats's ode, using intertextual revision to mark the aesthetic limits of memorial gestures, be they poetic or material. The past can be localized into poems, aesthetic objects, and memorials, but true loss extends beyond speech. Lorde revisits the thematic extremes of soft and hard materiality in Berlin—the tensions between the inscription of the plaque and the physical traces to which it refers, the offering of tangible earth that was sealed in the urn. Between these two material extremes, Lorde conveys her own and a larger shared sense of Berlin as both a refuge and a site of potential danger.[33]

OUT OF TIME AND PLACE IN EAST BERLIN

Between 1987 and her death in 1992, Lorde composed more poems that addressed themes of travel and return in Berlin. Her "Berlin years," as Schultz has called them, overlapped an era of sweeping change in Germany, in particular the dismantling of the Berlin Wall in 1989 and Germany's reunification in 1990. Lorde collected many of these poems into *The Marvelous Arithmetics of Distance*. Posthumously published, this collection offers a poetic bridge across Germany's epochal divide. But Lorde's post-1989 poems and writings pivot away from Cold War triumphalism and showcase her sense of wariness about how the *Wende*, the post-Wall "turn" in German history, would affect life in Berlin, especially for Afro-Germans and other people of color. Her works foreground the Berlin Wall as a site from which to recognize the symbolism and public feelings of historical estrangement in this period, and to draw broader attention to uncertainties and fears wrought in periods of seeming public revelry and progress. Lorde's skepticism during this period was centered on the waves of racially motivated violence against Afro-German and immigrant communities that were erupting on Berlin and other German streets. In a series of connected editorials, journal entries, and poems, she leveraged her critical insights against the bygone monumental backdrop of the border.

This intervention into the *Wende* period marks the poems in *The Marvelous Arithmetics of Distance*. While her Berlin poems in *Our Dead Behind Us* also obliquely deal with the division of the wall, these later poems reflect the historical challenges of reunification with a renewed focus on the former border. Beginning on November 10, 1989, Lorde reflected on her ambivalence in several journal entries, and she continued those reflections in early 1990 in a series of drafts for the poem "East Berlin."[34] She opens her published version with the declarative statement, "It feels dangerous now / to be Black in Berlin." The perspectival subject of this poem is disembodied and without a human subject, yet the poet's use of "it" makes her statement declarative and factual. Lorde's sense of the new geography of reunification is based on well-known urban landmarks, yet her narrator strays back and forth between the former West and East. Violence erupts in part from the rapid convergence of worldviews and legacies of previous lines of division:

> sad suicides that never got reported
> Neukölln   Kreuzberg   the neon Zoo
> a new siege along Unter den Linden
> with Paris accents   New York hustle
> many tattered visions intersecting.

> Already my blood shrieks
> through the East Berlin streets
> misplaced hatreds
> volcanic tallies rung upon cement
> Afro-German woman stomped to death
> by skinheads in Alexanderplatz[35]

Lorde's poetic mapping of "East Berlin" is a geopolitical anachronism, as the notion of "East Berlin" has become formally defunct in the reunified Germany. Her spaces within the poem separate areas that all lie in the former West Berlin (Neukölln, Kreuzberg, the zoo) to suggest dislocation amid the post-wall borderlines, which Lorde contrasts with her subsequent references to East Berlin's Unter den Linden and Alexanderplatz. The "tender forgiveness" subverting the border in her earlier poem gives way to a harsh concrete materiality in the post-wall era. The sidewalk, against the shadow of the ruins of the wall, becomes a scene of violence and disenfranchisement.

Though the wall is now partially dismantled and politically obsolete, Lorde sees it as a symbol of the continuing dangers that people of color face in Germany. In her poem, she gestures toward the pitfalls of historical change without full reconciliation between East and West Germany and its diverse peoples and violent history. She writes in the final stanza:

> Hand-held the candles wink
> in Berlin's scant November light
> hitting the Wall at 30 miles an hour
> vision first
> is still hitting a wall
> and on the other side
> the rank chasm
> where dreams of laurels lie.[36]

The stanza uses the word "wall" twice—capitalized to refer to the Berlin Wall itself, lowercased as a poetic symbol of a threshold separating temporalities and deeper truths. "The Berlin Wall" and "the wall" are joined as paired poetic sites. Again, Lorde views Germany through rituals of commemoration and the space of a dream, here physically represented as cast aside. She is wary of celebrations in light of the violence and the uncertainty of this time. The poem closes with "hollowness wed to triumph / differing from defeat / only in the approaching tasks."[37] These lines reaffirm the deep divisions that Lorde has traced in the city but do not offer finality. The possibility for transformation exists here, tethered to Berlin-based historical reconciliation and future action. For Lorde, "the approaching tasks" include an active poetics, with emphasis on persistent reflection rather than closure.

DREAMS AND DIFFERENCE

In October 1992, Lorde traveled to Berlin and gave a public reading in Schultz's apartment. A month later, she passed away in Saint Croix, after several prolonged bouts with cancer. The visit was documented in a bonus clip from Schultz's film *Audre Lorde—The Berlin Years* that shows Lorde seated by a table with a vase of sunflowers and an open notebook from which she reads her poem "1984." She provides some historical context about the poem, in which she imagines she becomes president of the United States, noting that George Orwell's vision of 1984 had inspired her to revise U.S. power relations. But she also said that the poem, like many of her others, was sparked by a dream—in this case, a dream on April 4, the anniversary of the assassination of Dr. Martin Luther King. She also reminded her listeners

PAUL M. FARBER

that this was a work in progress: "Now I really want some feedback about this poem. Because it's a dream and I feel different ways about it at different times."[38] Here, and across Berlin's historical divides, open spaces, and hiding places, revision not only nourished Lorde's work toward refinement and revelation but allowed her to remain situated within the creative process, spurred on by her dreams and the city.

Notes

1. Karla M. Hammond, "Audre Lorde: Interview," in *Conversations with Audre Lorde,* ed. Joan Wylie Hall, (Jackson: University Press of Mississippi, 2004), 32.
2. For more on expressive return, see Tayana Hardin, "Rituals of Return in African American Women's Twentieth Century Literature and Performance" (Ph.D. diss., University of Michigan, 2012).
3. Audre Lorde, "First Impressions," 1984, box 31, Audre Lorde Papers, Spelman College Archives (hereafter cited as Lorde Papers). My initial reading is based on the last unmarked edit of these drafts.
4. Nan Goldin, *The Ballad of Sexual Dependency* (New York: Aperture, 1986).
5. Amitai F. Avi-Ram, "Apo Koinou in Audre Lorde and the Moderns: Defining the Differences," *Callaloo* 26 (Winter 1986): 193–208.
6. All citations to drafts of this poem refer to Audre Lorde, "Berlin Is Hard on Colored Girls," box 31, Lorde Papers.
7. Melba Joyce Boyd, "Politics, Jazz, and the Politics of Aesthetics" in *From Black to Schwarz: Cultural Crossovers between African America and Germany,* ed. Maria Diedrich and Jürgen Heinrichs (East Lansing: Michigan State University Press, 2011), 262.
8. Lorde's use of "colored" may resonate with other such uses in the post–Civil Rights era. See Ntozake Shange, *For Colored Girls Who Have Considered Suicide / When the Rainbow Is Enuf* (1975; reprint, New York: Scribner, 2010).
9. For more on the dream spaces of Lorde's poems, see Gloria Hull, "Living on the Line: Audre Lorde and Our Dead Behind Us," in *Changing Our Own Words: Essays on Criticism, Theory, and Writing by Black Women,* ed. Cheryl A. Wall (New Brunswick, N.J.: Rutgers University Press, 1989), 150–72.
10. All citations to the published poem refer to Audre Lorde, "Berlin Is Hard on Colored Girls," in *The Collected Poems of Audre Lorde* (New York: Norton, 1997), 375. The poem was originally published in *Our Dead Behind Us* (1986).
11. Throughout her poetry, Lorde draws her poetic imagery from actual experiences and imaginative gestures. She uses the perspective of "I" for herself and to embody witnesses for others. This demands readers' close and open consideration to meaning and subjectivity.
12. Lorde, "Berlin Is Hard," 375.
13. For more on the Berlin Opera, see "Music View; East Berlin Opera Nervously Awaits the Next Act," *New York Times,* June 24, 1990, www.nytimes.com; and Emily Pugh, *The Berlin Wall and the Urban Space and Experience of East and West Berlin, 1961–1989* (Ann Arbor, Mich.: ProQuest, 2008), 62.
14. Lorde, "Berlin Is Hard," 375.

15. Alexis De Veaux, *Warrior Poet: A Biography of Audre Lorde* (New York: Norton, 2004), 337.

16. Lorde, "Berlin Is Hard," 375.

17. Ibid. I learned about the reference to Schultz in a personal interview with her, December 2010.

18. For more on nightingales in poetry, see Jeni Williams, *Interpreting Nightingales: Gender, Class, and Histories* (Sheffield, U.K.: Sheffield Academic Press, 1997).

19. John Keats, "Ode to a Nightingale," in *Selected Poems and Letters of Keats*, sel. Robert Gittings, ed. Sandra Anstey (Oxford: Heinemann, 1995), 187–92. Lorde had read Keats critically while she was at Hunter College. See Hammond, "Audre Lorde," 32.

20. Brian Ladd, *The Ghosts of Berlin: Confronting German History in the Urban Landscape* (Chicago: University of Chicago Press, 2000), 151–52, 162.

21. Plötzensee Memorial pamphlet, undated, box 43, Lorde Papers.

22. Audre Lorde, journal entry, July 29, 1984, box 46, Lorde Papers.

23. Ibid.

24. All citations to drafts of this poem refer to Audre Lorde, "This Urn Contains Earth from German Concentration Camps," ca. 1985, box 31, Lorde Papers.

25. *Shoah*, dir. Claude Lanzmann (Paris: New Yorker Films, 1985). Writing about *Shoah*, Lanzmann said, "Making a history was not what I wanted to do. I wanted to construct something more powerful than that. And, in fact, I think that the film, using only images of the present, evokes the past with far more force than any historical document." See Claude Lanzmann, *Shoah: An Oral History of the Holocaust. The Complete Text of the Film* (New York: Pantheon, 1985).

26. All citations to this poem refer to Audre Lorde, "This Urn Contains Earth from German Concentration Camps: Plotzensee Memorial, West Berlin, 1984," in Lorde, *The Collected Poems*, 376–77. The poem was originally published in *Our Dead Behind Us* (1986).

27. For more on Reagan at Bitburg, see Geoffrey Hartman, *Bitburg in Moral and Political Perspective* (Bloomington: Indiana University Press, 1986).

28. Lorde, "This Urn," 376.

29. Ibid.

30. Ibid.

31. Ibid., 376–77.

32. Keats, "Ode on a Grecian Urn," in *Selected Poems*, 195. I thank fellow members of the critical poetry seminar at the Texas Institute for Literary and Textual Studies for pointing out this connection.

33. Other poems from *Our Dead Behind Us* that contain Berlin themes and imagery include "Diaspora" and "For Jose and Regina."

34. All citations to drafts of this poem refer to Audre Lorde, "East Berlin," 1989–90, box 25, Lorde Papers. All citations to published versions refer to Audre Lorde, "East Berlin," in *The Marvelous Arithmetics of Distance: Poems, 1987–1992* (New York: Norton, 1993), 50.

35. Lorde, "East Berlin," 50.

36. Ibid.

37. Ibid.

38. *Audre Lorde—The Berlin Years, 1984 to 1992*, dir. Dagmar Schultz (New York: Third World Newsreel, 2012). The DVD version includes this bonus clip and other special features.

PAUL M. FARBER

13
"But We Are Not the Same"
Generating a Critical Poetics of Diaspora

ALEXIS PAULINE GUMBS

To the average Grenadian, the United States is a large
but dim presence where some dear relative now lives . . .
Grenada is their country. I am only a relative.

Audre Lorde, "Grenada Revisited"

So much Black blood has been shed upon that land, I
thought, and so much more will fall. But blood will tell,
and now the blood is speaking.

Audre Lorde, *Apartheid U.S.A.*

I am hearing Audre Lorde's voice shrill above the wind. Shaking but unstop-
pable, she pointed out racism and classism in a white-dominated women's
movement and homophobia and sexism in the Black Power movement. How
do we remember her protest? Lorde's embodied theorization of the creative
power of difference has been widely researched. More recently, scholarship
has amplified her words on the crucial role of antiracism in neo-Nazi European contexts during the 1980s and 1990s. But critical work on Lorde's impact
as a theorist has rarely treated her articulations of solidarity, difference, intimacy, and accountability as a U.S.-born woman of Afro-Caribbean heritage,
who navigated her relationships with majority-black spaces that had been
(and continue to be) directly harmed by U.S. imperialism. Why not? She
chose to live out her days on the majority black island of Saint Croix, where
she was instrumental in founding an antiviolence women's organization.
She delayed the publication of *Sister Outsider* to write about the politics of
the invasion of Grenada, the first black socialist republic in the New World.[1]
She was a founding mother of Sisterhood in Support of Sisters (SISA), the

first organization to coordinate solidarity activities directly between black feminists in the United States and South Africa.

Although majority-black nation-states and communities of struggle feature prominently in her poetry and essays, they are often overlooked when scholars document Lorde's impact. Maybe we have been focusing on different differences. Maybe the imperialism Lorde was protesting has also shaped the marketability of her legacy and skewed it to center majority-white Western nations. Drawing on critical black diaspora studies and generating a poetic reading practice based on her theoretical work allows us to explore her black transnational feminist praxis, especially as it concerns majority-black spaces, to both interrogate and reconstruct diaspora as a complex political category of solidarity.

THE GENERATOR: A DIASPORIC READING PRACTICE

In 1989, Lorde, Gloria Joseph, and their community in Saint Croix survived the direct impact of Hurricane Hugo, a storm so severe that "the land almost gave up her name."[2] In the shambles of their home, without running water or electricity, Lorde wrote about their survival in her journal and in letters to distant loved ones. Her little-known "Hugo Letter" which appears in *Hell under God's Orders*, an anthology that she and Joseph compiled to document and theorize about the experience and aftermath of the hurricane, is a crucial site from which to generate a Lordeian diasporic reading practice, particularly if we look at tense as tension. One way of reading her essay is to pay attention to her words in the same way that the Saint Croix community learned to pay attention to the generators that were their only source of electricity in the aftermath of the storm: "There is a prevailing and insistent language of the generators that we all begin to learn. No matter what else is going on, in the midst of every conversation, one ear is always attuned to the coughs and spits that might mean the generator is struggling or missing, or about to run out of gas. Quick, quick, throw the switch before it stalls, or else it will be twice as hard to get started again!"[3] Reading Lorde as a generator of an alternative theory of power, the source of an embattled, overworked, and overdue black diasporic critique, requires a similar attunement. She does not simply spout transnational theory. She coughs. And spits.

Systems of oppression threaten the possible body politic, the community that must find, repair, and become itself after the storm. In Saint Croix

Lorde was not only living through the unnatural disaster of the U.S. government's response/nonresponse to the hurricane, but she was also fighting cancer. Her disdain for the way in which the government prioritized private institutions over human lives reveals her belief in presence as a political practice and permanence as a political fallacy, given the natural cycles of life: "Hurricane Hugo was a terrible natural disaster, but nature heals herself. It is what we inject into her like tumors that fester and grow loathsome without constant attention, refusing to self-destruct, because out of our twisted wisdom—some fantasy of bloodless immortality—we have created them as if they would last 1,000 years. But wind is our teacher."[4] Even before the hurricane, the festering institutions, mostly designed for oil extraction, that the United States had constructed in colonial Saint Croix were negatively affecting the majority-black local population. To Lorde, those capitalist institutions were a cancer, part of a long history of colonialism that had devastated the island and its original and then enslaved inhabitants for many generations.[5] The storm clarified that the state was not accountable to its black citizens as citizens but viewed them, at best, as collateral and, at worst, as liabilities in comparison to its fossil fuel holdings. The government took days to respond to the hurricane disaster, and even then its emphasis was on securing corporate property. Lorde describes the response as "man-made ugliness." Personnel arrived with M16s and "armored trucks, but no blankets, no cots, no emergency rations," even though "the first supermarket with food for sale [would] not open for another month." "Obviously the first and primary mission of the U.S. military upon arrival [was] to protect property. No matter what."[6]

The military response was traumatic not only because it threatened the lives of Lorde's loved ones and her community but also because it repeated a pattern of antiblack U.S. military actions, including the 1983 invasion of her mother's homeland, Grenada. After Lorde's lifetime, we can also see the decision to protect private property and abandon human life, especially black life, repeated in the 2005 nonresponse and military antagonism after Hurricane Katrina. If Lorde's writing about the response to Hugo and her theories about state violence in relationship to black life had been more widely discussed, scholars' and activists' discourse around Katrina might have benefited. By connecting hurricanes (not to mention the earthquakes in Haiti and Chile) to U.S. invasions in the Caribbean, Lorde previsions Naomi Klein's term *disaster capitalism* and offers a narrative of repeated violence. She offers a poetics of trauma that demonstrates not only her experience as part of a black collective of resident survivors of Hugo but also a wider collective experience of state violence, lack of accountability, and harm. The trauma reveals itself in "Hugo Letter" through repetition (the lament "no blankets, no cots, no emergency rations" appears almost verbatim on two consecutive pages) and by the breakdown of her verb tenses in her description of the violence she witnessed.[7]

> Drawn guns barring the road to the airport. Drawn guns protecting the road to Hess Oil, a private company with government contracts. Drawn guns in the hospital lot. A U.S. military M-16 shoved into her face stops my friend as she tried to go to her aged and disoriented mother, who is crying out for one scrap of familiarity, dignity, or help as she is being abruptly rushed into a military ambulance for evacuation to who knew where. She calls to her daughter, who cannot run to comfort her because of the M-16s barring her way.[8]

This passage eloquently describes the use of military force on a systemic and individual level, but it is also the only place in the essay in which Lorde struggles with tense agreement. From sentence to sentence, and sometimes within a sentence, she switches from past to present tense and back. Consider, for example, this sentence: "A U.S. military M-16 shoved into her face stops my friend as she tried to go to her aged and disoriented mother." Is the event happening in the past or the present? Or is it always happening? The scene, emerging with the cadence and timelessness of trauma, recalls slave narratives in which parents and children were torn from each other without mercy. It recalls the transatlantic slave trade itself. Listen to the generator when it stutters and starts. Lorde, an experienced essayist who spent years teaching composition in the City University of New York system, was not lazy about tense agreement. She was tense about the violence she was witnessing, a violence that agrees with itself so easily across time. In this passage, diaspora and trauma meet, and an act of terror has the power to break the solidarity of a mother and a daughter, of a community and itself.

I am distinguishing here between diaspora as an existing and continuing experience of falling apart and dispersal as the potential scattering of the fictions of nation-states, which create reproductive subjectivity by representing persistent trauma and criminalized desire. In this sense, diaspora is to dispersal as trauma is to terror. Trauma is an ongoing condition

ALEXIS PAULINE GUMBS

or state that refers back to an earlier violence, much in the manner of diaspora. Trauma is the best description of the ontological experience of diaspora. Although most theorists track diaspora through the movement of a set of people from one place to another, Lorde describes a version that is the experience of trauma caused by perpetual economic and violence-inflected displacement. Thus, an indigenous population that has been economically displaced and exploited is diasporic; the people's lives and their subjectivity have been dispersed, and they continue to fall apart. Think of Native Americans, Palestinians, and all of the black people in Africa. You are a diasporic subject if your livelihood has been stolen from you, and that includes the theft of your children and the theft of your parents and the theft of your body itself. Military coups, economic sanctions, resource grabs, and imposed debt are all methods of dispersal, how "First World" nations create diaspora as an ongoing condition. By means of the transatlantic slave trade, colonialism, and neoliberal globalization, they have caused sites in the Caribbean, Latin America, Africa, Southeast Asia, the Middle East, and so on to fall apart while increasing their own national capital, credit, and labor leverage. Of the many preconditions for diaspora, Lorde seems to be especially interested in daughters falling away from and into mothers, the Caribbean falling away from and into the global north.

RELATIVITY AND SOLIDARITY: THE EXAMPLE OF GRENADA

"Grenada Revisited: An Interim Report," is Lorde's definitive piece on solidarity in diaspora, and it tackles the most difficult location: the impossible home referent that cannot be home. At the beginning of the essay, she writes, "The first time I came to Grenada I came seeking 'home,' for this was my mother's birthplace and she had always defined it so for me."[9] Among U.S.-born black persons with Caribbean parents, this is a common notion. *Home* for an Afro-Caribbean family is not the United States of America. The harder lesson to embrace is that nowhere else is home either. Many Afro-Caribbean people endure a double diaspora. Born into the African diaspora, they have been redispersed by market forces, which have pushed them out of the Caribbean into the United States, Canada, or Europe. Yet colonialism and neocolonialism are not their heaviest baggage, as Lorde knew.

She went to Grenada seeking home, but she could not find it. On her first visit, she learned that the stories her parents had told her about it referred to a place that no longer existed or, overwritten by longing, may have never existed except in their memories. On her second visit, after the 1983 U.S. invasion of the first black socialist republic, she learned that Grenada could not be properly claimed by any black person. A home controlled by black people who refuse capitalism is a dream that is too dangerous for reality. As Lorde wrote, "what a bad example, a dangerous precedent, an independent Grenada would be for the peoples of Color in the Caribbean, in Central America, for those of us here in the United States."[10]

The Grenadian Revolution and the subsequent U.S. invasion were defining events in the development of Lorde's concept of diaspora. She told her colleague and comrade, the black gay genius Joseph Beam, that when she arrived in the United States after her visit to the nation, she worked on "Grenada Revisited" for seventy-two hours straight.[11] In it she makes one of her most enduring statements about the relationship of the U.S. nation-state to the global black diaspora. Explaining that racism is the primary U.S. export to the world, she offers this inventory: "The lynching of Black youth and shooting down of Black women, 60 percent of Black teenagers unemployed and rapidly becoming unemployable, the presidential dismantling of the Civil Rights Commission, and more Black families below the poverty line than twenty years ago—if these facts of American life can be passed over as unremarkable, then why not the rape and annexation of tiny Black Grenada?"[12] Lorde argues not for a biological diasporic relationship but for a strategic one. Black people in the United States are related to black people in Grenada because the United States is using the story of racism to steal power from all of us. She models the practice of how we can relate with love to our dear relative, our mere relatives, our not very near relatives. The first requirement is that we are honest about the fact that we are not all the same.

Black people in the United States paid taxes that funded a military invasion into Grenada. The invading army was disproportionately composed of black people, whom the government made responsible for killing the young revolutionaries and imposing an economic situation that, among other things, now means that people who live on an island that produces cocoa beans are required to import chocolate. Directly or indirectly, the imperialist racism that links black people in the United States to black people everywhere consistently puts groups of black people on opposite sides of a very dirty coin. As blacks in the United States, we consent again and again to violence against other black people, which is done in our name and usually without our knowledge. In both "Grenada Revisited" and her subsequent conversation with Beam, Lorde suggested that the deployment of a disproportionately black military force to the black republic of Grenada was also an experiment to see if black U.S. soldiers would fire on other black people. And they did.[13]

Lorde tells us, as a relative, that it doesn't have to be that way. We are related through racist systems that we do not control, and we can create solidarity only if we acknowledge our different relationships to power. She offers vision of diaspora in which our key concerns must be the terms under which we are related and the ways that our different relationships to power and access make us accountable. Her analysis prefigures what M. Jacqui Alexander and Chandra Mohanty, influenced by her ideas, later called a democratic transnationalism in which we are accountable to everyone oppressed by racism with a strategic solidarity that acknowledges the systems through which we meet each other.[14] This strategic diaspora is what Lorde herself later activated with the women of South Africa.

THE BLOOD IS SPEAKING: SOUTH AFRICA AND FLUIDARITY

In 1985, after listening to the United Nations' special session on the state of emergency in South Africa, Lorde wrote her own address to mobilize black people in the United States to divest from apartheid South Africa. By this time she was well attuned to blood. Her poem "Sisters in Arms" from *Our Dead Behind Us* (1986) is filled with imagery of dead and dying children brutalized by white South African police. It is not surprising, then, that in the speech "Apartheid U.S.A." (later published as a Freedom Organizing pamphlet by Kitchen Table Press), directed explicitly at an audience of U.S. blacks, she makes a blood connection between six-year-old children that South African police jail and murder, twelve-year-old Johannes kicked to death in front of his garden, "nine year old Joyce bleeding to death on her granny's floor," the slaughter of black children and youth in the roads of Sebokeng and Soweto, "white america's not so silent applause for the smiling white vigilante who coolly guns down four Black youths in the New York City subway," and white policemen who kill three black children over a "dispute over a can of coca-cola."[15] This litany of spilled blood was Lorde's way of convincing her black U.S.-based audience members that they and South Africans share a blood relation, one that has been imposed even if they have never chosen it. Her litany progresses into fury, ending with the 1985 murders of the members of the Philadelphia-based MOVE organization "because they were dirty and Black and obnoxious and Black and arrogant and Black and poor and Black and Black and Black and Black and Black. And the Mayor who allowed this to happen . . . he is Black, too. How are we persuaded to participate in our own destruction by maintaining our silences?"[16]

Lorde's discourse of blood shed and soaked up, her comprehension of a shared condition of expendability, links to what cultural anthropologist Diane Nelson calls "fluidarity," an intervention into solidarity that allows for an accountable connection without fixed identities.[17] The concept resonates with many of the terms that Lorde used to explore diaspora and solidarity, especially the crucial bodily fluids of blood and water. This fluidarity allows her to ask African Americans in the United States, "Do you even know which companies your money supports that do business in South Africa?" and "How long will it take to escalate our consciousness as Black people that this is *us*?"[18] Her poem "Meet" also demonstrates her desire for transatlantic reconnection based in political solidarity against systems of violence:

> women exchanging blood
> in the innermost rooms of moment
> we must taste of each other's fruit
> at least once
> before we shall both be slain.[19]

This blood connection, which she frames as the shared experience of expendability and violence as well as connection to femininity, the moon, and nature, generates the tangible sisterhood and the political and economic solidarity that she eventually discovered as a cofounding mother of SISA.

In chapter 8 of this book, Gloria Joseph describes the founding of SISA, an initiative to recognize the South African women's self-help movement as a form of resistance to economic apartheid. SISA built relationships with two organizations, the Zamani Soweto Sisters and the Maggie Magaba Trust; and the founding mothers, Zala Chandler, Johnnetta Cole, Audre Lorde, Andrée McLaughlin, and Barbara Riley, recruited a wide range of black feminists into the sisterhood, including Toni Cade Bambara and Joseph Beam. SISA's goals were both specific and fluid, as one of its first outreach letters demonstrates:

1. Childcare facilities: Neighborhood women grow gardens and cooperate in preparing community meals for children. Our aid would enable them to increase facilities, food, buildings, and supplies.

2. The Maggie Magaba Scholarship Fund.

3. Zamani Soweto Sisters: Literacy, Sewing and Knitting Cooperatives: Neighborhood women are encouraged to become self-productive. A project is underway for the construction of a building to house their education and training activities.

4. And offer a space for the other specific requests that South African women might make.[20]

SISA's economic acts of solidarity acknowledged both the crucial community building role of South African women and the responsibilities of U.S. black feminists who had access to capital. Like blood beating through the heart or answering the moon, the relationship required repetition to respond to the litany of violence that came from "being Black and Black and Black and Black." The sound of the heartbeat persists; waves hit the shore again and again. Say *Sisterhood in Support of Sisters in South Africa,* and listen. Every time you say those words, a bloodstream is replicated, a waterway is traveled. The words went to South Africa with intention and love and hope that something "other" is possible.

ON OUR WAY: GENERATING BRIDGE SPACE

In "On My Way Out I Passed over You and the Verrazano Bridge," published in her penultimate collection of poems, Lorde uses space to articulate the fragility and possibility of a threatened future.[21] She started writing this poem while she was literally existing between spaces: she was on an airplane returning to New York from California. The poem opens with the scene of Lorde's own home and her commute from Staten Island and goes on to link the threatened, unsustainable environment of Staten Island to a global relationship of racial and economic violence and finally to a vision for a working connection to the future. The poem makes this journey through a number of moves that emphasize the use of space as a formal poetic strategy and an opportunity for solidarity.

One move involves a strategy that became more frequent in her later poems and her *Undersong* revisions: she adds spaces within the lines of the poem.[22] Readers are charged with either passing over these spaces or making a bridge. The poem starts with "Leaving [*space*] leaving," with the space suggesting an interruption, a restart. Throughout the poem, Lorde chooses spatial language in which space becomes an action: "leaving," "holding," "circling," "lowering," "covering," "scanning." Her insertion of spaces and her placement of words around them conscripts the reader into the action of bridging. The consonance between "leaving" and "love" asks the reader, What is the relationship between loving and leaving?[23]

Lorde also provides a bridge between the general political situation of late capitalism and its manifestation in specific places. In two instances, she combines the concreteness of place with the strategy of internal line breaks:

> from the dull wharves of Tompkinsville
> to Zimbabwe   Chad   Azania
> oh Willie sweet little brother with the snap in your eyes
> what walls are you covering now[24]

The reader is left to piece together the bridges that connect these three places in Africa—a connection that must move across both space and time. Zimbabwe is the postcolonial name for the land borders that once demarcated colonial Rhodesia, while Azania is the precolonial name for a larger region of sub-Saharan Africa that eventually included Zimbabwe but not Chad. Azania is also a name that, starting in 1958, some black radicals used to rename South Africa and thus assert an anticolonial, antiapartheid vision. Zimbabwe and Chad are nation-states, but Azania is a memory and a vision. Zimbabwe and Chad were both colonized but not by the same European powers, and their revolutions and their postcolonial politics have been different. The bridge that Lorde uses to link these three places is the figure of a "little brother" with "visions of revolution" covering walls with graffiti.[25] The creativity of youth, the work of presenting an illegal counter-normative vision, make the connection.

Likewise, in the next stanza, Lorde writes:

> the once-Black now wasted old people
> who built Pretoria
> Philadelphia   Atlanta   San Francisco[26]

Here, the bridge between the spaces is the dynamic of forced labor, starting with Pretoria in South Africa and moving to three cities in different regions

ALEXIS PAULINE GUMBS

of the United States. But the spaces or cuts in Lorde's lines are not healed. The bridges are not visible enough to make the spaces irrelevant. Her strategy here makes the brokenness of the contemporary world visible. People fall through these spaces; but at a time when land is owned, invaded, neocolonially controlled, and environmentally endangered, they are also poetic interventions into the meaning of space.

With their foundational collection *This Bridge Called My Back*, Cherríe Moraga and Gloria Anzaldúa brought the concept of the bridge into the center of the work that was engaging women of color / "Third World" feminists and writers. In that book (to which Lorde was a crucial contributor), the bridge is a vexed social relationship across racial difference that requires perpetual sacrifice and ongoing pain among the most oppressed.[27] For Lorde, the question of the bridge is a question of relationship and status. The bridge *is* the social relationship. Throughout "On My Way Out," the bridges that connect locations and people are conceptually dirty and backbreaking. The commonalities of great cities include forced labor, occupation, and war; their differences are mapped by the production of profit through the labor and lives of people across space and time.

The gaps (I almost spelled it "gasps") in the poem are about the distance between the poet and the subjects of the poem, a request for the reader's collaboration in providing a bridge of accountability between people on opposite sides of a matrix of power. For example, consider the stanza that begins "Picture small-boned dark women / gun-belts taut over dyed cloth" and goes on to describe the revolutionary response of women in South Africa and the traumatic violence against them:

> which one
> saw her two-year-old daughter's face
> squashed like a melon
> in the pre-dawn police raids upon Noxolo
> which one   writes poems
> lies with other women
> in the blood's affirmation?[28]

In contrast to statements in the dominant press, which cast black South African women as a monolithic group, the stanza questions the poet's ability to reach or describe the lived experiences of these freedom fighters. She can only ask and seek to identify, only attempt to bridge the spaces. One of the ways in which she does this bridging work is through her body of activist poems. Though she has not seen her two-year-old daughter murdered through state violence, she has written poems about her nightmares sparked by the New York Police Department's murder of children in her community. The final question, "which one [*space*] writes poems," is interrupted by a space that mirrors a longing to connect and stand in solidarity with the women who are struggling against apartheid. Lorde's queer relationship to space, here demonstrated as a poetic engagement with the visibility of space as structure, extends beyond her diasporic solidarity work with Afro-German women, South African women, and the people of Grenada. It positions her as a theorist of transnational feminist potential in her poetic work. The poem raises questions that M. Jacqui Alexander also asks: "How do we continue to be rooted in the particularities of our cultural homes without allegiance to the boundaries of the nation-state, yet remain simultaneously committed to a collectivized politic of identification and solidarity?"[29]

Lorde's poetic relationship to location engages this survival question in both content and form. As she writes in the penultimate stanza of the poem:

> History is not kind to us
> we restitch it with living
> past memory   forward
> into desire
> into the panic   articulation
> of want   without having
> or even the promise of getting.[30]

The idea of restitching a different, perhaps quilted, relationship between space and time is a response to the unkindness of history to "us," the oppressed audience convened in Lorde's poem "A Litany for Survival."[31] In "panic [*space*] articulation," "On My Way Out" articulates both desperate need and the violence that it represents. It shows us that we have major gaps to bridge and no solid ground to walk on. The closest we come to filling the space are the two gasps, "oh love" and "oh Willie," which seek to create intimacy or accountability between the speaker and the person whom she addresses.[32] This poem produces desire and sketches a possible relationship, appropriately filled with blank, undetermined spaces; and Lorde ends it with a vision:

> And I dream of our coming together
> encircled   driven
> not only by love

ALEXIS PAULINE GUMBS

but by lust for a working tomorrow
the flights of this journey
mapless   uncertain
and necessary as water.[33]

This vision offers an epistemological moment beyond the poem in which what was "a route map" becomes "mapless [*space*] uncertain," a relationship to space that Lorde asks us to bridge for our own survival, "necessary as water."

Notes

1. Audre Lorde, *Sister Outsider: Essays and Speeches* (Trumansburg, N.Y.: Crossing Press, 1984), 176.
2. Audre Lorde, "Of Generators and Survival—Hugo Letter," *Callaloo* 14, no. 1 (1991): 72 (hereafter cited as "Hugo Letter").
3. Ibid., 80.
4. Ibid., 76.
5. Lorde's time in Saint Croix overlapped with her journeys back and forth to Germany for cancer treatment and her work to respond to that country's racism and neo-Nazism after the fall of the Berlin Wall. She may or may not have been aware of the Nazi rhetoric that compared Jewish economic networks to a cancerous capitalism, but it is clear here that, unlike the Nazis, she was comparing systemic, dominant, state-based systems to cancer, not a specific group of people.
6. Lorde, "Hugo Letter," 75, 74, 78.
7. Ibid., 74.
8. Ibid., 78–79.
9. Audre Lorde, "Grenada Revisited: An Interim Report," in *Sister Outsider*, 176.
10. Ibid., 179.
11. Joseph Beam, letter, 1986, Joseph Beam Papers, Black Gay and Lesbian Archive, Schomburg Center, New York Public Library (hereafter cited as Beam Papers).
12. Lorde, "Grenada Revisited," 180.
13. Joseph Beam, notes from an interview with Audre Lorde, 1987, Beam Papers.
14. M. Jacqui Alexander and Chandra Mohandy, eds., *Feminist Genealogies, Colonial Legacies, and Democratic Futures* (New York: Routledge), 1997.
15. Audre Lorde, *Apartheid U.S.A.* (New York: Kitchen Table, 1986), 7.
16. Ibid., 9.
17. Diane Nelson, *A Finger in the Wound: Body Politics in Quincentennial Guatemala* (Berkeley: University of California Press, 1999), 42.
18. Lorde, *Apartheid U.S.A.*, 10.
19. Audre Lorde, "Meet," in *The Collected Poems of Audre Lorde* (New York: Norton, 1997), 258.
20. SISA outreach letter, undated, Audre Lorde Papers, Spelman College Archives.
21. Audre Lorde, "On My Way Out I Passed over You and the Verrazano Bridge," in *Collected Poems*, 403–6.
22. Audre Lorde, *Undersong: Chosen Poems Old and New* (New York: Norton, 1993).

23. Lorde, "On My Way Out," 403–6.
24. Ibid., 404.
25. Ibid.
26. Ibid.
27. Cherríe Moraga and Gloria Anzaldúa, eds., *This Bridge Called My Back: Writings by Radical Women of Color* (Watertown, Mass.: Persephone, 1981). See also Gayatri Spivak, *A Critique of Postcolonial Reason: Toward a History of the Vanishing Present* (London: Harvard University Press, 1999).
28. Lorde, "On My Way Out," 405.
29. M. Jacqui Alexander, *Pedagogies of Crossing: Meditations on Feminism, Sexual Politics, Memory, and the Sacred* (Durham, N.C.: Duke University Press, 2005), 268.
30. Lorde, "On My Way Out," 405–6.
31. Audre Lorde, "A Litany for Survival," in *The Black Unicorn* (New York: Norton, 1978, 31–32).
32. Lorde, "On My Way Out., 403–4.
33. Ibid., 406.

ALEXIS PAULINE GUMBS

14
The Geopolitics of the Erotic
Audre Lorde's Mexico and the Decolonization of the Revolutionary Imagination

TAMARA LEA SPIRA

> Consistently and with passionate strength, the Poet Audre
> Lorde eviscerates, she sears away the layers of hypocrisy
> that baffle and annihilate too much of our lives.
>
> June Jordan, "Introduction at Academy of American Poets"
>
> What does it mean that a black, lesbian, feminist, warrior,
> poet, mother is named the State Poet of New York?
> It means that we live in a world of the most intense
> contradictions. And we must find ways to use the best we
> have—ourselves, our work—and to work with every fiber of
> who we are to make the reality-pursuit of . . . [our] visions
> irresistible.
>
> Audre Lorde, *A Litany for Survival: The Life and Work of
> Audre Lorde*

Introducing Audre Lorde at the Academy of American Poets in March 1977, June Jordan offered the kind of words that could only come from one great poet to another. Describing the emotional tenor and affective force infusing Lorde's work, Jordan argued that her poetry carries an "unforgettable intensity and light"; it is so fiery that it "sears away" the hypocrisies that enshrine our daily lives. "Hers is not an obscure nor a stingy offering of ephemeral, optional considerations you may or may not examine at your leisure," she continued. "Her work is a poetry to be used, to be guided by, *to be changed by, deeply.*"[1] Jordan's beautiful imagery captured Lorde's ability to tap into "those physical, emotional, and psychic expressions of what is deepest and strongest and richest within each of us."[2] She brought to the fore the degree to which Lorde's work beckons confrontation with one's contradictions, pains, and power, requiring that we all "scrutinize" our lives with an "intensity of light" so that we may truly live in service of social transformation.[3] In so doing, Jordan put into practice a central principle that stands as one of Lorde's most precious contributions to this service: the power of the erotic.

In the early 1990s, when Lorde was named State Poet of New York, she warned against the dangers of accepting accolades of individual merit: "We must find ways to use the best we have—ourselves, our work—to bridge those contradictions. This is the work of the poet within each of us. To envision what has not yet been, and to work with every fiber of who we are to make the reality-pursuit of those visions irresistible."[4] Viewing her own recognition with caution, she challenged the uncritical reception of platitudes that do not also acknowledge the larger communities of struggle that produce brilliance such as hers. In other words, she modeled the praxis of which she spoke when she called on us all to forge a vision of justice so "irresistible" that it must be heeded.

The epigraphs that open this chapter may seem to be an unlikely beginning for an essay that focuses on the way in which Cold War–era Latin America and the Caribbean served as crucibles for the development of some of Lorde's most visionary insights and theories. Yet they reveal the forms of radical accountability that are a hallmark of her legacy. Informed by her commitment to always acknowledge the communities of struggle that form us, this chapter shifts the purview of scholarship on Lorde from the geopolitical centers of the United States and Europe, concentrating instead on the force of her thinking as it developed at the fringes of U.S. empire. I explore her experiences in Mexico and Grenada, examining how her insights from those travels came to mediate her conceptions of the intimate economies of geopolitics and the erotic as a counter-hegemonic force. Far from being marginal, the Americas emerge as incredibly important sites for the development of her thoughts on the complex connections between affective economies and geopolitics. By accounting for these diverse genealogies, I challenge the fragmentations and dichotomizations that currently characterize U.S. women of color and transnational feminist analyses.[5] Such historiographical reframings are crucial because they open up new spaces for reconsidering cross-bordered solidarities and reanimate Lorde's commitment to interdependency and mutual struggle.

TAMARA LEA SPIRA

LORDE'S EXPERIENCES IN MEXICO: THE EROTIC AS POWER

Paging through *Zami, Sister Outsider,* and other examples of Lorde's work, I am struck by the extent to which she framed her address to encompass multiple communities of struggle. Systematically directing her attention to the broad web of communities in which she was enmeshed, she offered trenchant but loving critique. Addressing everyone—black men, white women, black women, her Grenadian brothers and sisters—she invited all into a shared project for collective survival. She believed that this ethos and a deep belief in interconnections had the potential to link us all in pursuit of justice.

In the opening of *Zami,* Lorde dedicated her work to all the women she had ever met or dreamt of, crediting them as the source for the "power behind [her] voice."[6] With this notion of radical interconnectivity in mind, we can begin to assess the importance of her time in Mexico as a young woman.[7] As *Zami* relates, in the early 1950s a sense of hopelessness and despair pushed her to leave the Communist-obsessed United States. Shortly after attending the funerals of Ethel and Julius Rosenberg, around whose case she had intensively organized, she arrived in Mexico City. She had just been fired from her dangerously toxic factory job, a job that may well have contributed to her premature death, where she had lied about productivity outputs in order to earn enough money to travel. Additionally, she had recently ended her relationship with her lover Bea, a bourgeois "mainline, white, monied" woman with whom Lorde had tried hard to connect yet who remained reserved, cerebral, and cold.[8]

In terms of *Zami*'s narrative progression, it is significant that Lorde's entry into Mexico was framed by U.S. capitalism, racism, and imperialism as well as ascetic sexual mores—a colonial separation of mind and body as they played out within the caricature-like figure of Bea. No longer able to stomach the McCarthyist purges, Lorde took the government's murder of the Rosenbergs as final confirmation that she could no longer survive the "hostile surroundings" of the United States.[9] Moreover, plagued by her long struggle to earn a decent living, she saw no lucrative economic future for herself on the horizon. As paranoia, Red-baiting, and economic recession expanded, an insidious sense of loneliness and alienation seeped into her most intimate interactions. Nowhere was this more compellingly emblemized than in her loveless affair with Bea, who managed her whiteness and sculpted petite body as carefully as she managed her theoretical and nonvisceral relationship to sex.[10]

Against this bleak backdrop, Lorde imagined Mexico to be the antithesis of the United States—a land "full of color and fantasy and delight, full of sun, music and song."[11] During the 1950s and 1960s, Mexico was the home of a leftist expatriate community whose members, fleeing Red Scare repression, were able to cross the border without a passport (although documents now reveal persistent joint U.S.-Mexican surveillance efforts to stop them).[12] As we learn in *Zami*, the cohort included white artists and intellectuals such as Alf, a friend of Audre's who went to Mexico City as a teenager to paint with Diego Rivera. Importantly, it also included black expatriates—painters such as Elizabeth Catlett and John Wilson as well as writers such as Willard Motley. These artists used complex aesthetic forms and intellectual traditions learned from their Mexican counterparts to produce comparative critiques of U.S. and Mexican racism and U.S. imperialism.[13]

Thus, for Lorde Mexico symbolized a different way of being, a space from which she might attain some breathing or "living room" away from the hegemonizing forces of the racist, heterosexist, xenophobic, and capitalist violence she had experienced in New York.[14] Mexico was a "beacon" that might keep her "steady." In *Zami*, it comes to signify a route to "hope," an affective state as much as a physical locale. Or, as Lorde put it simply, when she first arrived in Mexico, "I was happier than I'd been in what seemed like a very long time. What was even better, I was wholly conscious that I was."[15]

As we learn from *Zami*, Lorde's arrival in Mexico City was filled with wonders. Intrigued by its sights, smells, and sounds, she corrected her habit of looking down at her feet while walking. Now she wanted to take in everything around her. Emboldened by the sea of nonwhite faces, she felt able to walk with her head held high, which she described as a form of "profound . . . exhilarat[ion] . . . unlike any other experience . . . [she] . . . had ever known."[16] Such feelings were deeply connected to a new experience of racialization vis-à-vis the community in which she had found herself: "For me, walking hurriedly back to my own little house in this land of color and dark people who said *negro* and meant something beautiful, who noticed me as I moved among them—this decision felt like a promise of some kind that I half-believed in, in spite of myself, a possible validation."[17] She intuited the possibility of new modes of racial identification, an experience of herself as beautiful and validated, as a "promise" whose edges she could just begin to glimpse. Frequently people asked if she was *Cubana*, giving her a new vantage point into the significations of blackness that had

TAMARA LEA SPIRA

not been overdetermined by the particular violent U.S. racial histories she knew so well.[18] Her embodied physical presence among other African diasporic and indigenous communities broke her isolation, allowing her to rupture myths of white supremacy and move toward new forms of self-definition and -determination.

To properly attend to the complexities of Lorde's descriptions of Mexico as "exhilarating" and as filled with "color," "fantasy," and "delight," one must consider the historical context. On the one hand, such tropes may be read as consistent with a longstanding exotification at the heart of U.S. neocolonialism and imperial relations with Latin America. One might therefore read Lorde's language as both reflecting a romanticism rooted in this exotification and dangerously denying racism, slavery, and colonialism in Mexico. Simultaneously, however, the historical context reveals Lorde's awareness of a more complex panorama of racism, colonialism and U.S. imperialism. She evoked her aforementioned tropes directly after learning about the 1954 Brown v. Board of Education decision to desegregate schools. Several pages later she spoke of the genocide of colonization in Latin America, a horror that her lover Eudora described as a "holocaust."[19] Additionally, if we locate Lorde among a broader movement of black expats who used their experiences in Mexico to critique U.S. racism and imperialism, we see a more complicated picture. Far from simply feeding the U.S. imaginary of Latin America as "exotic," Lorde was issuing a powerful indictment of the joint forces of American racism and imperialism. This became a critical dimension of her later writings on U.S. imperial invasions in Asia, Central America, and the Caribbean as well as on U.S. involvement in upholding oppressive regimes in South Africa, Palestine, and elsewhere.

A more generous, historically contextualized reading therefore acknowledges Lorde's naïveté about her new surroundings, but not as an abnegation of her own complex relationship to Mexico as a tenuous U.S. citizen. Rather, living in Mexico allowed her to denaturalize the virulent forms of North American pre–civil rights racism in which she had been raised, shifting her point of entry into a struggle against racism, colonization, and imperialism that needed to cut across multiple intersecting vectors of power and geographical borders. In Lorde's descriptions of Mexico, we witness Lorde as she first began imagining the radical possibility of a shifting racial landscape outside the deadening forms of violent U.S. taxonomies of racial and sexual difference.

We also witness Lorde as she began to *remember*—that is, as she challenged the institutionally sanctioned amnesia that accompanied her uneven socialization into the U.S. nation-state. As a first-generation U.S. citizen, Lorde was scratching beneath ossified forms of feeling, subjectivity, and being that had trapped her in her subject position as a "North American." In so doing, she gave language to not yet accessible epistemologies, ontological modes of being, and affective states that had thus far been the overdetermined experiences of selfhood as a disciplined U.S. subject.

Importantly, then, Mexico came to mediate Lorde's relationship to Grenada as well as her own complex connections to her mother. For example, as she later reflected in an interview with Adrienne Rich, it was only after she had spent time in Mexico that she was able to access knowledge, memories, and feelings that connected her to the stories her mother told about life in Grenada.[20] Lorde's presence in Mexico triggered deep physical and psychic familiarity, allowing her to reach modes of self-definition that had eluded U.S. hegemonic forms. By destabilizing her subject position of belonging as a tenuous U.S. citizen and the delimited forms of selfhood it allowed, Mexico "remind[ed]" her that "we have recognized each other before"—to borrow a phrase from M. Jacqui Alexander's reflections on the complex intergenerational and transnational webs of "Third World" and queer of-color feminists.[21] Such relational, intergenerational modes of thinking about racialized subjectivity offer a touch point for modes of inhabiting life outside the ossified structures of U.S. histories of racial segregation and bodily control. "In this nourishing land of light and color in which [she] was . . . somehow home," Lorde was able to gain a foothold and come to know and locate herself in a new way. "Hope" appeared on the horizon of her consciousness, sparking possibilities for the prospect of alternative racial arrangements in which her legally sanctioned otherness was not simply a given.[22]

After a brief sojourn in Mexico City, Lorde moved slightly south to Cuernavaca, which had by the mid-1950s become a refuge for leftists, artists, and radicals. Among the people she encountered were nurses from the Lincoln Brigade in the Spanish Civil War, who had been granted citizenship by the Mexican government, as well as members of the Hollywood Ten and other activists who had protested the Rosenberg trial. And then there was Eudora, whose character reappears in *The Cancer Journals* but is absent from Lorde's Mexico diaries.[23] A white, working-class woman from Texas,

Eudora represented a world of sensuality, vitality, and Eros. Brash and experienced, tough yet tender, she was nearly thirty years Lorde's senior and the first woman that Lorde had ever heard describe herself as a "lesbian."[24] She was also the first to call Lorde "beautiful" and the first to speak openly about having a mastectomy, a detail later recounted in *The Cancer Journals*.[25] Moreover, she was the first woman from whom Lorde allowed herself to receive pleasure and with whom she grew bold and direct about her desire.

Eudora brought a new level of Eros into Lorde's life, in the true sense of the word. She personified "love in all its aspects—born of Chaos, and creative power."[26] Although she was an alcoholic and possessed by her own demons, she allowed herself to feel, often teasing Lorde about her "prudishness" and teaching her to not shy away from the intensity of emotion— no small detail to the "black feminist lesbian warrior poet" who would later teach future generations that "our silence will not protect us."[27]

As Lorde gathered the courage to admit her desire for Eudora, a transformation occurred. We learn in *Zami* that she felt her words "touch and give life to a new reality" within her, spurring the growth of "some half known self come to age." In a hauntingly beautiful passage about their first night together, she wrote, "I raised my eyes and found hers again, speaking a tenderness my mouth had no words for yet. She took my hand and placed it there, squarely on her chest. Our hands fell. I bent and kissed her softly upon the scar where our hands had rested. I felt her heart strong and fast against my lips. My lungs expanded and my breath deepened with the touch of her warm dry skin . . . My body took charge from her flesh."[28] Here, Lorde began to give name to a "tenderness" she felt emerging but for which she had not quite found the words. As we learn in her later poetry, such "tenderness" was "nameless and formless, about to be birthed, but already felt."[29] Eudora's mastectomy scar, a symbol of illness, became alive as her beating heart drew Lorde's lips. As Lorde's body "[came] to life in the curve of Eudora's arms," all that was numb became infused with vitality and feeling.[30] All sensual dimensions of life—lungs, breath, heart, touch— were heightened by this embrace.

The figure of Eudora thus came to symbolize life and Eros, chaos and creativity—a spectrum of sentience and emotion broader than Lorde had ever experienced before. The dead had come to life, as Lorde reinforced metaphorically in her anecdote about a June bug that she had killed hours before first sleeping with Eudora and that she found resurrected, crawling up her wall after their evening together.[31] Read in the context of Lorde's larger oeuvre, Eudora's persona triggered the birth of many of the most cherished elements of Lorde's work. Their union was poetry, connecting Lorde to the erotic currents of life. Their embrace opened a wellspring of love, solidarity, and joy. Lorde elegantly summarized such associations in the epigraph of a section on Cuernavaca: "*Eudora. Mexico. Color and light and Cuernavaca and Eudora.*"[32]

Living outside the strictures of racial-sexual otherness and alienation in Mexico helped Lorde embrace sexuality, vitality, and Eros. In *Zami* (and later in a conversation with Rich), she recounted the experience of being seized by an epiphany about her ability to harness this beauty and power.

> It was here in the breathtaking dawns and quick-hill twilight of Cuer-navaca that I learned that it is really easier to be quiet in the woods. One morning I came down a hill into the square at dawn to catch my [bus] ride to the District. The birds suddenly cut loose all around me in the unbelievable sweet warm air. I had never heard anything so beautiful and unexpected before. I felt shaken by the waves of song. *For the first time in my life, I had an insight into what poetry could be.* I could use words to recre-ate that feeling, rather than create a dream, which is what so much of my writing had been before.[33]

Lorde was suddenly seized by the knowledge of the tangible beauty of life that poetry can represent. Unlike a distant dream, the "rock experi-ences" out of which "poetry" is "carved" came to life, exploding in color, feeling, and sound.[34] As she marveled at this new potential, she was also immersed in the beauty around her: the sweet sound of birds, the falling and rising of light, the warm air on her skin. By fully experiencing herself as a sensual being, she had gained access to a larger cosmology of person-hood; she was no longer tied to the abstracted Cartesian individual pre-mised on the colonial division of body and mind.[35] The epiphany lay the foundation for her revolutionary thinking about the necessity of poetry as a vehicle for holistic social change. "I learned that day on the mountain," she later told Rich, "that words can match that [feeling], re-create it."[36]

Lorde's writing on Mexico therefore functions as an archive of the inti-mate economies of geopolitics in the early Cold War years. By temporar-ily leaving the United States, she learned that alternative social and sexual relations had the potential to challenge U.S. hegemony. Her experience became the groundwork for an antiracist, queer, feminist praxis that linked anticapitalist and antiracist movements with new forms of embodied sexuality, sentience, and emotion. When the hegemony of U.S. racial and sexual regimes were denaturalized and their grip on her imagination loosened, her creative and erotic forces were unleashed. As *Zami* reveals, this shift permanently affected her writing.

COUNTER-REVOLUTIONS OF THE SENSES: U.S. IMPERIAL BACKLASH AND THE RECOLONIZATION OF THE SUBJECT

As Lorde wrote in her now beloved essay "Uses of the Erotic," it is powerful to learn to recognize our potential as more complete beings in an oppressive world. For "[once] having experienced the fullness of this depth of feeling and recognizing its power, in honor and self-respect we can require no less of ourselves."[37] Lorde's experiences in Mexico brought her more fully into the knowledge that the essay traces. There she was able to imagine and embody new modes of feeling, revealing the erotic as a powerful force that could defend against—and transform—U.S. racial and sexual regimes, forever altering the ways in which she connected with herself and others.

Lorde's writing on 1950s Mexico helps us understand the potential of the erotic to subvert the subjectifying powers of U.S. state force in the early Cold War years; it locates erotic connection as a potential force for interrupting internalized forms of racism and imperialism structuring U.S. modes of compulsory heterosexuality. Yet in the years before her untimely death in 1992, the landscape of U.S. neo-imperial power had shifted significantly. In the wake of radical "Third World" movements for collective liberation, the United States had come to "stand . . . on the wrong side of every single battle for liberation taking place upon this globe."[38] Indeed, with the resurgence of refurbished modes of post–civil rights racism and U.S.-propagated crusades of counter-revolutionary violence across the "Third World," it became increasingly clear to Lorde and her contemporaries that, to quote June Jordan, a "natural order [was] being restored."[39] Furthermore, the 1990s occasioned dramatic shifts, as the neoliberal U.S. state and capitalism began to coopt radical queer, lesbian, and even transgender movements into the fold of more "flexible" forms of imperialism, white supremacy, conquest, and war making.

Nowhere was the link between the shoring in of U.S. hegemony and the reeling in of revolutionary dreams more powerfully articulated than by

Lorde, particularly in her writings about the 1983 U.S. invasion of Grenada. Emphasizing the relationship between physical and psychological aggression, her essay "Grenada Revisited" connected the clamping down of the New Jewell movement with the manipulation of the erotic self-determination of black communities across the hemisphere and globe. As Lorde demonstrated, the recolonization of the subject was codified formally through the psychological operations of the occupation forces (which she abbreviated as "P.S.Y.O.P.S.") and the relentless cultural imperialism of the U.S. military.[40] Thus, once more, she connected U.S. state force and a reassertion of white supremacy with the control of one's sexual and erotic self-determination.

More importantly, however, she also warned us that the battle for "bodies, hearts, and minds" would not simply remain in the hands of the U.S. government. She voiced concern about the extent to which African Americans, all communities of color, feminists, and queers were being called on in unprecedented ways to enact U.S. projects of imperialism and white supremacy. She argued that the United States was not primarily interested in quashing a specific revolutionary movement in Grenada, as devastating as that action was. Rather, its key interest was "the concern long expressed by the Pentagon as to whether or not Black soldiers could be gotten to fire upon other Black people."[41] In a grave warning to all communities of struggle, Lorde demystified the extent to which communities were being pitted against one another. Diagnosing a moment of danger, she begged everyone to resist the temptation to buy into the idea that capitalism, U.S. nationalism, or imperialism could ever provide freedom or justice for anyone. She marshaled her sharp words in the service of social transformation. Working to challenge the people's lulling amnesia, she cautioned that "nineteen eighty-four is upon us and doublethink has come home to scramble our brains and blanket our protests."[42]

These concerns about blanketed protests are an apt place to close this essay's reconsideration of Lorde's radical internationalist legacy and the ongoing work required to honor her memory. Today, more than twenty years after Lorde's death, we live in an era of neoliberal empire and, as many believe, at the brink of economic and ecological disaster. Wars are waged in the name of so-called sexual and gender liberation. Claims that we live in a post-race, post-feminist, postcolonial order are pretexts for reproducing white supremacy and empire. Once unthinkable asymmetries of wealth and power abound, and genocide is masked as liberal democracy and freedom.[43] As feminists, queers, indigenous people, black people, and communities of color become the literal and metaphorical foot soldiers of a U.S. neo-imperial order, we are lulled into believing that the status quo may serve us if only we work hard enough to ascend a hierarchy that we all know has been wrought by expropriation, slavery, colonial genocide, and bloodshed.[44] Within this context Lorde's visionary work creates a necessary counterpoint, reminding us once again of the forms of "erotic decolonization" and revolutionary social transformation toward which we must aspire.[45] Her sharp words and exemplary life beckon us to ponder these truths, as difficult as they may appear.

As Lorde lay in bed in Grenada, battling cancer, she felt deep clarity about the intricate connection between the diseases of racism, sexism, capitalism, and imperialism and the cancer in her body: "Visualizing the disease process inside my body in political images is not a quixotic dream. When I speak out against the cynical U.S. intervention in Central America, I am working to save my life in every sense. Government research grants to the National Cancer Institute were cut in 1986 by the exact amount illegally turned over to the contras in Nicaragua. One hundred and five million dollars. It gives yet another meaning to the personal is political."[46] Lorde was aware that the integrity of the world she would soon leave was interconnected with the integrity of her soul. As a U.S. citizen, she could not stand by in support of the contra wars any more than she could be complicit in the invasion of Grenada. A death order issued to the Sandinistas in Nicaragua or the New Jewell movement in Grenada was also a death order issued to her. In this vulnerable moment, she laid bare a key argument of this essay: that the reproduction of the U.S. state has always been predicated on the management and dampening of one's life force and the intrinsic right to erotic self-determination. Only with an integrated movement for decolonization, abolition, and racial, sexual, economic, and gender liberation can any of us be free.

Lorde reminded her readers that the power to reclaim these forces within is ours for the taking. The battle against U.S. imperialism is the battle against white supremacy is the battle against capitalism is the battle against homophobia is the battle against cancer. She wrote, "Sometimes we are blessed with being able to choose the time and the arena and the manner of our revolution, but more usually we must do battle where we are standing. The real blessing is to be able to use whoever I am wherever I am, in concert with as many others as possible."[47] Once more, her words beckon us to remember that interdependency, solidarity, and connection are the only means toward true belonging and survival. Now, as she wrote, "is a time for the real work's urgencies."[48]

Notes

1. June Jordan, "Introduction at American Academy of Poets," 1977, in June Jordan Papers, 1936–2002, MC 513, Schlesinger Library, Radcliffe Institute, Harvard University. The italics are mine.
2. Audre Lorde, "Uses of the Erotic: The Erotic as Power," in *Sister Outsider: Essays and Speeches* (Berkeley, Calif.: Crossing Press, 1984), 56.
3. Audre Lorde, "Poetry Is Not a Luxury," in *Sister Outsider*, 36.
4. *A Litany for Survival: The Life and Work of Audre Lorde,* dir. Ada Gay Griffin and Michelle Parkerson (New York: Third World Newsreel, 1995).
5. For more on the internationalist genealogies of the feminisms of black and U.S. women of color, see Cynthia Young, *Soul Power: Culture, Radicalism, and the Making of a U.S. Third World Left* (Durham, N.C.: Duke University Press, 2006); and Tamara Lea Spira, "Intimate Internationalisms: U.S. Third World and Queer Feminist Solidarity with Chile and Nicaragua," in *Feminist Theory* 15, no. 2 (2014): 119–36.
6. Audre Lorde, *Zami: A New Spelling of My Name* (Freedom, Calif.: Crossing Press, 1982), 3.
7. I tentatively use the word *woman* to describe Lorde because this is her language in *Zami,* although it is critical to note the complex way in which she constructs gender. For an important analysis on the "third gender" constructed by this generation of feminists of color, see Grace Kyungwon Hong, *Ruptures of American Capital: Women of Color Feminism and the Culture of Immigrant Labor* (Minneapolis: Minnesota University Press, 2006), vii–xxxiv.
8. Lorde, *Zami,* 147, 151.
9. Ibid., 149.
10. Ibid., 151.
11. Ibid., 147.
12. The FBI created a classification for what they called the "American Communist Group in Mexico." This created a pretext for a closer relationship with the División Federal de Seguridad, who collaborated in projects of joint surveillance. See Diana Anhalt, *A Gathering of Fugitives: American Political Expatriates in Mexico, 1948–1965* (Santa Maria, Calif.: Archer, 2001).
13. Lorde, *Zami,* 81. Examples include paintings that drew from muralist aesthetics and mass production techniques to depict the horrors of U.S. racism in a new light. See Rebecca M. Schreiber, *Cold War Exiles in Mexico: U.S. Dissidents and the Culture of Critical Resistance* (Minneapolis: University of Minnesota Press, 2008).
14. June Jordan, *Living Room: New Poems by June Jordan* (New York: Thunder's Mouth Press, 1985).
15. Lorde, *Zami,* 148, 174, 158.
16. Ibid., 154–57.

17. Ibid., 173.
18. Ibid., 154.
19. Ibid., 170. Much could be said of the holocaust analogy as a limit point for measuring atrocity, particularly from the context of the early 1950s. See, for example, Andreas Huyssen, "Present Pasts: Media, Politics, Amnesia," *Public Culture* 12, no. 1 (2000): 21–38.
20. Adrienne Rich, "An Interview with Audre Lorde," *Signs* 6, no. 4 (1981): 717.
21. M. Jacqui Alexander, "Remembering *This Bridge Called My Back*, Remembering Ourselves," in *Pedagogies of Crossing: Meditations on Feminism, Sexual Politics, Memory, and the Sacred* (Durham, N.C.: Duke University Press, 2005), 266.
22. Lorde, *Zami*, 168.
23. Audre Lorde, *The Cancer Journals* (San Francisco: Spinsters Ink, 1980), 35. As Alexis De Veaux notes in her biography of Lorde, Eudora is not mentioned in Lorde's letters about Mexico. For me the "reality" of Eudora's existence is not important. Rather, I am interested in what her figure allowed Lorde to work out, especially in regards to her theory of the erotic as power. See Alexis De Veaux, *Warrior Poet: A Biography of Audre Lorde* (New York: Norton, 2004), 380.
24. Lorde, *Zami*, 162. Eudora's persona deviates from the standard racialized, sexualized tropes of the North American who goes south to find romance and pleasure.
25. Ibid., 165. Rich, "An Interview with Audre Lorde," 717.
26. Lorde, "Uses of the Erotic," 55.
27. Lorde, *Zami*, 164. This trope appears many times in Lorde's work—for instance, in "The Transformation of Silence into Language and Action," in *Sister Outsider*, 36–44.
28. Lorde, *Zami*, 167.
29. Lorde, "Poetry Is Not a Luxury," 36.
30. Lorde, *Zami*, 169.
31. Ibid., 168.
32. Ibid., 161.
33. Ibid., 160. The italics are mine.
34. "Poetry is the way we help give name to the nameless so it can be thought. The farthest external horizons of our hopes and fears are cobbled by our poems, carved from the rock experiences of our daily lives" (Lorde, "Poetry Is Not a Luxury," 36).
35. "Since colonization has produced fragmentation and dismemberment at both the material and psychic levels, the work of decolonization has to make room for the deep yearning for wholeness, often expressed as a yearning to belong, a yearning that is both material and existential, both psychic and physical, and which, when satisfied, can subvert and ultimately displace the pain of dismemberment" (Alexander, "Remembering *This Bridge*," 283).
36. Rich, "An Interview with Audre Lorde," 716.
37. Lorde, "Uses of the Erotic," 55.
38. Lorde, "Learning from the 1960s," in *Sister Outsider*, 140.
39. June Jordan, "From Sea to Shining Sea," *Feminist Studies* 8, no. 3 (1982): 535–41. This was also the first poem in *Living Room*, 11–20.
40. Audre Lorde, "Grenada Revisited," in *Sister Outsider*, 182. In addition to interrogating, imprisoning, and torturing prisoners, the U.S. troops blared "Beach Boys rock group music, hour after hour" (185).
41. Ibid., 184.
42. Ibid.

43. Joy James, "The Dead Zone: Stumbling at the Crossroads of Party Politics, Geno-cide, and Postracial Racism," *South Atlantic Quarterly* 108, no. 3 (2009): 459–81.

44. I am indebted to Anna Agathangelou and Morgan Bassichis for our collective work on this question. See Anna Agathangelou, Morgan Bassichis, and Tamara Lea Spira, "Intimate Investments: Homonormativity, Global Lockdown, and the Seductions of Empire," *Radical History Review* 100 (Winter 2008): 120–44.

45. This phrase "erotic decolonization" is drawn from Alexander, *Pedagogies of Crossing*, in which she theorizes from the work of Lorde. It has also been taken up in Native American queer and Two-Spirit scholarship and praxis. See, for example, Quo-Li Driskill, "Stolen from Our Bodies: First Nations Two-Spirits / Queers and the Journey to a Sovereign Erotic," *Studies in American Indian Literature* 16, no. 2 (Summer 2004): 50–64.

46. Audre Lorde, "A Burst of Light: Living with Cancer," in *I Am Your Sister: Collected and Unpublished Writings of Audre Lorde*, ed. Rudolph P. Byrd, Johnnetta Betsch Cole, and Beverly Guy-Sheftall (Oxford: Oxford University Press, 2009), 149.

47. Ibid., 140.

48. Ibid.

III
WORK

15
The Critical Feelings of Audre Lorde, from the Standpoint of an Academic Minor

SARAH CEFAI

Sister Outsider is an expression of how Audre Lorde feels. The speeches and essays in the book present how the exercise of power makes her feel, along with the power of feeling in her thinking and writing—the power of Lorde's voice. This chapter explores the idea that the expression of feeling in *Sister Outsider* resonates with that of the split subjectivity, which manifests itself through the contradiction of becoming a feminist academic. The feeling of powerlessness, and the desire to find voice as Lorde does, shore up the demand for speech that can be identified with feminist academic discourse. Yet feminist academic speech is conditioned by the institutionalized relations of power and knowledge that accord with the interests of university stakeholders. Such relations produce a feminist subject "in conflict" because the very discourses that make possible a feminist analysis of power are also those that silence individual experience and curtail the possibilities of speaking in a singular voice. The feminist subject is least able to speak to the relations of power and knowledge that institutionalize her within a disciplinary milieu, even when it is precisely these relations that academia has trained her to critically analyze. In the feminist academy, *Sister Outsider* evokes a break with the paralysis that results from this contradiction. The notion of critical feeling is a way to conceptualize the crucial importance of feeling as it relates to evaluative judgment. Feelings are critical to Lorde's evaluation of the relation between feminist speech and silence, and this evaluative expression of the relation between what can and cannot be said allows us to think of Lorde's feminism in a transnational sense.

By drawing on the Foucauldian concept of enunciation, feminist cultural studies predisposes academia to scrutiny as practices of enunciation.[1] Less remedial than medial, cultural studies treats academic representation as itself a site for intervention, as an interface for thinking and doing. Feminist cultural studies mediates representations and other forms of expression to discover, identify, and analyze the palpable middle of normative living. Within this schema, those who subsist at the fringes of normative belonging learn how the outside opens new standpoints for struggle.

In the global emergence of the neoliberal university, feminism has become a term to describe a type of institutional labor (among other instantiations).[2] Nevertheless, readings of Lorde have signaled the desire for a feminism that is a collective practice of enunciation capable of undermining and revealing the violence of the assumed neutrality of governing discourses. In line with Gilles Deleuze and Felix Guattari's concept of the "minor literature," Lorde's enunciation "takes on a collective value" without representing a collective body of resistance.[3] Such counterintuitive thinking seeks to avoid the quandary of establishing feminist movement in and outside of the university system.

Having never been employed to teach or research feminist theory, and having never been part of a feminist collective (despite efforts to the contrary), I refer to my enunciation here as "minor." Collating "underdeveloped languages and oppressed sounds," I offer here an *"intensive* engagement" with Lorde's creative energy.[4] I wrote this chapter by way of stunted and stuttered speaking; I sought to recuperate something from a worn-out autonomy. I fought to find words in the conflict of living between national myopias; in the grind of precarious employment, fraying relationships, and transnational airplane spaces. I was deskless and always "moving into the sunlight."[5]

Academia is no minor literature. Speaking *as* feminist academics, we cite Lorde but do not speak *like her,* in her tongue, from her position of enunciation. Many are denied the very process of coming to voice about which so many of those whom we read write. Academic discourse affords its subjects the liberatory logic of critical discourse, but its institutional mastery denies the political creativity to which it remains adjacent. For those failed by liberal fantasies of "upward mobility, job security, political and social equality, and lively durable intimacy," *Sister Outsider* is not just

SARAH CEFAI

a source of conceptual insight into how identity relates to feeling and emotional knowledge.[6] It is comfort—a cushion or pillow—in relation to that process.[7] Expressing a revolutionary feminist imaginary, Lorde's writing buffers the contemporary subject from her disappointment, insisting that the collective is still out there, "to come."[8] Properly named *feminist* and full of the force of feeling, Lorde's transnational legacy is pulse, hope, broken heart, agitation, friendship, kindness, rage, disappointment, difficulty, the refusal to accept. It is not genre but "sense."[9] The legacy lives in the hands that hold copies of *Sister Outsider.*

> Readers of Lorde
> coat the spine of feminism with her courage
> with her layered meanings
> that we make in our layered readings
> of the struggle we encounter
> to be courageous
> like her.

This chapter engages the creative energy of *Sister Outsider* in the context of five subject positions used heuristically to imagine feminist academic subjectivity in its contemporary assemblage form: the subject of speech, the subject of collective knowledge, the subject of feminist difference, the subject of academic hierarchy, and the subject of neoliberal individualism. Feminist academics occupy and are occupied by these positions in various ways that condition their ability to make knowledge, including their ability to think critically and to be supported materially in that endeavor. These subject positions go some way in situating the split subjectivity or double bind of the feminist scholar who has experienced feminist academia as a space of compromise, confinement, and even violation. There is seemingly no escape from the paradox that feminism's epistemological authority is conditioned by, and indeed provides intellectual energy for, institutional norms that advance the very forms of subjugation that feminist thought opposes. The expression of silence, fear, anger, and the erotic in *Sister Outsider* echoes the taxonomy of critical feelings that express this affliction. The emotional labor required by this epistemological paradox is particularly acute at the entry into feminist academic subject positions—in postgraduate training, as an early career researcher who is under- or unemployed—a situation that reflects the condensation of power around liminal subjectivities.

How can I deal with the fear and anger and pain that pervade my life? This registers only elliptically as an academic question, if at all. In the process of reconciling my own critical and not so critical feelings with the capacities of antisexist, anti-homophobic, and antiracist knowledge, the way in which I live with fear and anger and pain presses into my dreams as much as it does into my capacity to analyze. How should I speak, what should I say, when, and to whom?

Lorde insists on the primacy of speech: "I have come to believe over and over again that what is most important to me must be spoken, made verbal and shared, even at the risk of having it bruised or misunderstood."[10] Speech wards off the fear that otherwise saps the potential of difference. Fear of speaking is a regressive horizon that orients its subjects toward what has already been. The subject of silence is the bearer of the potential difference that speaking could make but is also someone who is living with something bigger than herself. By putting fear into motion, speaking "is never without fear—of visibility, of the harsh light of scrutiny and perhaps judgement, of pain, of death."[11] Literature, philosophy, and art can cultivate ways to speak feeling that do not yoke realities to their liminal existence inside rubrics of acceptance.

A diagnosis of cancer led Lorde to diagnose her "silences" as what she "most regretted." Throughout *Sister Outsider* she refers to the silence of not speaking about racism's "constant, if unspoken, distortion of vision."[12] Anger and pain and fear are noises of distortion that can be clarified only through their expression. When Lorde expresses the noise, her experience of racism transforms the noise inside us. Her expression of pain expresses more than the singularity of racism's prejudicial violation. By expressing the psychic pain of the distortions of racism, Lorde renders her feeling into critical insight; it becomes indistinguishable from how she survives a force of representation bigger than her own. By foregrounding the qualities of feeling that accompany the unspoken, distorted visions of racism, critical feelings reverberate between Lorde and her readers, allowing the social distinctions that produce feelings of anger and pain and fear to vibrate.

Silence is a source of critical insight in my work and the only way I know to become (or unbecome) a feminist academic. Academics' names are synonymous with their speech. The risk of having what is important bruised or misunderstood is subject to the discursive proliferation of representations beyond individual control. The relations of power most pertinent to feminist scholars are likely to be those we exercise or are subordinate to in the university. Rather than speak as Lorde does, untenured academics and academics tethered to their tenure learn the Foucauldian craft of lining conversation with the difference between what is said and what is not. This speaking, while appearing not to, is characteristic of the interpenetration between sexuality and discourse that affects all knowledge.[13] As an institutional refusal of articulation, it creates the conditions of academic suffering. The duplicity of silence allows *Sister Outsider* to register as the potential of a collective rather than one that has form.

THE SUBJECT OF COLLECTIVE FEMINIST KNOWLEDGE

Lorde describes herself as a "sister outsider": belonging to a sisterly collective while retaining her singularity as a subject of marginal experience. With its status as collective, feminist speech joins individuated voices, marking an authorial trace that is both shared and painfully separate. The collective status of feminist knowledge is part of the feminist epistemological challenge to the masculinist ideal of the individual subject. Such a challenge to patriarchal ideas about gendered subjectivity entails consciousness of how we as women learn to "testify against ourselves, against our feelings." This process intervenes in the affective scripts that have taught women "to suspect what is deepest in ourselves," "to reject what is most creative."[14] To create the potential for trusting feeling, Lorde expresses her vulnerability in the world. It is the scene of something collective, allowing a "whole story" to vibrate within her "individual concern."[15] Where "people learn to distrust everything in themselves that has not been sanctioned, to reject what is most creative in themselves to begin with," minority subjects learn to distrust feeling as part of their subordination.[16] *Sister Outsider* raises consciousness not as a means to transcendence but as an embodied, creative practice of making available new relations of "self on self," as described in Foucault's ethics.[17]

The suspicion of feeling runs deep in Western epistemology and is particularly evident in the way in which, as a presence, the absence of feeling secures the disembodied abstraction of rational thought. In the closeted structure of knowledge, Lorde uses language to bring feelings into the open and recatalog social harm. Poetry is the most powerful form of language because the poetic voice is closest to feeling. Somewhere in the

poem's "emotional sentence" is the feeling, "the vital piece of information."[18] The creativity of writing a poem is an erotic act of breaking language into forms that register historical experience. By functioning as a
testimony of feeling to witness, poetry becomes a critical strategy for survival; it forges relations where elsewhere there were none.

The erotic nurtures "all our deepest knowledge." It expresses becoming;
it is a force that exists on the cusp of our arrival into ourselves, into speech,
into reciprocity: "[it] is a measure between the beginnings of our sense
of self and the chaos of our strongest feelings."[19] The testimonial of feminist thought allows self-reflexive subjects to engage the measure between
self and feeling. Feminist theory gathers agency where we sense it in the
loss of feeling, in the loss of self, at the edges of "the leprosy of egotism."[20]
The feminist agency of *Sister Outsider* is authorial in the sense that Lorde
risks herself through writing. By describing the erotic as "the power which
comes from sharing deeply any pursuit with another person," she states
that the truth of feeling lies in the collective. The erotic "is not a question
only of what we do; it is a question of how acutely and fully we can feel in
the doing."[21] The singular act of witnessing partial truths is made possible
by the erotic—the inexplicable connection to others we feel when we feel
something deeply.

THE SUBJECT OF FEMINIST DIFFERENCE

To become a subject of difference feminism, one must become a subject
of the emotional labor of difference, which means one must experience
firsthand the difference of being a person of color, being a lesbian, being
displaced. Lorde writes, "The erotic cannot be felt secondhand. As a Black
lesbian feminist, I have a particular feeling, knowledge, and understanding
for those sisters with whom I have danced hard, played, or even fought. This
deep participation has often been the forerunner for joint concerted actions
not possible before."[22] Her call for firsthand knowledge is not a foundational
clarion that equates ontological categories with knowledge or subjectivity.
Rather, firsthand knowledge privileges the erotic as the indeterminable connection between subjects of knowledge who are also subjects of difference:
"Difference is that raw and powerful connection from which our personal
power is forged."[23] Lorde does not ground her feminist politics on empathy with others but on working through the reproduction of hierarchies of

difference in how we *feel as*. Witnessing how feelings mark her as different—
as black, *as* lesbian, *as* feminist—she relates feelings with their social origins.
The feeling of anger—"the anger of exclusion, of unquestioned privilege, of
racial distortions, of silence, ill-use, stereotyping, defensiveness, misnaming,
betrayal, and co-optation"—is evaluative from a standpoint of difference.[24]
The rational norm of academic knowledge turns the emotional labor that
difference entails from a site of action into an object of knowledge.

Feminist theorists frame Lorde in ways that emphasize her experience of
difference. Katy King claims that "Audre Lorde's formulations of difference
have been particularly powerful in . . . [the] theoretical/practical elabora-
tion" of the race and class critique of white feminism.[25] Further acknowledgments include Donna Haraway's account of "oppositional consciousness,"
Teresa de Lauretis's description of the "shift in feminist consciousness," and
Rosi Braidotti's outline of the challenge presented to the whiteness of feminism by "ethnic and colonial thinkers."[26] In theorizations of identity they
position Lorde's writing as "multiple," "partial," "nomadic," and "intersec-
tional," notions that do not in themselves dislodge the norm of white subjectivity from the feminist subject. Rather, they point to the narrative framing
of difference feminism as a white Western feminist response to feminists of
color. From the standpoint of whiteness such framing marks difference as
a self-reflexive turn that is also a mode of incorporation. Suki Ali observes
how the narrative of feminism as "(homogeneous) white, middle-class and
Western women who are out to define the world" erases or reduces "the
writings of women of colour . . . to the role of critiquing the central emergent field."[27] Expressions of feeling by feminists of color are sanctioned
because they are different from the norm of whiteness figured by the academic subject of knowledge. This allows the norm, particularly as it is taken
up by white feminists, to go unchallenged. In the context of tacit whiteness
Lorde's voice is prone to appropriation as the voice of a black feminist.

The framing of difference as a demand placed on feminism and as feminism's demand appropriates the emotional labor undertaken by feminists
of color. The emotional labor of black feminists informs the critical capacity
of the "cultural politics of emotion," the "margin as a space of radical openness," and the "transformation of silence into language and action."[28] The
conditions of discursive reciprocity in a feminist academy with a mandate to
address its whiteness identify Lorde's expression of feeling as a black feminist.
Citing her expression of feeling *as* a feminist of color reassociates emotion

with black women, as seen in figures such as the "mammy" and the "angry black women."[29] In turn, the emotional labor of white scholars enters into a relation of exchange with the emotional labor of feminists of color without necessarily avowing the conditions of racial inequality that structure such an exchange.[30] The critical feelings of black feminist scholars risk being used to secure the emotional neutrality of the white feminist voice.

THE FEMINIST SUBJECT OF ACADEMIC HIERARCHY

By addressing her feelings as the properties of racist discourse, Lorde expresses the idea that feeling does not distinguish between the autobiographical and the structural. The structural aspect of critical feeling, which she relates partly through her discussion of the limitations of the feminist movement, is pertinent to academic hierarchy. Her discussion of silence resonates with my experience as someone seeking to become a feminist academic because both of our silences are conditions of being subordinated within an institution that has the power to narrate our value as subjects of knowledge.

Critiques of the subject of Western knowledge in feminist epistemology largely discuss identity outside the day-to-day realities of the university. Yet the intersection of class, race, gender, and sexuality affects who has to work harder to participate, find ways to speak, and be heard.[31] The minutiae of university hierarchy self-organizes through the interpersonal register of friendship that occludes the operation of identity (whiteness, masculinity, heterosexuality) in legitimizing knowledge.[32] Academic hierarchy is particularly fraught because its subjects exercise oppositional, nepotistic power but represent this power as meritocratic (racially, sexually neutral). Within the liberal sensibility of bourgeois culture and its antidiscrimination laws, speaking about relations of power is a demand for accountability, which may make speaking before the failure of accountability a harrowing experience.

According to Lorde, we as women are "attempting to examine and to alter all the repressive conditions of our lives."[33] By ensuring that to speak about resistance is always to speak from a position of privilege, the university obscures its repressive conditions. Academics are trained to know that, even if they are not empowered, they must speak as if they are. Academics who have "betrayed" themselves into "small silences," who are planning "some day to speak" or are waiting "for someone else's words," can use this undisclosed hypocrisy to their advantage, to overlook the disposition of others.[34] Because "we have been socialized to respect fear more than our own needs for language and definition," speaking takes courage. "Any discussion among women about racism must include the recognition and the use of anger. This discussion must be direct and creative because it is crucial."[35] But courage is not a quality in which academics are trained. Rather, academic subjection disciplines its subjects to defer to authority in every aspect of their intellectual enterprise and to fear authority as an expression of one's own fear of inadequacy. Precarious employment erodes the possibility for confident intellectual autonomy. Lorde's claim that "the master's tools will never dismantle the master's house" is very real in an environment in which we are invested in feminist academic spaces that provide the conditions of our own undoing.[36]

Criticism of the subject of contemporary feminism tends to turn away from the relations of power that subjugate the feminist academic within the academy.[37] The idea that fairness and transparency are not only academic norms but also uniquely important to feminist academia creates a paradox. Feminist academic subjectivity cannot reconcile the normative demand to acquiesce to power with the meaning of feminism as a collective concern for "teaching and professional/institutional relations of power, knowledge, and expertise."[38] Speaking forces alliance; it singularizes academic voice into *mine* and *yours*. Thus, universities exercise power while retaining forces that disappear from accountability. The hypocrisy of exercising the very relations of power that one also critiques is linked to the hypocrisy of white feminism that Lorde identifies in "The Uses of Anger: Women Responding to Racism" and "Age, Race, Class, and Sex: Women Redefining Difference."[39] We participate in the silence that cloaks the abuses of power that we witness. *Sister Outsider* is an allegory for a politics that is not possible and makes us feel close to a form of resistance we do not have.

THE FEMINIST SUBJECT OF NEOLIBERAL INDIVIDUALISM

In *The Managed Heart: The Commercialization of Human Feeling*, Arlie Russell Hochschild claims that performing emotion as a professional obligation disrupts employees' feelings. She explains that the subjection of employees through the subjugation of their emotions disrupts their sense of self; the "signal function" of emotion is "impaired when the private management of feeling is socially engineered and transformed into emotional labor for a wage."[40] More recently, the Marxist critique of emotional labor has developed in the study of cognitive labor, defined as "capacities for relationships, emotional aspects, linguistic aspects, [and the] propensity for care."[41] Second Wave feminists could not have anticipated the extent to which the *"baggage of female experience"* would render the social precariousness of cognitive labor structurally and quintessentially feminine.[42]

The emotional labor of feminist academic subjectivity is not limited to what is immediately recognizable as exchange for a wage. It is also normative.[43] For instance, fear of failure or paranoid thinking can overdetermine the senses. These critical registers of feeling ("what will others think?") engender a fear of others—states of solitude that revive and intensify lonely affects. A culture of emotional labor as the performance of emotional norms thwarts the ways in which feelings might be felt, making it difficult to recognize how we feel and who we are and thus how we want to be in relation to one another. This confusion of senses and self vibrates with the self-estrangement that Lorde describes as the consequence of living in a society that objectifies feeling.

In "Uses of the Erotic: The Erotic as Power," Lorde contrasts the deep feeling of the erotic with the "plasticised sensation" of pornography.[44] She critiques porn as a field of representation that grafts power onto bodies by shaping their unfeeling. This "instrumentalisation of feeling is a direct denial of the power of the erotic, for it represents the suppression of true feeling."[45] The pornification of feeling through sensation implicates a wider cultural campaign of misinformation about the social relations that feeling expresses. Practices of feminist academic enunciation riff the tension between the erotic and the pornographic, reengaging and estranging the subject in her feeling.[46]

In the neoliberal university, Lorde's critical feelings chime with the articulation of a feminist double consciousness. Feminist scholarship has a rank, value, and market situated in "relations between transformations in capitalism, new forms of governmentality and psychological experiences of working in the university."[47] This commodification hollows out the radical status of feminism as a necessarily social, cultural, epistemological, and political project, entangling feminism with the paternalism, exploitation,

SARAH CEFAI

nepotism, and cultural imperialism both facilitated and denied in adminis-
trative systems. As Lorde wrote:

> The principle horror of any such system which defines the good in terms
> of profit rather than in terms of human need . . . is that it robs our work
> of its erotic value, its erotic power and life appeal and fulfillment. Such
> a system reduces work to a travesty of necessities, a duty by which we
> earn bread or oblivion for ourselves and those we love. But this is tan-
> tamount to blinding a painter and then telling her to improve her work,
> and to enjoy the act of painting. It is not only next to impossible, it is also
> profoundly cruel.[48]

Erotic value is removed from Western knowledge through the epistemological separation of the science of sexuality from the erotic arts to enable
the biopolitical production of "sex."[49] This instrumental stance toward
feeling creates regard for "spontaneous feeling" as "sacred and precious."[50]
Feminist and queer philosophies have both questioned and restored erotic
value to knowledge.

In his discussion of post-democratic culture, Jeremy Gilbert claims that
expressing "at the level of pure desire . . . primarily a positive force, a collective potential for creative expression," popular cultures are also "incredibly limited, captured, commodified and territorialised almost at the point
of their emergence by the machinery of capital, commodity and state."[51]
Such an observation is pertinent to contemporary academic culture as an
enormous positive force territorialized at its point of emergence. This char-
acterization pertains even more specifically to feminist knowledge. The
erotic of feminism, its joy, is a specific target of what Deleuze has termed
"societies of control."[52] As Gilbert explains, "[for] capital, uncommodified
collective creativity is always dangerous, and the point of managerialist bureaucratisation is precisely to inhibit it, to destabilise it, to ensnare
it." He continues: "The very purpose of managerialist bureaucracy is to
frustrate the expression of that creative potential for collaboration which,
according to Deleuze . . . is the very stuff of joy . . . The expression of this
joy, of this positive desire and potential for connectivity, is also the very
stuff of revolution, and of democracy as such."[53] Feminist critical feelings
are histories of the present of feminist feeling, expressing such histories'
potential for collective action.

In *Sister Outsider*, Lorde asks us to consider "how the sensual locations of political marginality might provide an unpredicted energy for

reconfiguring power, identity, and collective knowledge."[54] In the academy, such collective action appears as a "cluster of promises," the "cruel optimism" that keeps us facing a feminist horizon.[55] The failure of the feminist academy to fulfill the promises of feminist epistemology quashes the joy of thinking and burdens the individual with unrealized collectivity. The distinction between spontaneous and instrumental feeling is ground down in the transformation from disciplinary society to societies of control. The erotic value of feminist knowledge must now be reinterpreted as a commodification of feeling by an academy that is precisely and contradictorily fearful of feeling's effects.

Cognitive capitalism extracts labor value from emotional relations but only recognizes labor output in the register of the economic.[56] Work for profit is the blindfold that blinds the painter and then requests her to paint. But it is also the act of painting. Work is part of what Cristina Morini calls "active life": "To bring into play emotions, sentiments, the whole of one's life outside work as well as territorial and social networks means, in fact, to make the whole person productive."[57] The academy extracts labor value from the emotional labor of difference while also allowing feminist discourse to disseminate "the capacity for humans to tend towards modification and their way of existing and *feeling* the world."[58] Importantly, the modes of feeling and existence that proliferate in published feminist discourse specifically omit the minor modes of suffering that thrive in active life as a consequence of academic labor.

The extraction of labor value is a condition of maintaining this distinction between what is said and what is not; it sustains the contradiction of feminist academic subjectivity in the neoliberal university. In active life and in print I would like to see the joy that we feel in doing feminist scholarship together. This is the joy in the writing of Audre Lorde. And it comes, as she tells us, only through articulation of the anger and pain and fear that rattles and clamors, that shackles and shakes us, that muffles and breaks our voices into our own. *Sister Outsider* holds out this promise of joy while drawing attention to the extent to which it has already been lost. An intensive engagement with Lorde's critical feelings registers something of this promise—the potential and positivity of her feminism, witnessed as past and passing, and as a promise then, that still is.

Notes

1. Meaghan Morris, *The Pirate's Finance Fiancée: Feminism, Reading, Postmodernism* (London: Verso, 1988).
2. For example, see Diane Elam and Robyn Wiegman, *Feminism beside Itself* (New York: Routledge, 1995).
3. Gilles Deleuze and Felix Guattari, *Kafka: Toward a Minor Literature,* trans. Dana Polan (Minneapolis: University of Minnesota Press, 1986), 16–27, 17.
4. Lauren Berlant, "'68, or something," *Critical Enquiry* 21, no. 1 (1994): 133.
5. Audre Lorde, *Sister Outsider: Essays and Speeches* (Berkeley, Calif.: Crossing Press, 1984), 58.
6. Lauren Berlant, *Cruel Optimism* (Durham, N.C.: Duke University Press, 2011), 3.
7. See also ibid.
8. "There isn't a subject; *there are only collective assemblages of enunciation,* and literature expresses these acts insofar as they're not imposed from without and insofar as they exist only as diabolical powers to come or revolutionary forces to be constructed" (Deleuze and Guattari, *Kafka,* 18).
9. Ibid., 20.
10. Lorde, *Sister Outsider,* 40.
11. Ibid., 43.
12. Ibid., 41, 42.
13. Michel Foucault, *The History of Sexuality,* vol. 1, *The Will to Knowledge,* trans. Robert Hurley (New York: Penguin, 1998).
14. Lorde, *Sister Outsider,* 102.
15. Deleuze and Guattari, *Kafka,* 17.
16. Lorde, *Sister Outsider,* 102.
17. Michel Foucault, *The History of Sexuality,* vol. 3, *The Care of the Self,* trans. Robert Hurley (New York: Penguin, 1990).
18. Lorde, *Sister Outsider,* 58, 82.
19. Ibid., 56.
20. T. Minh-ha Trinh, *Woman, Native, Other: Writing Postcoloniality and Feminism* (Bloomington: Indiana University Press, 1989).
21. Lorde, *Sister Outsider,* 56, 54.
22. Ibid., 59.
23. Ibid., 112.
24. Ibid., 124.
25. Katy King, "Audre Lorde's Lacquered Layerings: The Lesbian Bar as a Site of Literary Production," *Cultural Studies* 2, no. 3 (1988): 324.
26. Donna Haraway, *Simians, Cyborgs, and Women: The Reinvention of Nature* (New York: Routledge, 1991), 155; Teresa de Lauretis, *Technologies of Gender: Essays on Theory, Film, and Fiction* (Bloomington: Indiana University Press, 1987), 10–11; Rosi Braidotti, *Nomadic Subjects: Embodiment and Sexual Difference in Contemporary Feminist Theory* (New York: Columbia University Press, 1994), 147.
27. Suki Ali, "Introduction: Feminist and Postcolonial: Challenging Knowledge," *Ethnic and Racial Studies* 30, no. 2 (2007): 194.
28. Sara Ahmed, *The Cultural Politics of Emotion* (Edinburgh: Edinburgh University Press, 2004); bell hooks, "Choosing the Margin as a Space of Radical Openness," in *Women, Knowledge, and Reality: Explorations in Feminist Philosophy,* ed. Ann Garry and Marilyn Pearsall (New York: Routledge, 1996), 48–55; Gloria Anzaldúa,

Borderlands: The New Mestiza, La Frontera (San Francisco: Aunt Lute Books, 2007); Lorde, *Sister Outsider*, 40.

29. Kimberly Wallace-Sanders, *Mammy: A Century of Race, Gender, and Southern Memory* (Ann Arbor: University of Michigan, 2008); Sara Ahmed, *The Promise of Happiness* (Durham, N.C.: Duke University Press, 2010).

30. This critique extends more broadly to scholarship that benefits from but does not fully consider the conditions of academic knowledge production altered by black feminist thought. See Sue Campbell, "Being Dismissed: The Politics of Emotional Expression," *Hypatia* 9, no. 3 (1994): 46–64; Marilyn Frye, "The Possibility of Feminist Theory," in *Feminist Philosophy*, 34–47; and Elizabeth Spellman, "Anger and Insubordination," in *Feminist Philosophy*, 263–73.

31. Cherie Moraga and Gloria Anzaldúa, eds., *This Bridge Called My Back: Writings by Radical Women of Color* (New York: Kitchen Table Press, 1983).

32. This claim is based on experience in the Australian academy, where I gained my Ph.D.

33. Lorde, *Sister Outsider*, 128.

34. Ibid., 41.

35. Ibid., 44, 128.

36. Ibid., 110–13.

37. Rosalind Gill, "Breaking the Silence: The Hidden Injuries of Neoliberal Academia," in *Secrecy and Silence in the Research Process: Feminist Reflections*, ed. Róisín Ryan-Flood and Ros Gill (New York: Routledge, 2009), 228–44.

38. Berlant, "'68 or something," 125.

39. Lorde, *Sister Outsider*, 124–33, 114–23.

40. Arlie Russell Hochschild, *The Managed Heart: The Commercialization of Human Feeling* (Los Angeles: University of California Press, 1983), x.

41. Christina Morini, "The Feminization of Labour in Cognitive Capitalism," *Feminist Review* 87 (2007): 42.

42. Morini, "Feminization," 42.

43. "Performing and being recognized as emotionally authentic is just as important to the modern sense of being someone as understanding one's sexual identity is" (Lauren Berlant, "Starved," in *After Sex? On Writing Since Queer Theory*, ed. Janet Halley and Andrew Parker [Durham, D.C.: Duke University Press, 2011], 82).

44. Lorde, *Sister Outsider*, 53–59.

45. Hochschild, *Managed Heart*, 54.

46. Teresa Brennan, *The Transmission of Affect* (Ithaca: Cornell University Press, 2004).

47. Gill, "Breaking," 231.

48. Lorde, *Sister Outsider*, 54.

49. Foucault, *The History of Sexuality*, vol. 1.

50. Hochschild, *Managed Heart*, 22.

51. Jeremy Gilbert, "Moving On from the Market Society: Culture (and Cultural Studies) in a Post-Democratic Age," *opendemocracy.net*, July 13, 2012, www.opendemocracy.net.

52. Gilles Deleuze, *Negotiations, 1972–1990* (New York: Columbia University Press, 1990).

53. Gilbert, "Moving."

54. Berlant, "'68 or something," 133.

55. Berlant, *Cruel Optimism*, 24.

56. Morini, "Feminization," 40.

57. Ibid., 46.

58. Ibid., 45.

16
Audre Lorde and What Remains

CHANTAL OAKES

My head is a museum full of other peoples' eyes.
Audre Lorde, *A Birthday Memorial to Seventh Street*

As a woman of African descent living in northwest England, surrounded by the crumbling red-brick remnants of British industrial cotton manufacturing, their chimneys higher than church spires, I know that the value of African American literature and its effect on my generation of Black British intellectuals and artists cannot be underestimated. Despite cable television, multimedia platforms, and globalized communication, the availability of twentieth-century literature means that a place remains for the contextualized discourse of women from the African diaspora. I am an artist living among the pervasive stereotypical and shallow media visualization of peoples of African descent, whose lives are often depicted as influentially disruptive. Writings such as Audre Lorde's have given me the cultural tools I need to piece together a base on which to build a more sustainable foundation.

Historically, literature from the Caribbean has shaped the cultural conversations of women of African descent who live in Britain. In 1831, a Bermudian, Mary Prince, published a slim autobiography only forty-one pages long. *The History of Mary Prince* added fuel to the fire of the antislavery and abolition movements in Britain. Two decades later, in 1857, legitimate colonial enslavement had ended, and Jamaican Mary Seacole had published her own autobiography. *The Wonderful Adventures of Mrs. Seacole in Many Lands* is a vivid account of her experiences, and like Prince's, it was influential. Both books supported and developed a political redefinition of

Britishness that incorporated antislavery and shifted the nation's self-image toward cultural liberalism. By the mid-1900s, the voices of colonial European women, the English Creoles, were dominating the dialogue, crowding out the black women who had made space for critical discourse with British culture. Therefore, after 1940, a sizable first generation of creative black women living in Britain sought a reflection of themselves and their lives in the culture of the Caribbean.

Of all the black women authors who have used biographical fiction in their writing, Audre Lorde was one of the first to engage with postmodernism—not the "end of history" postmodernism typified by theorists such as Fredric Jameson and Jean Baudrillard but as a new presentation of biographical memory. In *Zami: A New Spelling of My Name* (1982), she produced what may have been the first example of African diasporic metafiction for women. *Zami* examined black women's histories from a contemporary artistic perspective, and its structure was biomythography—that is, a biographical text shaped by the drives of radical communities existing outside of mainstream consciousness, as black women mostly do, in both Britain and America.

According to Judith Butler, "the body *is* a historical situation."[1] Her comment goes beyond notions of power and economic wealth; for artists it also affects how we see and what we are encouraged "to see." Western cultures are highly visual, with a sophisticated framework for reading media that now verges on cynicism. Contemporary audiences distrust the mono-eye of the camera, for instance. The camera is a politicized tool that contains neither magic nor realism; instead it is a mediated concealment and highly influential in how women of African descent are seen and unseen. Black women characters in contemporary American television presentations are more likely than white women to use profanity, be physically violent, and therefore be more likely to be physically restrained, promoting the notion that black women are somehow morally inferior. Likewise, women of African descent are 75 percent less likely than white women to be shown as sexual and six times less likely to get an onscreen hug or kiss.[2]

In my work with a small group of black women artists, we appropriated the biomythographic form for our installation performance *The Queen and Mr Wooton*, a site-specific art piece for the Merseyside Maritime Museum in Liverpool. We were determined to show the fallacy of visual presumptions by using our character to express what the Portuguese call *saudade*—a

CHANTAL OAKES

strong and intimate feeling for "a presence," which is evoked through memory. The museum commissioned the project to commemorate the bicentenary of the abolition of the slave trades, and the performance was scheduled to take place during a weekend of events at the museum's Anthony Walker Lecture Theatre. Although our proposal for the project included predictable mentions of the sorrow and triumph of the African struggle, we had no intention of keeping to that brief. Commemoration, we decided, is for all the survivors.

The museum is located in a gigantic renovated brick warehouse beside the Albert Dock, part of Liverpool's once thriving waterfront. Liverpool played a huge part in the slave trades, which helped to finance the city's development and made its port for some time the second largest in the world. Perhaps it was inevitable Liverpool's political leaders voted against the Abolition Act. That moment in history, however, still resonates in the city's culture. Liverpool continues to be highly segregated: it is uncommon to see people of African descent in the city center, even though Liverpool is home to one of Britain's oldest African communities. (Its members were originally from Somalia.) It is the only city in the region with a long history of murderous antiblack protests, and this is why the African American experience and the biomythographic framework became key to the realization of our project.

Despite the city's Somali links, the museum wanted to focus exclusively on exploring the plight of Africans on British ships bound for the Caribbean and the Americas. Our proposal fit that parameter. Our plan was to reenact the story of Charles Wooton, a mariner from the Caribbean who, in the midst of an antiblack riot in Liverpool in 1919, was chased down to the dock by more than three hundred white men—Swedish, Irish, and English dock workers and mariners.[3] After he jumped into the water to escape, the mob stoned him to death. But instead of making Wooton our central character, we chose to visualize his murder through a fictional character, his partner and survivor.

Although Wooton may well have had a partner, her comments and reactions were not recorded. Thus, we had to invent her. The incident took place in 1919 during the silent movie era, so we trawled through film media of the time to find references to black women. To begin to build this fictional character, we needed to discover how black women of the era acted and spoke through the visual. Yet even though Britain was at the forefront of early filmmaking, and we did learn how to make a film that would look as if had been produced in 1914, we found no visual references to black women.

Undeterred, we went to the dock to take some photographs and to get a physical sense of the place. Pockets of the architectural layout remain unchanged, and being in the place made it easier for us to imagine the context of our character's life. During our first visit, Maria Paul, the actor who would play our character, convinced a security guard to show us around an old empty warehouse; and the next day we convened again at the dock, this time equipped with torches. In the hundred years since the Wooton incident, few if any black men have worked on the Liverpool waterfront. Because the security guard was a man, Maria decided to bring along a male friend. Even though he had lived in Liverpool all his life, he was among the first black men in years to explore these huge crumbling dockside buildings, their broken windows open to the wild sea air. Inside, we walked over rubble and a clutter of old plastic wrappings and descended a flight of stairs to the first level below ground. The warehouse ran under us for another two or three levels to the water's edge (now flooded by rainwater) and up six or more low-ceilinged levels that offered views across the harbor into the Irish Sea. The guard's friends shouted jokes through the broken windows that sat just below ground-floor level, windows that threw no light into the cavernous space, but we were invisible to them and the jokes quickly ended.

Each chamber of the warehouse was larger than a football pitch. With his torch, the guard pointed out the huge, heavy, rusted metal rings on the concave wall of each bay. He told us, in a hushed voice, that these were for chaining enslaved Africans. Some in our group were tempted to believe him, but I already knew that the rings were, in fact, resting tethers for the horses and mules that had pulled trolleys of goods through the warehouse. However, before I could share my thoughts, the guard had changed the subject. Unexpectedly, he told us that he came into the buildings regularly to take photographs of ghostly beings, and he showed us some pictures on his digital camera. Before we knew it, we found we had agreed to switch off our torches for a moment so that he could take some more shots into the blackness. "There is one," he said, and we gathered around to look at the square of luminous screen that was not even powerful enough to light his face. We saw tiny flecks of brilliant light in the blackness, iridescence

CHANTAL OAKES

emitted by the wings of flying creatures. I did not speak; I was already smarting from my sense of failure at being unable to contradict his story about the tethering stations—a story, I worried, that Maria's friend would retell.

Perhaps sensing our ambiguity about his photography project, the guard swiftly changed tack, showing us a photograph on the camera in which he was posing with one of the Cheeky Girls, a picture taken while he was on holiday somewhere sunny.[4] When we switched our torches back on, we saw that he looked a lot happier in that photo than he did now. We made a general decision to go upstairs into the light of day and take some publicity photographs. By doing this, we missed the chance to ask him what he knew about the reality of Liverpool's part in the slave trade, what stories he had been told by his fathers and their fathers, and why he was seeking out ghosts in these old buildings. We did invite him to come and see the performance, but we already knew that he would not be there.

We also knew that the museum's commissioning committee, curators, and regular visitors as well as newspaper reporters would probably not be there. This left us free to create what we wanted, yet our freedom meant that we had a great amount of responsibility. According to Butler, gender is an "identity instituted through a *stylized repetition of acts,*" a "constructed identity, a performative accomplishment which the mundane social audience, including the actors themselves, come to believe and to perform in the mode of belief."[5] But, what if that construct is hollow: an imposition visually reenacted rather than a ritual agreed to at *any* stage? What if we have come to believe, for instance, that because we see black women being angry in performance, they are therefore only believable in performance when they are angry?

The biomythographic framework is an expression of the complexities that confound these varieties of expectations, and we needed support for our thinking because we were going to perform something that had never been enacted in Liverpool: the displayed physicality of our character's memories. Black people are aware of a gaze laden with notions of otherness whose constant repetitions interfere with life chances and even health. Yet a black actor must find ways to survive being herself, as she really is, while being looked at. This is the only way to give any performance believability. We discovered that the film we had made, which explored a character and her reactions to the news of how her partner had died, was not enough. Though we had spliced archival footage into original material, constructed a soundtrack, and tinted the film to match films of the era, it was only when we placed the actor in front of the screen that the art installation began to live.

The knowledge that we and the actor used and placed inside the biomythographic framework was an aggregate of other practical research we had undertaken during issue-led creative projects with various local communities of African descent. During the performance, the actor spent most of her time cleaning the numerous items that surrounded her, while the film played in the background. As with all performed material, the performance exuded a sense of reportage: the act of looking is culturally driven, with implications for both textual description and notions of the relationship between audience and actor in performance. When women of African descent entered European consciousness, and when they became half of the African diaspora, their metaphoric and physical site was the Caribbean, rather than Plymouth Rock or the Liverpool docks. From this position our character's cleaning actions, which Western medicine might diagnose as obsessive compulsive disorder, become part of a psychic or spiritual cleansing ritual.

The following appeared on the installation's publicity:

> THE QUEEN AND MR WOOTON
> *An installation performance exploring the dilemma—*
> *what would you do in retaliation to racial violence?*
> Using a historical incident to engage with you in this debate,
> we find Cecelia Wooton has three of the rocks that killed
> her partner—What do you think she should do with them?[6]

More recently, a 2005 act of racial terrorism—random in nature, ugly in method—has deeply affected the black women and men of Liverpool. Anthony Walker was killed by two young white men, cousins, who drove an ax into his head as he accompanied his white girlfriend to a bus stop. He bled to death before help could arrive. This time, the law (unable to arrest even one person out of the three hundred or more who had attacked Charles Wooton) found and convicted the murderers and then convicted three more who had helped them evade justice. Walker's mother has said she needed to find forgiveness because it was hate that had killed her son. His girlfriend refused that option. Because she felt that he was still a part of her life, she texted him on the day the two men were convicted. It seemed the natural thing to do, she said.

Art is not made without a context. It needs appropriate examples of how others have dealt with similar historical and contemporary issues and seeks work that demonstrates how to critically question cultural meanings and actions while acknowledging that valuing experiences includes knowing what molds them. In this way, the biomythographic framework, long after Audre Lorde's influence first reached the Black British avant-garde, continues to encourage black women artists to explore, define, and understand our history as something more complex than a countercultural force.

Notes

1. Judith Butler, "Performance Acts and Gender Constitution: An Essay in Phenomenology and Feminist Theory," *Theatre Journal* 40, no. 4 (1988): 519–20. The italics are mine.
2. Robert M. Entman and Andrew Rojeck, *The Black Image in the White Mind: Media and Race in America* (Chicago: University of Chicago Press, 2000), 240.
3. *What Remains* is the film shown within the installation performance titled *The Queen and Mr Wooton* (www.afro-culture.com/wooton.html). Audio was taken from Mark Christian's lecture at the Merseyside Maritime Museum, Liverpool, November 14, 2007 (www.liverpoolmuseums.org.uk/podcasts).
4. The Cheeky Girls is a pair of twins originally from Romania, now living in Britain, whose 2002 hit, "The Cheeky Song (Touch My Bum)," was written by their mother.
5. Butler, "Performative Acts," 520. The italics are mine.
6. This text also appears in a slightly revised form on the artist's website (www.afro-culture.com).

17
The Cicadas of Courage
Let Us Perform Audre Lorde

CHRISTIANA LAMBRINIDIS

In the academy, we all live in conceptual worlds that become corporeal or tangible by means of the scholarship we produce and participate in. How does a Hellenic playwright teach an African American poet? How does Socrates inspire a feminist seminar on translation? Why is theater important as a paradigm that cocreates contexts within which time ceases to be conceptual and truth is discernible through multiple and simultaneous perceptions of a city? In my scholarship and thought about Audre Lorde, I have sought to establish a connection among inspiration, empowerment, and the triumph over prejudice through creative writing and translation. What follows here is a parable, in the classic Socratic tradition, which narrates how we can enlighten canons by hosting pedagogical paradigms between the Hellenic and the African American.

What if the Muses did not inhabit ethereal memory but descended to the earth to mobilize women into a rebellion against voicelessness? What if a black poet of Caribbean descent met them and took it on herself to change the song of the cicadas—not surveillance of obedience but instruction for empowerment? What if language were theater and within its chthonic auditorium time acquired race, gender, and class? Questions demand answers, and answers can be given as parables.

The asphalt is rising to eye level. High temperatures cause audible noises. The soles of shoes shriek, and shadow begets frantic hunts. The hill is steep, built to the rim with apartments that see with blind eyes, eyes that never will be like Teiresias'.[1] Down the hill, under a plane tree, a philosopher walks accompanied and befriended. His gait is quick, his knowledge vivacious. The riverbed is hospitable, the day accepting. Up the hill there is no repose. Down the hill, the fragrance of fresh leaves envelopes the passerby, lulls the afternoon. The stones along the river soothe the feet. A venerable alliance exists between water and flesh. Baby frogs leap among the reeds; a few meters away, a lemon grove sighs with relief. The cicadas announce month and heat. The omnipotence of weather formulates conditions, but the philosophic parables seem inaudible.[2]

Up the hill, geopolitics have perched in a seminar room built to replace the neglect of the parables—better, to create new ones that may transliterate the sagacious song of the cicadas. Noise is noise. Philosophy is reiterated, transposed, viewed differently. Ambience is achieved through natural light and the comfortable executive furniture of a postwar era. Cultural institutions rush to new eras, new walks, new solidarity. The pedagogue is indigenous yet educated in the halls of Ivy League schools. She has proposed a reinvention of an Athenian seminar for inhabitants of up the hill and down. Under her laureled achievements, much respected by the Athenians, she will provide new respite. There will be no need for nostalgic musings about the river Ilissos and its archaic endeavors.[3] Geopolitics through culture are efficient, speedy, transformative, everlasting.

Two mornings a week, three hours at a time, translators and translators-to-be congregate to search for ways or alternatives to themselves and each other. Athens is brimming with transitions in the arts, in academia, in politics. Yet the writing of women threatens the publishing houses, threatens even the writers themselves if they happen to be women—as if the modern version of the cicadas' relentless song is not irrelevant but hidden inside words; as if the ceaselessly expected and revered Muses will abandon their humanistic surveillance if women are found to be their followers. Feminism may be a basis for activist consciousness, but it is not the basis for the Hellenic intellectual and artistic world of the early 1990s. The seminar assumes a mediating position, and what is not visible, audible, acceptable, speakable is hosted in the realms of translation.

Within the seminar we learn not to be afraid of women because we are women. Feminist pedagogical practices are engaged, and identity is discussed, practiced, and understood as a self-defining topos. We come from

Greek and go to American English. Some of us were raised in English. Most of us learned foreign languages in schools outside our bloodlines. We read a lot, we love literature, and we want to learn from each other and our experiences, from text and its practices, from writers and their métiers. To do so, we reinvent translation as an emancipating force that enables us to become actors, directors, and devisers of change—first our own. The annual allocation of time can be spent with δημιουργία (*demiourgia*)—consciousness, intellect, and literary activism.

Although the hosting cultural institution presses for an analytical curriculum, as the pedagogue, I discuss the benefits of an improvisational approach to learning and practice. Because of the excellent results achieved during the previous year, I am temporarily left to my own devices. I give the students an experiential writing assignment that will eventually link the class to the democratization of thought and practice that Audre Lorde's work stands for. I say, "Find an object that solidifies your own relationship with the mother tongue. Bring it to class and translate your own story through the found object." Now many items fill the seminar table—private, personal, revered, taken out of hiding or context. A batiste pouch is the most unexpected. The umbilical cord of a student lies in it. The student has taken it out of her mother's bedroom drawer. We are taken aback by the somatic archive. The sight is deformity, the student's action rebellious. The object-subject has been dragged out of maternal memory, brought to the collective yet almost public space of the feminist seminar. An inarticulate language asks for articulation, collective and personal; it asks for translation into a communicative form. The voicelessness of the pouch speaks a story of origins that escapes the mnemonic trace and may reconstruct the relationship between the Muse and the cicada, aided by a metaphoric marsupium—a peculiar afterlife within life. Is the birth destined to be ruled by the mother's omnipotence? Is it a psychosocial bondage brought in to break or strengthen the oligarchy of Hellenic maternal structures?

Between inarticulate words and articulated intention, a self-narrated consciousness and a translating-self claim an exceptional theater. In the blinding light of the city, screeching players seek to define origins as insistent as the cicadas and as physical as the sun. Without a sound but with literary cymbals, Audre Lorde materializes, as writers do when readers are in need of their utterances. Defiant, celebratory of intended words, "Poetry Is Not a Luxury" makes itself known around the table. The text is distributed,

CHRISTIANA LAMBRINIDIS

and the discussion ferments: "The quality of light by which we scrutinize our lives has direct bearing upon the product which we live, and upon the changes which we hope to bring about through those lives. It is within this light that we form those ideas by which we pursue our magic and make it realized."[4]

Enter the oracular elements of the sun and envelop the teaching landscape. A sun within a sun allows for an uninhabited space. Could it be that Socrates is taken aback? The students become startled and confused about their allegiances, intellectual and national. In Greece, poetry is celebrated and accepted as divine gift, as a tradition of Homer. Can anyone become a poet? Is the poetry within us as women a secret to be shared? How can we allow the African American to undermine our position on the Hellenic, especially when the writer is not white and she is a lesbian? None of the students have identified themselves according to sexuality or race. In ancient Greece, identities were explored inwardly because race was not yet examined as a variable, because empowering scholarship about women's writing was not yet available. Now Lorde's words are a path-opening compass. Slowly the students recognize that the desire to be included in the canons of inspiration battles racial prejudice. The stumbling block is sexuality. *Lesbian* is an unforgivable word, doomed to perish outside of thought and practice. Even within a mutually accepted feminist curriculum, to study the words of a lesbian woman is not acceptable. There is so much literature to choose from; why do we have to focus on a black lesbian poet? The cicadas' song turns irascible.

Bodies and minds shut down. Crossing over has gone too far; I was expected to deviate to alternative, more expected routes. The new light within light around the seminar room has vanished, and trust has cracked audibly and cacophonously. I do not make any efforts to defend positions but distribute instead another writing exercise that will enable the students to bring themselves experientially, philosophically, to the words of the poet: "*Locate* the hiding regions of yourself within the limits of your physical body. Translate Audre Lorde, as a Hellenic translator, and trace the inmost censorship you have accepted and/or cocreated to survive systems possibly hostile to your existence." The poet's essay has called out the multilayered suppression between the self the students know they had and the one they didn't, between what was assumed to be safe and what was not, between the corporeal ramifications they possessed and the ways in which they have been led to conceptualize the ethereal ones. The students, encouraged to think for themselves in both the seminar and the literary texts, hesitantly yet gradually accept the words of the poet. Following her advice and her impetus has enabled them to feel accepted for what they can do, for how they think.

The transition from an Anglo-Saxon construct of performing, understanding, and using language—so much disputed in the prevalent socialist ethos of the day—to an African American philosophical practice of defiance and acceptance has intrigued the students and engaged their will. To liberate the spirit, one needs to exercise the mind in daily practices of empowerment. The philosophic walks by the river bank develop an alternative alertness of thought as a constant of life. What do you hear when you hear? What do you speak when you speak? We take into account the tongues of mothers, with a need, a demand almost, to articulate what insists on being articulated. Almost in whispers, which grow stronger in sound and resolution, we accept that mothers also have played a silencing role, along with fathers, aunts, uncles, sisters. What is the language you choose to use when none of the words seem willing to cooperate with you in voicing yourself? Where are the nonwords of words?

Here Audre Lorde becomes relevant, essential. In writing their own texts while translating hers, the students recognize that they are supported. They are understood and respected in their own time of writing. The essay before them clearly explains what the writer knew before they have discovered it. As they bring her words to theirs, an unexpected kinship is formed, a kinship of spirit, militancy, and compassion. It happens before fear for sexuality and race can intervene further. It happens because the reality of alliance is greater than the reality of fear.

Hellenic words are relevant to the soul and the intellect. Where are the cicadas located? Do you hear their endless song buzzing within their surveilling connection to the Muses? Do the cicadas stay within the theater of language; do they leave when a foreign language is at play; do they return with African American? Does Audre Lorde assume the position of the philosopher beyond her own just denunciation of "the white fathers," or does she transform into a Muse determined to change the metaphysical relationship between the conditioned surveillance performed by the cicadas on artists?[5]

CHRISTIANA LAMBRINIDIS

Language is theater: light, sound, body, memory, space, meaning.

Language keeps within it chthonic secrets between those who speak and those who do not.

Language is power: those who speak exercise it; those who do not are deprived of it.

Language is mother tongue and state tongue: performance between the two is politics.

When it is used for the benefit of the people, it presses life into remarkable achievements. When it is used against the people, it deprives hope of hope.

When you speak language, you understand language.

When you do not speak language, you find other means to understand.

POSTSCRIPT

I taught at the Professional Translation Annual Seminar, a collaboration with the Hellenic American Union in Athens, between 1991 and 1995. Writing about the experience years later has brought back memories of the women (and later men) who comprised it, some of whom still keep in touch with me. Our objective was to become proficient in translation practices and use these exact practices to fight fear and prejudice, first our own, while achieving high academic and literary goals. The seminar's graduates branched into literature, labor activism, socially conscious science, cultural diplomacy, and academic graduate degrees in comparative literature, interpretation, and translation. We gave presentations of our work at Sorbonne Nouvelle in 1993, at Aristotle University in 1993, and at the United Nations in Vienna in 1994. We engaged creative writing as a form of multileveled inquiry and contextualized the process of understanding ourselves and each other (within and beyond the boundaries of the seminar) through the triple sieve of race, gender, and class. Audre Lorde was invaluable because her work exemplified the impetus and the applied outcome of that impetus. She became a potent political tool of transformation from the personal to the collective and the collective to the personal.

Lorde's *The Cancer Journals* (sections of which seminar members translated into Greek in class) gave voice to the performance we created, "A Breast Beyond" (2003). Ten years later, I worked with a woman, Dimitra Argyriou, a creative writing student of mine, who had fought with the Communists as a partisan during the Civil War that had torn Greece apart (1945–49). Dimitra had survived a mastectomy and, at the age of seventy-five, matched her own experience to Lorde's with potent texts of her own. She showed, in the theater, how to annihilate the foe called cancer.

"Poetry Is Not a Luxury" proved to be a critical text with illiterate women at the borders of Greece, Turkey, and Bulgaria because it enabled them to physically write their stories. With them I did not discuss Lorde's sexuality. We did discuss race, not as an obstacle but as a vehicle of understanding exclusion—a reality they faced daily in their lives due to their illiteracy. Fatima Gallaire's play *Princesses* (*You Have Come Back*) brought the French-Algerian context to the Muslim minority in western Thrace during a project I facilitated about mothers and daughters at the borderlands.[6] I was able to create a bridge between Islam and Christianity, between Greeks and Turks, beginning with the reading of this play, which we translated in class and which was presented by a member of the seminar. Although the language of the play was not Turkish, its themes—coming home, the choice of a Muslim woman not to try to convert her Christian lover to Islam, her defense of that choice against the female elders of her village—engaged the women of this minority community and triggered the mutual respect that was essential to building trust and cooperation.

In 2002, along with women from the translation seminar, I founded Collective Feminist Translation Group, which continued to employ the principles of the seminar as it worked to found the first feminist publishing series in Greece.[7] The series includes books that are today widely read by women all over the country. We proved that professional training can build intellect, activism, and inspiration for creating unbiased lives beyond and within transnational boundaries of gender, race, and class. The initiative of individuals, a belief in people and their intellectual capacity for survival, surmounted the obstacles and geopolitical agendas of structures and state that are forever battling between Hellas and Greece.

CHRISTIANA LAMBRINIDIS

Notes

1. In Greek legend, Teiresias was a blind prophet from Thebes. See Sophocles, *Oedipus Rex* (any edition); and *The Greek Myths: The Complete and Definitive Edition*, ed. Robert Graves (London: Penguin, 2011).

2. "Socrates: The story is that once upon a time these creatures were men—men of an age before there were any Muses—and that when the latter came into the world, and music made its appearance, some of the people in those days were so thrilled with pleasure that they went on singing, and quite forgot to eat and drink until they actually died without noticing it. From them in due course sprang the race of cicadas, to which the Muses have granted the boon of needing no sustenance right from their birth, but of singing from the very first, without food or drink, until the day of their death, after which they go and report to the Muses how they severally are paid honor among mankind, and by whom. So for those whom they report at having honored Terpsichore in the dance they win the Muse's favor, for those that have worshiped in the rites of love the favor of Erato, and so with all the others, according to the nature of the worship paid to each. To the eldest, Calliope, and to her next sister, Urania, they tell of those who live a life of philosophy and so do honor to the music of those twain whose theme is the heavens and all the story of gods and men, and whose song is the noblest of them all" (Plato, *Phaedrus*, in *The Collected Dialogues of Plato*, ed. Edith Hamilton and Huntington Cairns, trans. R. Hackforth (Princeton: Princeton University Press, 2002), 504–5.

3. Ilissos (Ιλισσός, Ειλισσός), one of the two rivers of Athens, was considered to be sacred in antiquity. The ancient Greeks believed that the Muses lived along its banks and erected an altar in their honor (βωμός των Ιλισιάδων). A poplar tree was close to the site, which Socrates frequented with his students.

4. Audre Lorde, "Poetry Is Not a Luxury," in *The Audre Lorde Compendium* (London: Pandora, 1996), 95.

5. Ibid., 97.

6. Fatima Gallaire, *Princesses (You Have Come Back)*, trans. Jill Macdougall, in *Plays by Women: An International Anthology*, ed. Catherine Temerson and Françoise Kourilsky (New York: Ubu Repertory Theater Publications, 1988), 2:166–221. The borderland project was conducted under the auspices of the George Seferis Chair for Modern Greek Studies, Harvard University.

7. The series, whose title translates as "women's writing + theory/literature/philosophy," was published by Kochlias Editions.

18
Inscribing the Past, Anticipating the Future
Audre Lorde and the Black Women's Movement in Germany

PEGGY PIESCHE

> Poetry is not only dream and vision; it is the skeleton architecture of our lives. It lays the foundations for a future of change, a bridge across our fears of what has never been before.
>
> Audre Lorde, "Poetry Is Not a Luxury"

In 2012, when Black German women marked the twentieth anniversary of Audre Lorde's passing, we were not only commemorating her life and impact as a poet, theorist, and activist in the Black American women's and lesbian movements but were paying homage to her special connection to us and our twenty-five-year-old movement. Lorde was closely tied to the beginning of the Black lesbian women's movement in Germany, whose protagonists shared her vision of a diasporic Black activists' network beyond national borders. This connection is made clear in the 2012 anthology *"Euer Schweigen schützt euch nicht": Audre Lorde und die Schwarze Frauenbewegung in Deutschland* (which translates as *"Your Silence will not protect you": Audre Lorde and the Black Woman's Movement in Germany*).[1] The anthology collects poems, essays, interviews, short stories, and scholarly work by Lorde, Maisha Eggers, Katharina Oguntoye, May Ayim, and other contemporaries, with the goal of recapturing and contextualizing a key moment in Black political, cultural, and academic activism, one that entwined intellectual endeavor, grassroots feminism, antiracist engagement, and creative labor. The book offers a critical and appreciative perspective of Lorde's Black mobilization in Germany, activism that in the long run resulted in a transnationally connected movement. This movement worked through a collective process of self-definitions, historical documentation, and political interventions.[2]

In the mid-1980s, the two most important Black German organizations were founded: Initiative of Black Germans (ISD), now known as Initiative of Black People in Germany (1985); and Afro-German Women (ADEFRA), now known as Black Women in Germany (1986). These groups enabled or supported numerous activist conferences, events, organized protest actions, and publications, as Maisha Eggers and I have begun to document.[3] Like Lorde, whose passionate essays, poems, and speeches emphasized the power of language, the Black women's movement in Germany has been closely tied to finding a language. Lorde considered language a means of resistance. For her, speaking was a challenge to mainstream white heteronormative silence. In her pathbreaking essay "The Transformation of Silence into Language," she described the necessity of speaking out, regardless of the risks.[4] She knew about the power of self-definition and the articulation of the self. Self-definitions, such as "Black, lesbian, female, poet, theorist, mother, and activist," themselves claimed a counter-history within the culture and politics of white heteronormative silence that had denied such marginalized voices. Finding a language became a means to struggle toward a collective identity as *we*.

In 1984 Lorde was a guest professor at the John F. Kennedy Institute at Berlin's Free University. The Black lesbian women who attended her seminars and lectures formed the core group of this *we*: feminists such as Katharina Oguntoye and Katja Kinder, poets such as Nzingha Guy St. Louis and Raja Lubinetzki, activists such as Katja Kinder and Jasmin Eding, scholars such as May Ayim. Our *we* even extended beyond political borders. When Ina Röder Sissako invited Lorde to come to East Berlin, her West German brothers and sisters argued that the visit would be too risky. But Lorde said, "Of course I will come. If my Afro-German Sisters and Brothers can live there every day, I should be able to visit there for a few hours and demonstrate my connection with them."[5] After an impressive lecture before a mixed audience of Blacks, migrants, and whites, she engaged Black audience members in a special meeting so that she could learn about their lives and work in an environment marked by rightwing and neofascist attacks. She had encountered a situation in Germany that she saw as familiar and that she was also analyzing in her own work. At the same time, by interacting with Black Germans in East Berlin at a time of extreme racism, she shaped a template for Black antiracist interventions in Germany that were from the start premised on transnationalism.

In the face of society's silence and denial, the process of self-recognition, self-realization, and community building is both powerful and harrowing. Lorde repeatedly pointed out that her work required both questioning and learning. In these exhilarating and painful encounters with Black German women, she drew their challenges, insights, and questions into the context of Black diasporic discourses. The intensity of that mutual process has only recently become clear, and I hope someone will undertake a detailed research project that follows its growth. In 1986, in her foreword to *Showing Our Colors,* Lorde described how important the meetings with Black Germans had been for both her personally and the activist movement in the United States.[6] She understood that her encounters with Black women in Germany was part of a process that had allowed her to find an aspect of herself as she entered into conversation with Black communities beyond her own. Such overarching, transdiasporic experiences can be traced back not just to her own writing during the 1980s but also to the literary (knowledge) production of other Black authors—for instance, Ana Herrero Villamor, May Ayim, and Raja Lubinetzki—whose work has both reflected and anticipated a maturing Black movement and sense of identity.[7]

In 1983, when Nzingha Guy St. Louis published her first volume of poetry from the perspective of a Black lesbian (*Gedichte einer schönen Frau,* which translates as *Poems of a Pretty Woman*), her work was seen as a novelty.[8] Today, as the contributors to this book have demonstrated, Black women writers in Germany are vocal and powerful. The impressive work of Black women in Germany and Audre Lorde's transnational legacy force us to further address and investigate questions of epistemic contextualization. Yet questions remain. How can we deal with an academic archive that has mostly ignored Black literary and cultural interventions in Germany? How can we reconstruct the manifold relations between the pioneering agency of the young Black lesbian movement and other Black German communities and actors? How can we write the history of the Black lesbian movement's impact on the white German feminist movement? These are only a few of the questions that a commemoration of Lorde's influence should prompt us to ask and investigate.

Notes

1. Peggy Piesche, ed., *"Euer Schweigen schützt euch nicht": Audre Lorde und die Schwarze Frauenbewegung in Deutschland* (Berlin: Orlanda Frauenverlag, 2012).
2. Also see Katarina Oguntoye, May Ayim, and Dagmar Schultz, eds., *Farbe bekennen: Afro-deutsche Frauen auf den Spuren ihrer Geschichte* (Berlin: Orlanda Frauenverlag, 1986), translated by Anne V. Adams as *Showing Our Colors: Afro-German Women Speak Out* (Amherst: University of Massachusetts Press, 1991).
3. On the importance of Black women and lesbians within this network, see Maisha M. Eggers, "Transformationspotentiale, kreative Macht und Auseinandersetzungen mit einer kritischen Differenzperspektive: Schwarze Lesben in Deutschland," in *"Euer Schweigen schützt euch nicht,"* 85–96.
4. Audre Lorde, "The Transformation of Silence into Language and Action," in *The Audre Lorde Compendium: Essays, Speeches, and Journals* (London: Pandora, 1996), 11–15.
5. Quoted in Ina Röder Sissako, letter to Peggy Piesche, July 2012.
6. Audre Lorde, "Foreword to the English Language Edition," in Opitz et al., *Showing Our Colors,* vii–xiv.
7. See selections in Piesche, *"Euer Schweigen schützt euch nicht."*
8. Nzingha Guy St. Louis, *Gedichte einer schönen Frau* (Berlin: Lorez, 1983).

Afterword

STELLA BOLAKI AND SABINE BROECK

A project such as the one we have undertaken in this book relies on the telling of multiple histories or herstories—some private, some public—that are hard to document or have been largely overlooked in the academy. Its existence has a special fragility, and we hope that by engaging with these formerly scattered histories readers will help to consolidate their various meanings. After all, the process of archive making is, ultimately, one of meaning making. But it is also a democratic process, a way of opening up material to wider audiences, a way of starting a conversation. In the epilogue of *Zami*, Lorde describes her life as having increasingly become "a bridge and field of women," and we would like to think the same of our own collaborative journey in this book.[1] The more we learn about Lorde's transnational legacies, the more we become aware of the need to continue solidifying and sharing the impact of her life and work.

We hope this book will lead other scholars to carry out that work. In Europe, which was in many ways the starting point and predominant focus of our project, there are more contexts to explore. In Spain, for example, after "Uses of the Erotic" was translated by the queer-feminist collective Lesbianas Sin Duda in its fanzine *Non Grata* in 1997, Lorde's work spread throughout young activist groups linked to autonomous feminist and queer collectives. Carmen Romero Bachiller has explained that this pattern can be understood within the particular development of feminism in Spain. During the 1980s and 1990s, the eruption of differences between and within women was mostly discussed around the issue of sexuality; despite the discriminatory situation of the nation's Romani people, "it was not [until] . . . the turn of the century that the issue of race and ethnicity arose in the public feminist arena, due to the increasing impact of transnational immigration." The translation of Lorde's major works, along with Gloria Anzaldúa's and Barbara Smith's, has certainly contributed to the development of critical diasporic and postcolonial awareness in the Spanish context; but Lorde's specific contribution to such awareness merits detailed consideration.[2]

In an interview included on the DVD version of *The Berlin Years*, Dagmar Schultz mentions meeting Serbian women from Kosovo during the annual "Women in Black" peace conference in 1992. In the following year, these women developed a magazine that quoted Lorde in translation, a remark that was displayed on women's kitchen walls in many villages. Schultz also notes a surge of interest in Italy. In May 2006, the Fuoricampo Lesbian Group in Bologna, Italy, organized and hosted an international conference, "The Value of Difference: The Significance of Audre Lorde's Thinking Today." In 2012, *The Berlin Years* was screened at the Torino GLBT Film Festival. *Sister Outsider, The Cancer Journals,* and *A Burst of Light* have been translated into Italian by Margherita Giacobino and Marta Gianello Guida; and in May 2014 the Milan-based publishing house Il Dito e la Luna published them as a single volume under the title *Sorella Outsider.* The press also publishes a series, Officine T. Parole in corso (edited by Giacobino) that features lesbian fiction and essays translated from English, French, and Spanish. Il Dito e la Luna is not the only Italian press interested in Lorde: Edizioni ETS published a translation of *Zami* in 2014.[3] As Lorde's work continues to be translated, it will reach many more audiences and circles and generate interesting questions about translation, readership, and the role of publishing houses in disseminating her work and legacies.

Although several of the chapters in this book focus on Lorde's influence in Germany, more work needs to be done to detail the responses of other people of color living in Germany at the time of early Afro-German mobilization, such as Asian and Caribbean women. In Germany and elsewhere, Lorde acknowledged these women in her work and her activism. As she herself once asked, "Who are they, the Black German women of the Diaspora?" Certainly today, many members of the Initiative of Black Germans

(ISD) identify as "Black" irrespective of national and ethnic differences, emphasizing a shared political project of resistance against marginalization.[4] As we have seen throughout the book, Lorde critically reflected on the significance of such political gestures. Yet a more systematic exploration of her legacy will provide a broader portrait of her impact on Afro-European sisterhoods.

Similarly, why does a Palestinian and Muslim poet such as Suheir Hammad list Audre Lorde and June Jordan among her main influences?[5] Hammad was born in Jordan but grew up in New York around black people. In the preface of her collection of poems *Born Palestinian, Born Black* (1996), she offers the following "usages of the word 'black'":

> Black   like the coal diamonds are birthed from
>   like the dark matter of the universe
>   the Black September massacre of Palestinians
>   the Arabic expression "to blacken your face"
>   meaning to shame.[6]

Alongside the echoes of Lorde's work in this passage (her poem "Coal" and the phrase "coming out blackened and whole" in *Zami*), Hammad's use of "Black" in relation to "the other / Indians in England, Africans in America, / Algerians in France and Palestinians in Israel" resonates with Lorde's reflections in *A Burst of Light*, where she considers the advantages and possible limitations of using the term to refer to either a cultural or a political identity.[7] We find similar echoes in relation to Lorde's concerns with illness, cancer, and racialized bodies (in *The Cancer Journals* and "A Burst of Light") in recent breast cancer narratives and memoirs that extend her transnational perspectives, such as Evelyne Accad's *The Wounded Breast: Intimate Journeys through Cancer* (2001).[8]

In two essays from *Sister Outsider*, "Sexism: An American Disease in Blackface" and "Man Child: A Black Lesbian Feminist's Response," Lorde expressed the hazards of patriarchal hegemonic masculinity as manifested in black men: "The Black male consciousness must be raised to the realization that sexism and woman-hating are critically dysfunctional to his liberation as a Black man because they arise out of the same constellation that engenders racism and homophobia."[9] In "Man Child," drawing on her own experience of raising her son Jonathan with her then partner Frances, she broadened the discussion to a reconceptualization of the role of parents and the family. With the exception of brief references, our volume has

STELLA BOLAKI AND SABINE BROEK

not reflected on Lorde's legacies for white and black heterosexual, queer, or transmen in different contexts or examined their specific place within transnational and global narratives of sisterhood. However, a brief sample of her work, including the essays just mentioned, show that she had much to say about these issues.[10]

Before spending time in Europe in the 1980s, Lorde visited Russia in 1976, at the invitation of organizers of the "African-Asian Writers Conference," sponsored by the Union of Soviet Writers. *Sister Outsider* includes her "Notes from a Trip to Russia" that covers this two-week period (she stayed in Moscow and then went to Uzbekistan for the conference) and reflects on socialism as well as on solidarity between oppressed people and the "deference and unpleasantness she received as an American."[11] As regards the latter, Lorde was invited as an observer rather than as an active participant, and she was surprised that conference delegates from African, Asian, and Middle Eastern nations made no mention of the struggles of Black Americans. Concerning socialism, she noted, "It's not that there are no individuals who are nationalists, or racists, but that the taking of a state position against nationalism, against racism is what makes it possible for a society like this to function." But, she added, "the next step in that process must be the personal element . . . for without this step socialism remains at the mercy of an incomplete vision, imposed from the outside. We have internal desires but outside controls." Thus, even though she opened her essay with "for a while, in my dreams, Russia became a mythic representation of that socialism which does not yet exist anywhere I have been," she found contradictions that she reiterated in her private reflections on Cuba, following her visit there in 1985 as part of a delegation of black women writers.[12]

As this range of contexts shows (and we could also have mentioned South Africa, the Caribbean, Latin America, Australia, and New Zealand), Lorde is a truly transnational figure, and her work has far-reaching legacies. Our wish is that it will inspire readers to continue documenting her impact and locating her work in relation to the broader transnational questions that our contributors have posed.

Notes

1. Audre Lorde, *Zami: A New Spelling of My Name* (London: Sheba, 1982), 255.
2. Carmen Romero Bachiller, personal communication, September 2013. See Audre Lorde, *La hermana, la extranjera* (Madrid: Horas y horas, 2002); and Audre Lorde, *Zami: Una biomitografía* (Madrid: Horas y horas, 2010). For an articulation of the intersection of non-normative gender and sexuality positions, racial-diasporic ones, and class differences in Spain, see Raquel (Lucas) Platero, ed., *Intersectiones: Cuerpos y sexualidades en la encrucijada* (Barcelona: Melusina, 2012).
3. Audre Lorde, *Sorella Outsider. Gli scritti politici di Audre Lorde*, trans. Margherita Giacobino and Marta Gianello Guida (Milano: Il Dito e la Luna, 2014); Audre Lorde, *Zami. Così riscrivo il mio nome*, trans. Grazia Dicanio, ed. Liana Borghi (Pisa: Edizioni ETS, 2014).
4. For an exploration of Germany as both a diasporic and postcolonial setting, see Kien Nghi Ha, Nicola Lauré al-Samarai, and Sheila Mysorekar, eds., *Re/Visionen: Postkoloniale Perspektiven von People of Color auf Rassismus, Kulturpolitik und Widerstand in Deutschland* (Münster: Unrast, 2007); Cathy S. Gelbin, Kader Konuk, and Peggy Piesche, eds., *AufBrüche: Kulturelle Produktionen von Migrantinnen, Schwarzen und jüdischen Frauen in Deutschland* (Königstein im Taunus: Ulrike Helmer, 1999); and Carmen Faymonville, "Black Germans and Transnational Identification," *Callaloo* 26, no. 2 (Spring 2003): 364–82. *Macht der Nacht: Eine Schwarze Deutsche Anthologie* (which translates as *Power of the Night: A Black German Anthology*), was published in 1991 and 1992 by the Munich ISD and includes texts by Asian Germans such as Sheila Mysorekar.
5. See Marcy Jane Knopf-Newman, "Interview with Suheir Hammad," *MELUS* 31, no. 4 (Winter 2006): 77; and Nathalie Handal, "Drops of Suheir Hammad: A Talk with a Palestinian Poet Born Black" *Al Jadid* 3, no. 20 (Summer 1997), www.aljadid.com.
6. Suheir Hammad, *Born Palestinian, Born Black* (Brooklyn, N.Y.: UpSet Press, 2010), 12.
7. Lorde, *Zami*, 5; Hammad, *Born Palestinian*, 12. Also see this book's introduction.
8. On these books, see Therí A. Pickens, *New Body Politics: Narrating Arab and Black Identity in the Contemporary United States* (New York: Routledge, 2014), esp. chap. 5; and Mary K. DeShazer, *Mammographies: The Cultural Discourses of Breast Cancer Narratives* (Ann Arbor: University of Michigan Press, 2013), chap. 2.
9. Audre Lorde, "Sexism: An American Disease in Blackface," in *The Audre Lorde Compendium: Essays, Speeches, and Journals* (London: Pandora, 1996), 116.
10. See Andrew J. Young's "Are You Doing Your Work? White Transmen Holding Ourselves Accountable to Audre Lorde's Legacy," and Chris Rupertus's "Audre Speaks: Lordean Lessons for a White Man." Both are included in the Audre Lorde Forum on *The Feminist Wire*, http://thefeministwire.com/2014/03/afterword-standing-lordean-shoreline.
11. Audre Lorde, "Notes from a Trip to Russia," in *The Audre Lorde Compendium*, 94.
12. Ibid., 84, 75. On Cuba, see Alexis De Veaux, *Warrior Poet: A Biography of Audre Lorde* (New York: Norton, 2004), 347.

STELLA BOLAKI AND SABINE BROEK

NOTES ON CONTRIBUTORS

SARA AHMED is a professor of race and cultural studies and director of the Centre for Feminist Research at Goldsmiths, University of London. Her research is concerned with how bodies and worlds take shape and how power is secured and challenged in both every-day lives and institutional cultures. Her many publications include *The Cultural Politics of Emotion* (Edinburgh University Press, 2004) and *Willful Subjects* (Duke University Press, 2014). Currently, Ahmed is working on *Utility: The Uses of Use,* which tracks the history of the idea of use across a range of domains, including design and material culture, evolutionary theory, and political and ethical theory; and *Living a Feminist Life,* which draws on everyday experiences of being a feminist and focuses on the importance of renewing feminism as a mode of critique, a form of disobedience, and a way of challenging power.

STELLA BOLAKI is a lecturer in American literature at the University of Kent, where she is affiliated with the Centre for American Studies; the Centre for Gender, Sexuality, and Writing; and the Centre for Postcolonial Studies. She studies contemporary American literature and culture, with a focus on multiethnic and transnational writing, disability studies, and medical humanities. Bolaki is the author of *Unsettling the Bildungsroman: Reading Contemporary Ethnic American Women's Fiction* (Rodopi, 2011) and has published in journals such as *Textual Practice, Mosaic, Symbiosis,* and *MELUS.* She is currently completing a monograph, *Illness as Many Narratives: Arts, Medicine and Culture* (forthcoming from Edinburgh University Press) that explores the complex contributions of illness narratives (in a range of media and forms) to contemporary culture and the emergent field of the critical medical humanities.

SABINE BROECK is a professor of American studies and black diaspora studies at the University of Bremen. She has served as director of the university's Institute for Postcolonial and Transcultural Studies and as president of the Collegium for African American Research (CAAR). Her teaching and research address the intersections of race, class, gender, and sexuality; issues of black diaspora studies; and the decolonial critique of transatlantic modernity. Currently, Broek is studying the impact of transatlantic slavery and the culture and regime of enslavism on white modernity, including theories of human liberation, such as those in feminism. Her book *Gender and Anti-Blackness* is forthcoming from SUNY Press.

SARAH CEFAI is a fellow in media and communications at the London School of Economics and Political Science, where she focuses on feminist, queer, postcolonial, and indigenous critique as politics of feeling. Her work on affective politics has appeared in the journals *Gender, Place and Culture, Somatechnics, Rhizomes,* and *Participations.* Cefai is currently writing a monograph that reimagines the conditions of possibility for feeling in Western thought via the feminist intervention of the body, and she is also developing new research on Australian mediascapes.

CASSANDRA ELLERBE-DUECK is a diversity marketing manager for the city of Mannheim and a member of the Black Diaspora in Germany Scholars Project, funded by the German Research Foundation. After studying at Université Paris 8 and Ludwig-Maximilians University, she received a Ph.D. in comparative culture studies / anthropology from Ghent University. Between 2007 and 2010 Ellerbe-Dueck served as a postdoctoral research fellow at the University of Southampton. Her essays appear in *Afroeurope@ns: Cultures and Identities,* edited by Marta Sofía López (Cambridge Scholars Publishing, 2008), and the journal *African and Black Diaspora.*

PAUL M. FARBER is a scholar of American and urban studies. He earned a Ph.D. in American culture from the University of Michigan and is currently a postdoctoral writing fellow at Haverford College. He has also served as a doctoral fellow in the history of African Americans and Germans/Germany at the German Historical Institute in Washington, D.C., and has taught in the urban studies program at the University of Pennsylvania. Farber has contributed to several books, including *This Is the Day: The March on Washington* (Getty, 2013), *Re-Made: Reading Leonard Freed* (Steidl Verlag, 2013), and *Kodachrome Memory: American Pictures, 1972–1990* (powerHouse, 2013). He has also coedited a special issue of the journal *Criticism* focusing on the HBO series *The Wire.* Presently, he is working on a book-length study of representations of the Berlin Wall in American art, literature, and popular culture since 1961.

TIFFANY N. FLORVIL studied at the University of Wisconsin–Madison and the University of South Carolina, where she received her Ph.D. in European history. She is currently an assistant professor of history at the University of New Mexico, where she specializes in the histories of post-1945 Germany, the African diaspora, comparative women's and gender studies, and the study of emotions. Florvil is working on a book titled *Making a Movement: A History of Afro-Germans, Emotions, and Belonging.*

KATHARINA GERUND teaches American studies at Friedrich-Alexander University, where she coordinates the interdisciplinary doctoral program Presence and Tacit

Knowledge. She has held fellowships at Bremen University and in the Bavarian American Academy's postgraduate research program at Yale University. She specializes in African American literature and culture, postcolonial theory, diaspora studies, gender studies, and popular culture (especially contemporary film and TV series). Gerund is a coeditor of *Pirates, Drifters, Fugitives: Figures of Mobility in the U.S. and Beyond* (Winter, 2012) and has recently published a monograph, *Transatlantic Cultural Exchange: African American Women's Art and Activism in West Germany* (Transcript, 2013).

ALEXIS PAULINE GUMBS is a queer black troublemaker, a black feminist love evangelist, and a prayer poet priestess. She earned a Ph.D. in English, African, and African American studies and women's and gender studies from Duke University. Gumbs has published widely on Caribbean women's literature and is currently touring with her interactive oracle project "The Lorde Concordance," a series of rituals that mobilize the life and work of Audre Lorde as a dynamic sacred text. She is the author of an acclaimed collection of poems, *101 Things That Are Not True About the Most Famous Black Women Alive* (Scribd, 2012). Works in progress include the poetry collection *Good Hair Gone Forever,* a scholarly monograph on diaspora and the maternal, and an educational resource titled the *School of Our Lorde.*

GLORIA I. JOSEPH is professor emeritus at Hampshire College. She has taught and lectured around the world on issues of education, racism, feminism, and social justice and has helped to found several organizations, including Sisterhood in Support of Sisters in South Africa (SISA). Joseph has published three books, including (with Jill Lewis) *Common Differences: Conflicts in Black and White Feminist Perspectives* (South End Press, 1981), and her essays have appeared widely in books and journals. She became Audre Lorde's partner toward the end of Lorde's life, and her multilensed biography of Lorde, *The Wind Is Spirit: The Life, Love, and Legacy of Audre Lorde,* is forthcoming from Villarosa Media.

JACKIE KAY is a professor of creative writing at Newcastle University. Her first collection of poetry, *The Adoption Papers* (1991), won the Forward Prize, a Saltire Award, and a Scottish Arts Council Book Award. In addition to poetry collections, she has published novels for adults and children as well as short-story collections. Her most recent books include *Red Dust Road* (2010), a memoir about meeting her Nigerian birth father, which was shortlisted for the 2011 PEN/Ackerley Prize. In 2006, Kay was named a Member of the Order of the British Empire in honor of her service to literature.

MARION KRAFT teaches English and women's studies at the Oberstufen-Kolleg of the University of Bielefeld and has also served as a visiting literature professor at the University of Osnabrück. She is the author of *The African Continuum and Contemporary African American Women Writers—Their Literary Presence and Ancestral Past* (Peter Lang, 1995) and a coeditor of *Schwarze Frauen der Welt—Europa und Migration* (Orlanda Frauenverlag, 1994). Kraft has translated Audre Lorde's poems into German and has also published several essays on women's literature, black women's culture, racism, and the Afro-German experience.

CHRISTIANA LAMBRINIDIS is the founding director of the Athens-based Center for Creative Writing and Theater for Conflict Resolution. She now lives in Amsterdam, where she continues her work as a playwright, scholar, teacher, essayist, editor, and activist. In 2002 Human Rights Watch honored her with the Lillian Hellmann and Dashiel Hammett Award. Editor of Greece's first feminist publishing series (an imprint of Kochlias Editions), Lambrinidis has also cofounded the organization (W)rightful with women, refugees, and members of the Turkish minority in Thrace. (W)rightful focuses on restoring dignity through writing and performance and is affiliated with the international Women's World Organization for Rights, Literature, and Development. Her writings appear in *Theatre and Democracy,* edited by Ravi Chaturvedi (Rawat, 2008).

ZEEDAH MEIERHOFER-MANGELI is a feminist activist, educator, consultant, and politician who serves on the advisory boards of the Conflict, Security and Development Group at King's College London and the African Leadership Center in Kenya. Her focus is on women, peace and security, transformative leadership, and social justice in pre- and post-conflict environments; and she is particularly interested in issues concerning young women and girls. Meierhofer-Mangeli has worked as a regional and international consultant for the Swiss police force; the Rwandese, Indian, and Nigerian military; and the Ugandan and Liberian parliaments. She has co-edited (with Shelley Berlowitz and Elisabeth Joris) *Terra Incognita? Der Treffpunkt Schwarzer Frauen in Zürich* (Limmat Verlag, 2014).

RINA NISSIM is an activist, naturopathic gynecologist, and publisher. After completing her training in nursing in 1972, she helped create Dispensaire des Femmes, a pilot women's health center in Geneva. She has since worked with women and health groups in the United States, Central America, Brazil, and India. After her first book *Mamamélis* (Pandora, 1986) became a bestseller, she founded Editions Mamamélis, which publishes health-related books as well as French translations of authors such as Audre Lorde and Adrienne Rich.

CHANTAL OAKES is founding member of Kitchen Sink, an artist-led project supporting the development of diversity in the arts in northwestern England. A writer and an artist, she focuses on developing methodologies to record histories from the perspective of the African diaspora. Her works investigate representations of seemingly concrete ages, situations, and visual ideas. By contesting the division between memory and experience, she explores documentation and questions of re-presentation. Recent work includes the short story "The Weight of Four Tigers" in the forthcoming anthology *Closure* (Peepal Tree Press, 2015) and a solo fine art show "Elephants," as part of the In Certain Places program based in Preston, Lancashire. Currently she is also compiling an illustrated book about Lancashire's black history with the Harris Museum and Art Gallery.

LESTER C. OLSON is a professor of communication at the University of Pittsburgh who specializes in visual rhetoric, rhetorical criticism, and public address. He has an abiding interest in silence, human rights, and rhetoric on social justice. His current book-length project focuses on Audre Lorde, and his essays about her public advocacy have appeared in journals and on websites such the *Quarterly Journal of Speech, Philosophy and Rhetoric, The Literary Encyclopedia,* and *The Feminist Wire.* He has also contributed chapters to *American*

Voices (Greenwood, 2005), *Queering Public Address* (University of South Carolina, 2007), *The Responsibilities of Rhetoric* (Waveland, 2009), and *Standing in the Intersection: Feminist Voices, Feminist Practices in Communication Studies* (SUNY, 2012).

PRATIBHA PARMAR is a filmmaker who has spent more than twenty years bringing fresh perspectives to stories of women, minorities, and social issues. Her work includes the documentaries *Place of Rage* (1991), *Khush* (1991), *Warrior Marks* (1993), *The Righteous Babes* (1998), and *A Brimful of Asia* (1999) and the feature film *Nina's Heavenly Delights* (2006). Parmar's most recent production is *Alice Walker: Beauty in Truth* (2013), the first film biography about the writer and activist Alice Walker. Her films have been screened widely at international film festivals and broadcast in many countries, and she has received the San Francisco Frameline Film Festival Life Time Achievement Award and the Visionary Award from the One in Ten Film Festival. Parmar is also the coauthor and editor of several books, including *Charting the Journey: Writings by Black and Third World Women* (Sheba, 1988).

PEGGY PIESCHE is a literary and cultural studies scholar who works at the Academy for Advanced African Studies at Bayreuth University. Her focus includes critical race and whiteness studies, black feminist studies, diaspora and translocality, and the performativity of memory cultures. Her books include *AufBrüche. Kulturelle Produktionen von Migrantinnen, Schwarzen und jüdischen Frauen in Deutschland* (Ulrike Helmer, 1999), *May-Ayim-Award: Erster Internationaler Schwarzer deutscher Literaturpreis* (Orlanda Frauenverlag, 2004), *Mythen, Masken und Subjekte. Kritische Weißseinsforschung in Deutschland* (Unrast, 2005, 2009), and *"Euer Schweigen schützt euch nicht." Audre Lorde und die Schwarze Frauenbewegung in Deutschland* (Orlanda Frauenverlag, 2012). Piesche is currently working on a book-length project that explores how diaspora is negotiated through notions of race and digitalized collective identities.

DAGMAR SCHULTZ is an activist, author, and filmmaker who focuses on feminist studies, antiracist social work, women's health care, and cultural competence in the psychiatric care of migrants and minorities. In 1974, she cofounded the Feminist Women's Health Center in Berlin—the first of its kind in Germany—and the women's press Orlanda Frauenverlag. As director of the press, she edited *Macht und Sinnlichkeit: Ausgewählte Texte von Audre Lorde und Adrienne Rich* (1986), which introduced Audre Lorde and Adrienne Rich to German readers, and has also released *Die Quelle unserer Macht: Gedichte* (1994), a bilingual edition of forty-two poems that Lorde selected during her last summer in Berlin. More recently, Schultz has produced the award-winning documentary *Audre Lorde—The Berlin Years, 1984 to 1992*. She was awarded the 2011 Margherita von Brentano Prize for work that furthers the equal rights of women in academia.

TAMARA LEA SPIRA is an assistant professor of queer studies at Western Washington University. A social justice activist, she is also a scholar of Latin American and critical race feminist studies. While serving as a research scholar at the Beatrice Bain Research Center at the University of California, Berkeley, she coordinated the collective project

"Archiving 1960s and 1970s Third World, Indigenous and Anti-Colonial Women's and Queer Transnational Solidarities." Her writings appear in journals such as the *Radical History Review, Identities, Feminist Theory, NACLA Journal of the Americas,* and *E-misférica.* Spira is currently completing her first book, a study of feminist and queer memories of 1970s anticolonial revolutions.

GLORIA WEKKER is professor emeritus in the Department of Gender Studies at Utrecht University. A poet and cultural anthropologist, she is the author of *The Politics of Passion: Women's Sexual Culture in the Afro-Surinamese Diaspora* (Columbia University Press, 2006), for which she received the 2007 Ruth Benedict Prize from the American Anthropological Association. She is currently working on *White Innocence: Paradoxes of Colonialism and Race,* a collection of essays about the white Dutch psyche (forthcoming from Duke University Press).

INDEX

Burrows, Vinie, 44

"A Burst of Light" (Lorde), 5; death in, 14; female networks in, 10; French edition of, 88; Germany in, 7; hope in, 16; racialized body in, 228; on racism, 102–3; Switzerland in, 11; the transnational in, 6

A Burst of Light (Lorde): blackness in, 228; Italian edition of, 227

Butler, Judith, 208; on gender, 211

But Some of Us Are Brave (anthology), 42

Caloz-Tschopp, Marie-Claire, 90

camera, as politicized tool, 208

Campe, Sandra, 36; Ökodorf Sieben Linden project of, 37

Campt, Tina, 141

cancer, state-based systems as, 175n5. See also Lorde, Audre: cancer

The Cancer Journals (Lorde), 5, 6, 28, 92n1; Eudora in, 182–83; French edition of, 88; German edition of, 122; Greek translation of, 220; Italian edition of, 227; racialized body in, 228

capitalism, disaster, 165–66

"Caribbean Women" (conference, Saint Croix, 1986), 13

Castillo, Elaine, 35–36, 38

Catlett, Elizabeth, 180

Cavarero, Adriana, 7

Center for Black Women's Perspectives (AFRA, Vienna), 69

Central America, U.S. intervention in, 187

Centre Evolutif Lilith (Marseille), 89

Césaire, Aimé: Discourse on Colonialism, 24

Charting the Journey (anthology), Lorde's interview in, 12, 74–84

Cheatom, Ria, 32, 122–23

civil rights movement, Lorde's role in, 62

Clayton, Frances, 86

"Coal" (Lorde), 228

Cold War: geopolitics of, 184; U.S. state power during, 185

Collective Feminist Translation Group, 220

Collins, Patricia Hill, 36

colonialism: effect on nations, xi; lesbian descendants of, 92

colonization: fragmentation following, 189n35; genocide in, 181

common sense, racialized, 129

Comrades (South African rebels), 106

"Conference of Caribbean Women Writers" (Saint Croix, 1986), 13

"Conference on the Contemporary Urgencies of Audre Lorde's Legacy" (Toronto, 2013), 35

conservatism, international, 80–81

contras (Nicaragua), U.S. funding of, 187

Conversations with Audre Lorde (2004), 3

cosmopolitanism: and human difference, 113; Lorde on, 112

creative writing: empowerment through, 214; multileveled inquiry in, 219

creativity: collective, 203; Lorde's, 161, 194, 195; women's, 136

Crenshaw, Kimberlé: intersectionality theory of, 36, 124

Crichlow, Warren, 31

critical whiteness theory, 36

Cuba, Lorde's visit to, 229

Cuernavaca, Lorde in, 182

cultural studies, feminist: mediation of representation, 194

cultures, American: transnational context of, 2

Cvetkovich, Ann, 14

Dahomey, women warriors of, 49

Davis, Angela, 99, 132

decolonization: erotic, 186, 190n45; wholeness in, 189n35

de Kom, Anton, 68

de Lauretis, Teresa, 199

Deleuze, Gilles, 203; on minor literature, 194

De Veaux, Alexis, 3, 6, 154, 189n23

D-Flame (hip-hop artist), 72n33

diaspora: as category of solidarity, 164; "First World" creation of, 167; Lorde's concept of, 168; ontological experience of, 167; preconditions for, 167; trauma in, 166–67. See also African diaspora

"Diaspora" (Lorde), 162n33

diasporic communities, black: Afro-German women's, 144; British, 212; common ancestries of, 141; European, 2; German, 124, 125, 132; links among, 59; Lorde and, 5–6, 9–10, 15; of Mexico, 181; power in, 8. See also African diaspora

diasporic studies, power in, 18n28

124, 136-37, 178; estrangement, 148,
149, 152; female kinship, 141; feminist
academics, 194; forms of knowledge,
129; identity, 148; intersectionality, 36,
67, 124; justice, 178; language, 222;
optimism, xii; parenthood, 228; primacy
of speech, 196; socialism, 229; solidarity,
188; survival, xii; U.S. hegemony, 185-86;
women's creativity, 136
—cancer, 31, 61–62, 89, 111, during
Hurricane Hugo, 165; neo-imperialism
and, 187–88; treatments, 6–7, 9, 11, 32,
86, 175n5. See also *The Cancer Journals*
—celebrations and memorials for, 4; in
Lesbia magazine, 86; London (1993), 24;
New York (1993), 16n16
—conference participation: "African-Asian
Writers Conference," 229; "Black
Woman Writer and the Diaspora," 114;
"Caribbean Women: The Historical
and Cultural Ties That Bind," 13;
"Conference of Caribbean Women
Writers," 13; "The Dream of Europe,"
5, 23–26, 25; "I Am Your Sister," 111;
International Feminist Book Fair,
74, 75–78, 79, 85; National Women's
Studies Association, 111; Women 150
Writers' Week, 12–13, 116; "World
Lesbian and Gay Conference," 110;
"World Women's Conference," 27
—connections: to black diaspora, 5–6, 9–10,
15, 114-15; to German culture, 28
—creative process of, 161, 194, 195
—crossing of boundaries, 2, 4
—death of, 29, 35
—democratizing thought of, 216
—diasporic reading practice of, 164–67
—engagement with racism, x–xi, 11
—factory work of, 179
—family: children, 34, 228; mother, 47, 49,
58, 62, 182
—francophone academic interest in, 90
—friends and associates: Afro-German
women, 27–29, 30–31, 43, 138–44; Ayim,
123, 141; Ellerbe-Dueck, 55–57, 59–60;
Emde, 139; Hügel-Marshall, 7, 123,
138; Kay, 74–84; Kraft, 41, 42, 135, 140,
142–43; Kuzwayo, 39n12; Meierhofer-
Mangeli, 94–101; Nissim, 85–86;

Oguntoye, 139, 142, 143; Parmar, 74–84;
Schultz, 27–30, 61, 65, 85, 130; transnational, 4, 7–14, 68–69, 118; Wekker,
57–59, 60–62, 83
—global consciousness of, 6, 126
—identification with Holocaust victims, 155
—influence, 164; on Afro-European sisterhood, 228; on Black British avant-garde,
213; in Italy, 227; on queer movement,
90; in Spain, 226; transnational, 33, 124;
on white women's consciousness, 36
—influence of Afro-German women on,
144n5
—interactions with Europe, 4–6, 8, 14,
23–26
—interdisciplinary writing of, 148
—interviews, 32, 33; in *Charting the Journey*,
12, 74–84; with Kraft, 42, 46–54; *Spare
Rib*, 12
—knowledge production by, 5
—legacies, 1–2, 5, 14; accountability in, 178;
conferences on, 35; in Germany, 132; in
A Litany for Survival, 15; for men, 229;
radical internationalist, 186; transnational, xi, 2, 3, 5, 15, 16, 195, 224, 226,
229
—modes of identification, 149
—multiple identities of, 110–11, 137, 148, 151
—organizing principles of, 1
—poetry: activist, 174; Berlin-based, 148–61,
162n33; Berlin Wall in, 151, 153–54, 156,
160; bridge spaces in, 171–75; dreams in,
160, 161n9; the erotic in, 178; imagery of,
161n11; site-specific production of, 151;
spaces in, 172; Staten Island in, 171;
theories of, 46–47, 133n21, 136, 137, 138,
189n34; transnational feminism in, 174;
word placement in, 172; Zimbabwe in, 172
—practice of enunciation, 194
—public advocacy of, 109, 119n3, 137
—public literary production of, 148
—reading of Keats, 162n19
—reception of, 4, 14; in French-speaking
Europe, 88–92; in West Germany,
122–32
—responsibility as African American
woman, 10
—revision by, 148–61; revisitation practices
in, 149

Ravensbrück (female concentration camp), 157

Reagan, Ronald: visit to Bitburg cemetery, 156, 162n27

Reagon, Bernice, 47

relation, politics of, 130

return, expressive, 161n2

Rich, Adrienne, 88, 184; *Macht und Sinnlichkeit*, 28, 87, 96, 123; on white solipsism, 129

Rivera, Diego, 180

Robles, Ellin, 60

Rollins, Elizabeth Lorde, 34

Romani, Spanish: discrimination against, 227

Romero Bachiller, Carmen, 226–27

Rosenberg, Ethel and Julius, 179

Rowe, Aimee Carrillo, 125; on differential belonging, 131; on feminist alliances, 127; on transracial feminism, 130

Rowell, Charles H., 13

Ruf, Waltraut, 122

Russia, Lorde's visit to, 229

Saint Croix: colonial relationship with U.S., 13, 18n53, 165; during Hurricane Hugo, 164–66; Lorde's residence in, 13–14, 109, 116, 152, 163, 175n5

Saint Croix Women's Coalition, 13

saudade (presence), 208–9

Scheffer-Zbinden, Barbara, 99

Schokofabrik (Chocolate Factory, Berlin), 145n18; Lorde's reading at, 138

Schültheiß, Hella, 142

Schultz, Dagmar, 3–4; on Afro-German movement, 128–29; association with Lorde, 27–30, 61, 65, 85; in "Berlin Is Hard on Colored Girls," 154, 162n17; on coalition politics, 128; confrontation with her whiteness, 130; on "Dream of Europe" conference, 23–25; editing of *Macht und Sinnlichkeit*, 123; editing of *Showing Our Colors*, 8, 127; at Free University of Berlin, 28; at Hamburg women's conference, 42; *Hope in My Heart*, 30; on Lorde's Berlin years, 158; Margherita von Brentano award of, 33; meeting with Serbian women, 227; publication of Lorde, 87; "Racism and Sexism" seminar, 137. See also *Audre Lorde—The Berlin Years*

"Scratching the Surface" (Lorde), 111, 115

Seacole, Mary: *The Wonderful Adventures of Mrs. Seacole in Many Lands*, 207–8

Sedgwick, Eve, 129

self-definition, power of, 223

self-determination: Lorde's, 181; through the erotic, 186, 187

Seroke, Joyce, 102

sexism: black male, 228; in German society, 64

"Sexism: An American Disease in Blackface" (Lorde), 111, 228

shame, white, 129–30

Sheba (feminist publisher), 79–80, 84

Shotwell, Alexis, 124; on racial awareness, 129–30; on solidarity, 131

Showing Our Colors. See *Farbe bekennen*

silence: feminist, 193, 200; in *Sister Outsider*, 196–97

Simmons, Aishah Shahidah, 4

sisterhood: coalitions with men, 110; in combatting of oppression, 110; and community, 112; contingent, 119; diasporic, 113–16; diversity in, 115; global, 124; Lorde's advocacy of, 15, 94, 109–19, 123; performative, 109–19; transatlantic, 116; transnational, 116–18; transnational male role in, 229

"Sisterhood and Survival" (Lorde), 115

Sisterhood in Support of Sisters in South Africa (SISA), 10; founders of, 170; goals of, 170–71; Lorde's work with, 12, 39n12, 52–53, 103–5, 114, 116, 163–64; purpose of, 103

Sister Outsider (lesbian group), 57–58, 59, 73n37, 83; Wekker in, 60

Sister Outsider (Lorde), x, 56, 111; anger in, 199; creative energy of, 195; critical feeling in, 193–204; difference in, 198–99; emotional knowledge in, 194–95; the erotic in, 195, 198; feminist agency of, 198; French edition of, 88, 91; Italian translation of, 227; Lorde's legacy in, 195; political allegory of, 201; promise of joy in, 204; publication of, 163; "self on self" in, 197; silence in, 196–97; travels in, 112

"Sisters in Arms" (Lorde), 169

slave trade, transatlantic, 9, 166; Liverpool's role in, 209, 211

"The Uses of Anger" (Lorde), 50, 90, 98, 201; French translation of, 91
"Uses of the Erotic" (Lorde), 48, 60; on pornography, 202; Spanish edition of, 226. *See also* the erotic

Venster, Mea, 60
Vereniging Ons Suriname (Surinamese organization), 67
Vietninghoff, Aletta von, 32
violence, counter-revolutionary, 185
violence, racial: in Europe, 24; in Germany, 10–11, 158; political solidarity against, 170
violence, state: relationship to black life, 165–66
violence against women, optimism concerning, xi
visual culture, Western, 208

Walker, Alice: on black feminism, 82
Walker, Anthony: murder of, 212–13
Weed, Susan: *Wise Woman Herbal for the Childbearing Year*, 87
Wekker, Gloria, 35, 38; academic career of, 60; activism of, 60; association with Lorde, 57–59, 60–62, 83
What Remains (film), 213n4
whiteness: Afro-German women's envy of, 139; of Berlin, 126; critical, 36; perspective of universality on, 129; primacy of, 130; as social construct, 131

white supremacy, postcolonial reproduction of, 186
Wiedenroth-Coulibaly, Eleonore, 128, 138
Williams, Kim Hester, 31
Wilson, John, 180
Wolpert, Betty, 103–4; *Awake from Mourning*, 103; Les Quelles home of, 105–6
women: testimony against themselves, 197; violence against, xi
women, aboriginal, 118; experience of erasure, 117
women, Serbian: at "Women in Black" peace conference, 227

women, Swiss: insularity of, 11
"Women in Black" peace conference (1992), 227
Women of Black Heritage (WBH, Switzerland), 97, 99
women of color: in American usage, 80; cross-diaspora connections of, 36; dichotomizations in study of, 178; differences among, 44–45; feminists, 188n7, 199; forced sterilization of, 91; internationalist genealogies of, 188n5; literature by, 41, 42
Women 150 Writers' Week (Melbourne, 1985), 12–13, 116
women's writings: Afro-German, 1, 3; threat of, 215
women warriors, of Dahomey, 49
Wooton, Charles, 209
"World Lesbian and Gay Conference" (third, 1979), Lorde's speech at, 110
World March of Women (alter-globalist movement), 91
"World Women's Conference" (Copenhagen, 1980), 27
Wright, Michelle M., 140

Yemanjá (goddess), 47

Zamani Soweto Sisters (self-help group), 10, 103–4, 170; visit to England, 104–6
Zami (Lorde), x, 57; Afro-Caribbean identity in, 13; Bea in, 179; as biomythography, 208; blackness in, 180–81; black women's histories in, 208; dedication of, 179; difference in, 4; epilogue of, 226; the erotic in, 48–49; French edition of, 88; German edition of, 28, 122; hope in, 182; interconnectivity in, 179; Italian edition of, 227; Mexico in, 180, 183–85; myths in, 49; naming in, 49; narrative progression of, 179; self-identification in, 183; women-bonding in, 140
Zami (organization), 73n37
Zekina, Gabriele, 37
Zimbabwe, in Lorde's poetry, 172